CompTIA Network+®
Self Study Guide, 2e

Anthony Chiarella

CompTIA Network+®
Self Study Guide, 2e

Anthony Chiarella

THOMSON

DELMAR LEARNING™

Australia • Canada • Mexico • Singapore • Spain • United Kingdom • United States

CompTIA Network+ Self Study Guide, 2nd edition
Anthony Chiarella

Vice President, Technology and Trades SBU:
Alar Elken

Editorial Director:
Sandy Clark

Senior Acquisitions Editor:
Steve Helba

Senior Development Editor:
Michelle Ruelos Cannistraci

Marketing Director:
Dave Garza

Senior Channel Manager:
Dennis Williams

Marketing Coordinator:
Stacey Wiktorek

Production Director:
Mary Ellen Black

Production Manager:
Andrew Crouth

Production Editor
Stacy Masucci

Senior Editorial Assistant
Dawn Daugherty

Library of Congress Cataloging-in-Publication Data

Chiarella, Anthony.
    CompTIA Network+ self study guide / Anthony Chiarella.—2nd ed.
        p. cm.
    Includes bibliographical references and index.
    1. Computer networks—Examinations— Study guides. 2. Electronic data processing personnel—Certification. I. Title: CompTIA Network plus self study guide. II. Title.
    TK5105.5.C48228 2006
    004.6'076—dc22
                                                2005008179

ISBN: 1-4180-0933-4

NOTICE TO THE READER

Publisher does not warrant or guarantee any of the products described herein or perform any independent analysis in connection with any of the product information contained herein. Publisher does not assume, and expressly disclaims, any obligation to obtain and include information other than that provided to it by the manufacturer.

The reader is expressly warned to consider and adopt all safety precautions that might be indicated by the activities herein and to avoid all potential hazards. By following the instructions contained herein, the reader willingly assumes all risks in connection with such instructions.

The publisher makes no representation or warranties of any kind, including but not limited to, the warranties of fitness for particular purpose or merchantability, nor are any such representations implied with respect to the material set forth herein, and the publisher takes no responsibility with respect to such material. The publisher shall not be liable for any special, consequential, or exemplary damages resulting, in whole or part, from the readers' use of, or reliance upon, this material.

BRIEF CONTENTS

DETAILED CONTENTS

PREFACE

INTRODUCTION

Whether you are a student studying for the Network+ exam for the first time or a Networking professional that has yet to become Network+ certified, this book is for you. This book is a technical reference guide that will assist you in taking the Network+ exam.

PREREQUISITES

To best use this study guide, you should have some previous knowledge of computer concepts. This study guide has all of the information you need to pass the Network+ exam. However, it does not enter into great detail of the topics covered. It will not bring you from a beginner's level to an intermediate level without the assistance of additional material. It is assumed that you have a basic understanding of computers and basic networking concepts.

WHY I WROTE THIS BOOK

Many Network+ study guides are comprehensive books that can and sometimes are used as courseware to teach networking concepts. This book, on the other hand, is written in such a way that you will be able to use it to simply pass the Network+ exam. When I set out to write this book I had one goal in mind: making my readers certified. I have taken many technical certification exams and know how to study for them and pass them. One method I use to study for exams is to find all the information in a book that I feel is pertinent and write it down in a separate notebook. Then I study from the notebook. This is essentially what I did for you.

The chapters in this book are clear, concise, and to the point. The technical information in this book is geared toward the test objectives stated on CompTIA's web site.

ABOUT THE NETWORK+ CERTIFICATION

The exam was created to define the skill standards for networking professionals in 1997. In 2005 the objectives were revised again. The *CompTIA Network+ Self Study Guide*, 2nd edition, has been updated to reflect the new 2005 Network+ objectives.

The exam is computer–based, and there are three general types of questions given on the Network+ exam. They include *multiple choice*, which requires the examinee to select one option that best answers the question or completes the statement; *multiple response,* which requires the examinee to select more than one option that best answers the question; and finally, *sample directions,* which requires the examinee to read a statement or question and select only the option(s) that represent the best answer(s).

TAKING THE TEST

When you are prepared for the exam you must register for exam N10-003 with Thomson Prometric or Pearson VUE, the two learning companies that offer the exam. To learn how to register and the current cost of the exam, contact one of these companies to learn the closest location where you can take the exam. Thomson Prometric is located on the web at www.prometric.com. Pearson VUE is found on the web at www.vue.com.

TEST OBJECTIVES

The exam is broken into four domains. Each domain covers several areas of the exam. The domains and their objectives are shown here:

NETWORK+ EXAMINATION OBJECTIVES

Domain 1.0 - Media and Topologies

1.1 Recognize the following logical or physical network topologies given a diagram, schematic, or description:

> Star
> Bus
> Mesh
> Ring

1.2 Specify the main features of 802.2 (Logical Link Control), 802.3 (Ethernet), 802.5 (token ring), 802.11 (wireless), and FDDI (Fiber Distributed Data Interface) networking technologies, including:

> Speed
> Access method (CSMA/CA (Carrier Sense Multiple Access/Collision Avoidance) and CSMA/CD (Carrier Sense Multiple Access/Collision Detection))
> Topology
> Media

1.3 Specify the characteristics (e.g., speed, length, topology, cable type) of the following cable standards:

> 10BASE-T and 10BASE-FL
> 100BASE-TX and 100BASE-FX
> 1000BASE-T, 1000BASE-CX, 1000BASE-SX, and 1000BASE-LX
> 10GBASE-SR, 10GBASE-LR, and 10GBASE-ER

1.4 Recognize the following media connectors and describe their uses:

> RJ-11 (Registered Jack)
> RJ-45 (Registered Jack)
> F-Type
> ST (Straight Tip)
> SC (Subscriber Connector or Standard Connector)
> IEEE 1394 (FireWire)
> Fiber LC (Local Connector)
> MT-RJ (Mechanical Transfer Registered Jack)
> USB (Universal Serial Bus)

1.5 Recognize the following media types and describe their uses:

> Category 3, 5, 5e, and 6
> UTP (Unshielded Twisted Pair)
> STP (Shielded Twisted Pair)
> Coaxial Cable
> SMF (Single Mode Fiber) optic cable
> MMF (Multimode Fiber) optic cable

1.6 Identify the purpose, features, and functions of the following network components:

> Hubs
> Switches
> Bridges
> Routers
> Gateways
> CSU/DSU (Channel Service Unit/Data Service Unit)

NICs (Network Interface Card)

ISDN (Integrated Services Digital Network) adapters

WAPs (Wireless Access Points)

Modems

Transceivers (media converts)

Firewalls

1.7 Specify the general characteristics (e.g., carrier speed, frequency, transmission type, and topology) of the following wireless technologies:

802.11 (Frequency hopping spread spectrum)

802.11x (Direct sequence spread spectrum)

Infrared

Bluetooth

1.8 Identify factors that affect the range and speed of wireless service (e.g., interference, antenna type, and environmental factors).

Domain 2.0 – Protocols and Standards

2.1 Given an example, identify a MAC address and its parts.

2.2 Identify the seven layers of the OSI (Open Systems Interconnect) model and their functions.

2.3 Identify the OSI (Open Systems Interconnect) layers at which the following network components operate:

Hubs

Switches

Bridges

Routers

NICs (Network Interface Cards)

WAPs (Wireless Access Points)

2.4 Differentiate between the following network protocols in terms of routing, addressing schemes, interoperability, and naming conventions:

IPX/SPX (Internetwork Packet Exchange/Sequence Packet Exchange)

NetBEUI (Network Basic Input/Output System Extended User Interface)

AppleTalk/AppleTalk over IP (Internet Protocol)

TCP/IP (Transmission Control Protocol/Internet Protocol)

2.5 Identify the components and structure of IP (Internet Protocol) addresses (Ipv4, Ipv6) and the required setting for connections across the Internet.

2.6 Identify classful IP (Internet Protocol) ranges and their subnet masks (e.g., Class A, B and C).

2.7 Identify the purpose of subnetting.

2.8 Identify the differences between private and public network addressing schemes.

2.9 Identify and differentiate between the following IP (Internet Protocol) addressing methods:

> Static
>
> Dynamic
>
> Self-assigned (APIPA (Automate Private Internet Protocol Addressing))

2.10 Define the purpose, function and use of the following protocols used in the TCP/IP (Transmission Control Protocol/Internet Protocol) suite:

> TCP (Transmission Control Protocol)
>
> UDP (User Datagram Protocol)
>
> FTP (File Transfer Protocol)
>
> SFTP (Secure File Transfer Protocol)
>
> TFTP (Trivial File Transfer Protocol)
>
> SMTP (Simple Mail Transfer Protocol)
>
> HTTP (Hypertext Transfer Protocol)
>
> HTTPS (Hypertext Transfer Protocol Secure)
>
> POP3/IMAP4 (Post Office Protocol version 3/Internet Message Access Protocol version 4)
>
> Telnet
>
> SSH (Secure Shell)
>
> ICMP (Internet Control Message Protocol)
>
> ARP/RARP (Address Resolution Protocol/Reverse Address Resolution Protocol)
>
> NTP (Network Time Protocol)
>
> NNTP (Network News Transport Protocol)
>
> SCP (Secure Copy Protocol)
>
> LDAP (Lightweight Directory Access Protocol)
>
> IGMP (Internet Group Multicast Protocol)
>
> LPR (Line Printer Remote)

2.11 Define the function of TCP/UDP (Transmission Control Protocol/User Datgram Protocol) ports.

2.12 Identify the well-known ports associated with the following commonly used services and protocols:

20	FTP (File Transfer Protocol)
21	FTP (File Transfer Protocol)
22	SSH (Secure Shell)
23	Telnet
25	SMTP (Simple Mail Transfer Protocol)
53	DNS (Domain Name Service)
69	TFTP (Trivial File Transfer Protocol)
80	HTTP (Hypertext Transfer Protocol)
110	POP3 (Post Office Protocol version 3)
119	NTP (Network Time Protocol)
143	IMAP4 (Internet Message Access Protocol version 4)
443	HTTPS (Hypertext Transfer Protocol Secure)

2.13 Identify the purpose of network services and protocols (e.g., DNS (Domain Name Service), NAT (Network Address Translation), ICS (Internet Connection Sharing), WINS (Windows Internet Name Service), SNMP (Simple Network Management Protocol), NFS (Network File System), Zeroconf (Zero configuration), SMB (Server Message Block), AFP (Apple File Protocol), LPD (Line Printer Daemon), and Samba).

2.14 Identify the basic characteristics (e.g., speed, capacity, and media) of the following WAN (Wide Area Networks) technologies:

Packet switching
Circuit switching
ISDN (Integrated Services Digital Network)
FDDI (Fiber Distributed Data Interface)
T1 (T Carrier level 1)/E1/J1
T3 (T Carrier level 3)/E3/J3
OCx (Optical Carrier)
X.25

2.15 Identify the basic characteristics of the following Internet access technologies:

xDSL (Digital Subscriber Line)
Broadband Cable (Cable modem)
POTS/PSTN (Plain Old Telephone Service/Public Switched Telephone Network)
Satellite
Wireless

2.16 Define the function of the following remote access protocols and services:

RAS (Remote Access Service)
PPP (Point-to-Point Protocol)
SLIP (Serial Line Internet Protocol)
PPPoE (Point-to-Point Protocol over Ethernet)
PPTP (Point-to-Point Tunneling Protocol)
VPN (Virtual Private Network)
RDP (Remote Desktop Protocol)

2.17 Identify the following security protocols and describe their purpose and function:

IPSec (Internet Protocol Security)
L2TP (Layer 2 Tunneling Protocol)
SSL (Secure Sockets Layer)
WEP (Wired Equivalent Privacy)
WPA (Wi-Fi Protected Access)
802.1x

2.18 Identify authentication protocols (e.g., CHAP (Challenge Handshake Authentication Protocol), MS-CHAP (Microsoft Challenge Handshake Authentication Protocol), PAP (Password Authentication Protocol), RADIUS (Remote Authentication Dial-In User Service), Kerberos, and EAP (Extensible Authentication Protocol)).

Domain 3.0 - Network Implementation

3.1 Identify the basic capabilities (e.g., client support, interoperability, authentication, file and print services, application support and security) of the following server operating systems to access network resources:

UNIX/Linux/Mac OS X Server
Netware
Windows
Appleshare IP (Internet Protocol)

3.2 Identify the basic capabilities needed for client workstations to connect to and use network resources (e.g., media, network protocols, and peer and server services).

3.3 Identify the appropriate tool for a given wiring task (e.g., wire crimper, media tester/certifier, punch down tool, or tone generator).

3.4 Given a remote connectivity scenario comprised of a protocol, an authentication scheme, and physical connectivity, configure the connection. Includes connection to the following servers:

> UNIX/Linux/MAC OS X Server
> Netware
> Windows
> Appleshare IP (Internet Protocol)

3.5 Identify the purpose, benefits, and characteristics of using a firewall.

3.6 Identify the purpose, benefits, and characteristics of using a proxy service.

3.7 Given a connectivity scenario, determine the impact on network functionality of a particular security implementation (e.g., port blocking/filtering, authentication, and encryption).

3.8 Identify the main characteristics of VLANs (Virtual Local Area Networks).

3.9 Identify the main characteristics and purpose of extranets and intranets.

3.10 Identify the purpose, benefits, and characteristics of using antivirus software.

3.11 Identify the purpose and characteristics of fault tolerance:

> Power
> Link redundancy
> Storage
> Services

3.12 Identify the purpose and characteristics of disaster recovery:

> Backup/restore
> Offsite storage
> Hot and cold spares
> Hot, warm, and cold sites

Domain 4.0 - Network Support

4.1 Given a troubleshooting scenario, select the appropriate network utility from the following:

> Tracert/traceroute
> ping
> arp
> netstat
> nbtstat
> ipconfig/ifconfig

winipcfg

nslookup/dig

4.2 Given output from a network diagnostic utility (e.g., those utilities listed in objective 4.1), identify the utility and interpret the output.

4.3 Given a network scenario, interpret visual indicators (e.g., link LEDs (Light Emitting Diode) and collision LEDs (Light Emitting Diode)) to determine the nature of a stated problem.

4.4 Given a troubleshooting scenario involving a client accessing remote network services, identify the cause of the problem (e.g., file services, print services, authentication failure, protocol configuration, physical connectivity, and SOHO (Small Office/Home Office) router).

4.5 Given a troubleshooting scenario between a client and the following server environments, identify the cause of a stated problem:

UNIX/Linux/Mac OS X Server

Netware

Windows

Appleshare IP (Internet Protocol)

4.6 Given a scenario, determine the impact of modifying, adding, or removing network services (e.g., DHCP (Dynamic Host Configuration Protocol), DNS (Domain Name Service), and WINS (Windows Internet Name Service), for network resources and users.

4.7 Given a troubleshooting scenario involving a network with a particular physical topology (e.g., bus, star, mesh, or ring) and including a network diagram, identify the network area affected and the cause of the stated failure.

4.8 Given a network troubleshooting scenario involving an infrastructure (e.g., wired or wireless) problem, identify the cause of a stated problem (e.g., bad media, interference, network hardware, or environment).

4.9 Given a network problem scenario, select an appropriate course of action based on a logical troubleshooting strategy. This strategy can include the following steps:

1. Identify the symptoms and potential causes.
2. Identify the affected area.
3. Establish what has changed.
4. Select the most probable cause.
5. Implement an action plan and solution including potential effects.
6. Test the result.
7. Identify the results and effects of the solution.
8. Document the solution and process.

CHAPTER TO OBJECTIVE MATRIX

The following matrix shows the chapters that cover each objective.

Domain 1 Obj.	Chapter	Domain 2 Obj.	Chapter	Domain 3 Obj.	Chapter	Domain 4 Obj.	Chapter
1.1	1	2.1	4	3.1	7	4.1	9
1.2	3	2.2	2	3.2	7	4.2	9
1.3	3	2.3	4	3.3	9	4.3	9
1.4	2	2.4	4	3.4	7 & 8	4.4	7
1.5	2 & 3	2.5	5	3.5	8	4.5	9
1.6	2 & 8	2.6	5	3.6	8	4.6	9
1.7	2	2.7	5 & 8	3.7	8	4.7	1, 2, 9
1.8	2	2.8	5	3.8	1	4.8	9
		2.9	5	3.9	1	4.9	9
		2.10	4	3.10	8		
		2.11	4	3.11	8		
		2.12	4	3.12	8		
		2.13	8				
		2.14	6				
		2.15	6				
		2.16	8				
		2.17	8				
		2.18	8				

BOOK OUTLINE

This textbook contains nine chapters and one appendix. Each chapter has at least twenty knowledge-based questions which will prepare you for the exam. The answers to those questions are listed in the appendix. Below is a brief summary of each chapter.

- *Chapter 1, Introduction to Networking* explains the basic concepts associated with networking computers and lays the foundation for the rest of the book.

- *Chapter 2, Open Systems Interconnect (OSI) Model* covers one of the most popular standards associated with networking. This is a highly testable chapter. You should not continue on until you are completely confident you understand the concepts associated with Chapter 2.

- *Chapter 3, Project 802 and Layer 2 Protocols* describes additional standards that the networking community follows. Some of the concepts here include Ethernet and Token Ring, which are very popular network implementations.

- *Chapter 4, Network Protocols* describes what a protocol is and lists the protocols you will need to learn about to prepare for and pass the exam. The most popular protocol, TCP/IP, is discussed in Chapter 4, among others.

- *Chapter 5, Network Addressing* explains how an administrator would set up a network with an addressing scheme associated with the protocol being used. Important topics such as the TCP/IP addressing scheme and subnetting a network are described within.

- *Chapter 6, Routing and WAN Protocols* describes how multiple networks would be connected together in what is considered an intranet or Internet. There are specific components and protocols that are used to make this work successfully.

- *Chapter 7, Network Operating Systems* explains the popular operating systems used in networks today. You will learn about Windows 2000, Windows NT, Apple, NetWare, and UNIX.

- *Chapter 8, Supporting a Network* explains many of the services needed to successfully support a network. Some of those services include DHCP, DNS, NAT, and Security.

- *Chapter 9, Troubleshooting a Network* is one of the most important chapters since the Network+ exam places significant emphasis on the ability to diagnose and solve a problem. Be sure to pay attention to some of the techniques I have included, but feel free to develop your own for real-life situations.

FEATURES

At the end of each chapter there is a **Knowledge Test** where you will be presented with at least twenty questions and answers. This will provide you with the ability to quiz yourself as you go through the book. You should take the test after you read the chapter and again after you finish the book to see how well you retain the material. As a side note, write your answers on a separate sheet of paper so the next time you take the Knowledge Test, the answers are not next to the questions. Throughout each chapter *Test Tips* will assist you in studying specific objectives. They will generally appear after a subject that is more likely to be on the exam than others. However, I have also started several sections with a *Test Tip* to forewarn you that the material about to be read is of an important nature. This book also contains a glossary for hard-to-remember terms with simplified definitions, as well as an index.

ACKNOWLEDGEMENTS

First and foremost, I would like to thank my family for allowing and helping me to pursue all of my endeavors. Next, I would like to thank all of the folks at Delmar including:

>Michelle Ruelos Cannistraci
>Stacy Masucci
>Steve Helba
>Greg Clayton
>Dawn Daugherty
>Dave Garza
>Benj Gleeksman
>Andrew Crouth

Finally, I'd like to thank you for reading this book.

ANTHONY V. CHIARELLA

ABOUT THE AUTHOR

Anthony Chiarella is the president of TJC Consulting and a technical instructor. He teaches classes that range from basic computer architecture through WAN services and design. Mr. Chiarella holds dual platform engineering certifications from Microsoft, as well as Novell, and is certified in several other technologies including Cisco (CCNA), Citrix (CCA), A+, and Network+, Security+, and CTT+. He has been certified as a trainer by Microsoft (MCT) and currently holds the Certified Novell Instructor (CNI) certification by Novell. He has earned both his BA and his MA from the State University of New York, Empire State College.

His other works published by Thomson Delmar Learning include:

- *Internetworking with Cisco and Microsoft Technologies*
- *Lab Manual: Internetworking with Cisco and Microsoft Technologies*
- *Instructor's Guide to Internetworking with Cisco and Microsoft Technologies*
- *CCNA Self Study Guide, 2e*
- *CCNA Video Series*
- *Network+ Video Series*
- *Network Fundamentals Video Series*

CHAPTER 1

Introduction to Networking

OBJECTIVES

After reading this chapter you will be able to:

- Understand the different types of networks.
- Design networks.
- Define the difference between a physical and logical topology.

INTRODUCTION

Chapter 1 will introduce some of the basic networking concepts needed to pass the Network+ exam. Many of the chapters beyond Chapter 1 are built upon the concepts learned within. In this chapter you will learn some of the basic terminology used in networking, such as what a *topology* is (physical layout of a network) and what it is used for. The basic network topologies currently used will then be described, as well as some basic network services.

1.1 NETWORKING AND ITS BENEFITS

A network generally consists of a group of entities linked together (not necessarily computers). For example, a hotel chain can be considered a network of hotels, a telephone network consists of a series of switching stations linked together, and a group of people associated with one another for some reason or other is a network of people.

Computer networking is based on the same premise. Computers are linked together in groups that will facilitate the sharing of common information among one another. Regardless of location, computers in the same network give the appearance of being close to one another. It is safe to say that they are logically together, even if they are not physically together.

BENEFITS OF A COMPUTER NETWORK

The primary benefits of having a computer network are:

- Sharing resources
- Sharing information
- Centralized administration

Shared resources come in many different forms. For example, a printer shared by all users in a network is an example of a network resource. An example of shared information may include an on-line library or an employee handbook accessible by all users. However, in some circumstances there is a fine line that divides sharing resources from sharing information. For example, a document may be considered a resource although it is sharing some form of information. However, you must keep in mind that at times, although a resource may seem like information and information may seem like a resource, there is a difference between the two. It is more important to be able to see how shared information or a shared resource can be similar to one another rather than it is to find the difference between the two.

Sharing Resources

Current organizations are able to share both hardware (printers, etc.) and software (applications) between users without decreasing employee efficiency. Resources can be shared between employees who sit right next to each other, or who work in different time zones.

Sharing Information

As explained earlier, a resource and information can sometimes take on the same characteristic as one another. For example, consider sharing a spreadsheet of all employees' weekly schedules. This can be construed as both sharing information (schedule of hours to work) and sharing a resource (the actual document being shared). If the organization were using a program that was specifically tailored to the scheduling of employees rather than an ordinary spreadsheet, then it would be considered sharing information. Because the scheduling program itself is a form of *groupware* it would be a resource in this instance. The data, stored within the program, would be the shared information. Groupware allows a group of users to collaborate on a particular project.

Sharing information on a network is not as straight forward as circulating the hard copy of a spreadsheet or document for employees to read. Making the same information available on the network requires dedicated services running on the network. Such services include database services, electronic mail services, and Internet services. These services, which are the most popular network services, are discussed here:

- **Database Services.** Database services are extremely important in the Information Age. They allow for the timely access to huge amounts of data. For example, a corporation with thousands of employees can maintain their personnel records without having to utilize a single filing cabinet. All of the data is stored in a central location.

- **Electronic Mail (E-mail) Services.** E-mail services allow employees to share information effectively and efficiently. Many companies rely on e-mail as much as they do on their phone systems. There are many functions of e-mail programs that will allow for the sharing of information. For example, the first is simply sending and receiving e-mail between users. Next, you can access *newsgroups* through e-mail programs. Newsgroups allow for threaded discussions, and are used by groups of people who have a common interest.

- **Internet Services.** Internet or web services allow a company to set up and distribute information to the rest of the world. However, it is possible to set up private web services so information is only viewed and used by the employees within the company. For example, an organization may set up web services on the company network and post the employee handbook on the internal website so employees can have access to it whenever they may need it. This would reduce the cost of printing and allow for changes made to the document to be viewed almost immediately. Internal web solutions are considered *Intranets*. Another popular web solution is called an *Extranet*. An extranet is where a company allows an "external" company to access their private Intranet. This practice is popular for companies that have contracts with one another where they are allowed access to each other's data for, say, ordering supplies.

Centralized Administration

The third benefit of having a network in an organization is centralized administration of the resources and information that will be shared among users. Centralized administration consists of locating all of the resources within close proximity (physically or logically) of one another to simplify the administration of the network. For example, if there were twenty users on the same network, it would be easier for a network administrator to have all users save data to one shared hard disk drive. This would allow him to only have to back up one computer, rather than twenty.

Centralized administration does not stop at backing up data; it also means having a central focus point for user accounts, security, and administration of the entire network. This central focus point usually consists of one administrator or a small (relative to company size) group of them. This ensures that the flow of information moves smoothly. This allows the other employees of the company to focus on his own work with the confidence that his data will be there in the morning.

1.2 BASIC COMPONENTS OF A NETWORK

There are several components involved in the communication process that justify the existence and govern the communication process of a computer network. These components pertain to the passage of information in any network, regardless of whether it is a network of computers, hotels, or people. The three components include having something to share, having lines of communication to pass the shared information from one entity to the next, and abiding by a specific set of rules that will govern the communication process. All three of these components must be in place for a network of any kind.

Sharing

As discussed earlier, sharing can consist of sharing resources or sharing information. In either case, to justify the existence of a network, something has to be shared.

Line of Communication

A line of communication is comprised of some form of transmission media. Transmission media consists of *bound media* (wire) and *unbound media* (wireless) that allow networked components to remain in contact with one another. A bound technology refers to signals that are transmitted within the confines of a cable. Two examples are copper wire, which transmits electrical signals, and fiber optic wire, which transmits signals composed of light.

An unbound transmission consists of data that is sent from one point to another without being confined to a wire, thus wireless transmission. Some wireless technologies include microwave, infrared, and radio frequencies.

Rules

For successful networking to take place, many rules must be followed and specific guidelines be met. Rules for networking are governed by *protocols*. A protocol is an agreed-upon format of signals for sending data between two components. For components to communicate successfully, they must all be following the same rules or using the same protocol in the network.

1.3 NETWORK COMPUTING MODELS

A network computing model defines the processing method that computers in a network use to complete a processing task. There are three network computing models that will be described within. The first model is *centralized computing*. This type of processing is most popular with mainframes. *Distributed computing*, which is most popular within a *client/server* environment, is the next model discussed. The term client/server simply means that two computers work together in a way that allows one computer to request data (client) and the other to provide data (server). The third type of processing defined is *cooperative computing*, which consists of multiple machines working together to complete the same task.

CENTRALIZED COMPUTING

Centralized computing uses a central computer with a powerful processor to complete all processing tasks. The central computer, in most cases, is wired to a series of stations identified as *dumb terminals*, see Figure 1-1.

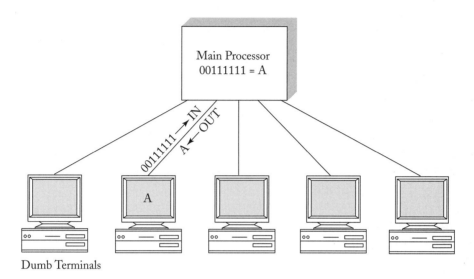

Dumb Terminals

Figure 1-1. *Centralized Computing*

A dumb terminal does not have the ability to process any information. It is responsible for providing users with access to the central computer's storage and processing capabilities. The central computer polls each dumb terminal to determine if there is any information that needs to be processed. If there is data instructions to be processed, the central node will gather and process the information.

DISTRIBUTED COMPUTING

Distributed computing is the term used to identify the processing type used in a network where each machine is capable of processing its own information. The workstations that users sit at are more than capable of processing complex sets of data instructions. There are several network configurations that fall into this category. They are *client/server, peer-to-peer, server based*, and *front-end/back-end*.

Client/Server

A client/server network consists of two primary components: servers and clients. A *server* is a computer with the primary responsibility of servicing requests as they arrive. So, in essence, a server is a provider. The *client*, on the other hand, consists of any computer on the network that submits requests to the server.

Server. As described, the server is a computer, however the computer acting as the server has an additional service running. The server service is a network service built into the operating system. The server service helps differentiate a *desktop operating system (OS)*, such as Windows 2000 Professional, from a *Network Operating System (NOS)*, such as Windows 2000 Server.

 Test Tip: The server service is used to service requests.

Network operating systems come in many different varieties from a diversified group of vendors. Several of them are listed below:

- Microsoft Windows NT Server
- Microsoft Windows 2000 Server
- Microsoft Windows 2003 Server
- Novell Netware
- UNIX
- Linux
- Apple

There are many different roles for a server in a network today. Some of the roles of servers in a network include, but are certainly not limited to:

- Directory Services. This service provides for the authentication of users in a network. One of the core services of a server in a client/server configuration is user log-ons. The servers maintain a listing of specific rights and permissions to use, be given, or to be withheld from users. These rights and permissions define the users' access capabilities in a network. Network administrators are usually given more rights and permissions than typical users.

 Test Tip: Directory services are the core of a client/server network.

- Application Services. These services provide users with the capability to run applications from designated servers in the network.
- File Services. File services allow users to store data in a central location.
- Print Services. This service allows for the ability to enable printing in a networked environment so users can print, regardless of whether or not they are physically connected to the printer.
- Web Services. Web services allow a server to host web sites.

- E-mail Services. These services provide users with the ability to send and receive e-mail. Often, e-mail services are an add-on product that must be purchased separately from the network operating system.

Client. The client in a client/server environment is normally a PC-based workstation. The term workstation is often used when identifying a computer used by a worker in a business. Like the server, a client is normally a service running within an operating system. Client computers use desktop operating systems rather than network operating systems.

The client does not have to consist of a complete desktop operating system, although in many cases it does. For example, Novell's client, which is called Client 32, is not an operating system. It is loaded onto a PC that is currently running a desktop operating system and takes control of the networking functions of the operating system. The client service for Windows 2000 is a built-in component of the operating system.

Here is a list of desktop operating systems and client software that can be loaded onto any computer, provided that it meets the minimum hardware requirements found in the operating system's documentation:

- Microsoft Windows 95, 98, 98 SE, ME

- Microsoft Windows NT Workstation

- Microsoft Windows 2000 Professional

- Microsoft Windows XP

- Novell Client 32 (Client 32 comes in different versions for each of the popular operating systems)

- UNIX

- Linux

- Apple

All client workstations in a network provide the same basic services. These services consist of:

- The ability to connect to the server through network services.

- They have local security mechanisms, which are based on the vendor. Some local security mechanisms include password policies and file system permissions.

- They provide authentication to the network through some type of a log-on window. Authentication can also consist of logging on to the local client rather than the network.

Peer-to-Peer

In a peer-to-peer network, the basic premise of distributed computing is the same. There are both requesters and providers that have the capability of processing their own information. However, there are some definite distinctions between the two, such as each computer acting as both a client and a server. This is true of some of the client/server operating systems already discussed. For example, all of the Windows products previously discussed have the ability to be both a client and a server. As a matter of fact, when any Windows 2000 machine is turned on, both the workstation and the server service are running, allowing for a true peer-to-peer configuration straight out of the box. Microsoft products refer to a peer-to-peer network as a *workgroup*.

The major difference between a client/server network and a peer-to-peer network is that there are no directory services available for users to authenticate to and be given or denied permissions to resources on the network in a peer-to-peer. There can, however, be servers in a peer-to-peer network. The servers in a peer-to-peer network normally provide file, print, and application services. There are additional characteristics that make peer-to-peer networking different from client/server networking. They are listed in Table 1-1.

TABLE 1-1. PEER-TO PEER VS. CLIENT/SERVER

PEER TO PEER	CLIENT/SERVER
No directory service	Directory service
No centralized administration	Centralized aministration
Ten computers or less	At least 10 computers
No real security	Many security options
Low administrative overhead	High administrative overhead
Low cost	High cost

Server Based

Server based is a hybrid of centralized computing and distributed computing. It has remnants of centralized computing because all processing tasks can be completed by the server, yet there is a client program that interfaces with the server, which represents the client/server environment. In many instances the client is more than capable of processing its own data. However, in this configuration the goal is to allow the client to run specific programs from the server.

The server service is called *terminal services*. Clients open a connection to the server and execute programs that are installed on the server. In this type of network it is important to have a very powerful server because the program the user is executing is loaded into the memory of the server, and the server's processor is completing most of the data instructions. However, it seems as though the user is running the program. The programs running on the server are called *sessions*.

Each user running a program on the server has a separate session open. The server allocates resources to each session and runs them independently of one another. Because each program receives a set of resources, the server must have an abundance of RAM and, preferably, multiple processors.

Front-End/Back-End Designs

This type of network design is used in specialized networking applications such as large databases, indexing services, web services, e-mail services, or a combination of them. The term front-end is used to describe a workstation or server that is running a program that will eventually interface with another server called the back-end. For example, a company is using a database to maintain records of purchases. A user, sitting at a workstation, is adding records to a database. The workstation being used to add the number of purchases to the database is the front-end (the users interface into the back-end). The database is the back-end.

The company's database is designed to update a second database (located at corporate headquarters) every night at midnight. Coincidentally, all ten of the company's stores are updating the database server at headquarters at approximately the same time. Once this process begins, the database in the store begins to perform the role of front-end processor, and the server at headquarters is the back-end.

COLLABORATIVE COMPUTING

Collaborative computing is a spin-off of distributed computing. This network computing model consists of multiple machines working together to accomplish the same task. Applications, complex databases, and other programs are being developed to use multiple machines to complete processing tasks cooperatively.

1.4 NETWORK TYPES

There are several types of networks in the industry that are governed by such bodies such as the Institute for Electronics and Electrical Engineers (*IEEE*). Networks are often categorized by size. The types of networks that will be discussed within are Local Area Networks (LANs), Campus Area Networks (CANs), Metropolitan Area Networks (MANs), Wide Area Networks (WANs), and Virtual Local Area Networks (VLANs).

 Test Tip: The Network+ exam gives scenarios of how a network is set up, and you should understand what type of network you are dealing with in the question.

LOCAL AREA NETWORK (LAN)

A local area network (or LAN) is a small grouping of computers in comparison to the other standards to be defined. The size of a LAN is usually confined to one building or a floor within a building. Often, a LAN is installed in a small- to moderate-size company. Local area networks provide users with high bandwidth because they are on the same type of shared media (see Figure 1-2).

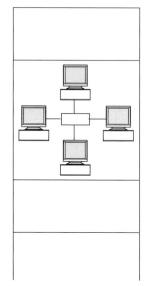

Figure 1-2. *LAN Within a Building*

CAMPUS AREA NETWORK (CAN)

Campus area networks (or CANs) are normally located where two or more LANs need to be connected together. A CAN is normally geographically larger than a LAN and often maintains a link between two or more buildings. A good example of a CAN is a college campus with several buildings connected together with a high-speed link (see Figure 1-3).

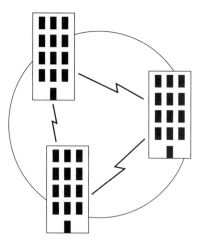

Figure 1-3. *Campus Area Network*

When installing a CAN, the media that links the buildings together, in most cases, is owned or requested to be installed by the company or school. *Bandwidth*, which is the data capacity of the medium, in a CAN is going to be high on each end of the CAN (at each LAN), but can become slower crossing the link that connects the LANs together since this interface becomes the bottleneck for all data crossing the link (see Figure 1-4).

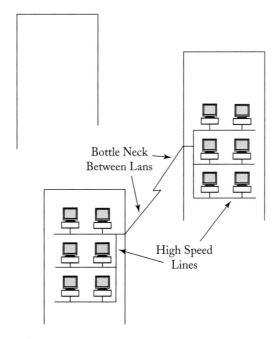

Figure 1-4. *Bottleneck Between LANs*

METROPOLITAN AREA NETWORK (MAN)

Metropolitan area networks (MANs) are defined as being larger than a CAN, yet within the limits of a metropolitan city. Campus area networks are often linked together through a MAN. The cabling for a MAN is often leased (for a recurring monthly fee) through a local telecommunications provider or *local exchange carrier (LEC)* servicing the local calling area, also known as the *Local Access Transport Area (LATA)*. Figure 1.5 shows an example of a MAN within a LATA.

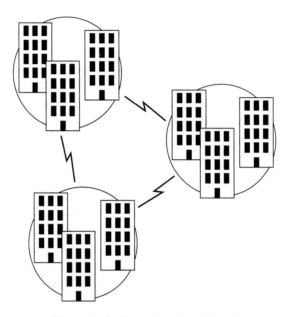

Figure 1-5. *Metropolitan Area Network*

If there is a problem associated with the wire, it becomes the LEC's responsibility. Bandwidth in a MAN is going to be limited to the connection speeds of the lines available through the LEC. If the LEC offers high bandwidth interconnectivity between sites, then a bottleneck is less likely. However, in most cases the LAN speeds will be faster than the MAN speeds, creating a bottleneck possibility at the MAN. Remember, the higher the bandwidth, the higher the cost of the service.

WIDE AREA NETWORK (WAN)

A wide area network (WAN) is a series of connections that span large geographic areas. WANs are often nationwide, and they can cross international boundaries. The

Internet falls into the WAN category and is often identified as a Global Area Network (or GAN) because it spans the entire globe (see Figure 1-6).

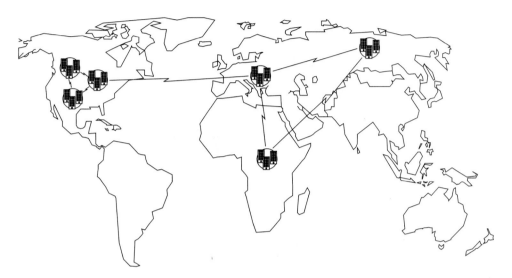

Figure 1-6. *Wide Area Network*

Often, the cost of the WAN is related to the amount of bandwidth requested. The WAN provider will charge a monthly fee for the service. Any problems with the wire are the responsibility of the provider. The WAN service providers are often defined as *inter-exchange carriers (IXC)*, and they connect multiple LATAs together (see Figure 1-7).

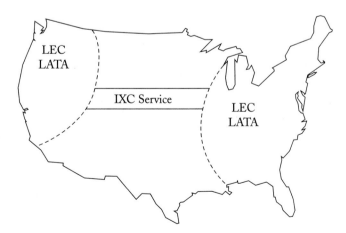

Figure 1-7. *Inter Exchange Carrier*

Currently, the bandwidth available on WAN links often causes a bottleneck between sites, and it is advisable to keep applications and services local to users if at all possible. Different WAN services are available in different locations of the world.

VIRTUAL LOCAL AREA NETWORK (VLAN)

Virtual local area networks (or VLANs) are becoming extremely popular. A VLAN provides the ability to place workstations that may not be within the same LAN into a logical group of computers that have some of the same characteristics of a LAN. However, workstations do not need to be on the same cable and may be geographically separated from one another. This is useful in some instances where users who may be located in different buildings have the same connectivity requirements. For example, assume that several users spread out between three LANs are assigned to a month-long group project. The users, regardless of their physical LAN locations, can be placed into the same VLAN for the duration of the project. Neither the users' workstations nor the users themselves would have to physically move from building to building. Figure 1.8 shows several users physically located in a CAN but virtually in a LAN, hence the term VLAN.

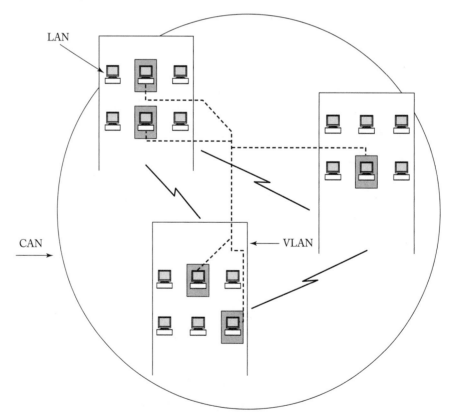

Figure 1-8. *Virtual Local Area Network*

1.5 NETWORK TOPOLGIES

The word "topology" simply means configuration or functional design of a set of elements. A network topology is the functional design of the components of a network. There are two topologies to be concerned with: physical topology and logical topology. A *physical topology* describes how the network cables are laid out. A *logical topology* describes how the data accesses and travels on the medium. This section of the chapter deals with the physical topology.

PHYSICAL TOPOLOGY

As already explained, networks can be categorized by several different methods. They have been described as processing models as well as LANs, CANs, MANs, etc. Now they will be described based on the layout of their wire. In other words, how the machines in the physical network physically connect with one another. When examining the topologies themselves, realize that these topologies can pertain to the nodes within a LAN, or even LANs within a WAN.

The most popular physical topologies are: bus, star, ring, mesh, and hybrid. These topologies, their advantages and disadvantages are described below:

Bus Topology

A bus topology consists of having all nodes connected to a single cable, often called a backbone or a trunk, in an open-loop fashion (the ends of the wire are not connected together). Figure 1.9 shows a bus network.

 Test Tip: Terms to look for are "open loop" and "in a series."

Star Topology

A star topology consists of having all nodes wired through a central device (see Figure 1-9).

 Test Tip: Terms to look for are "scalable," "easy to troubleshoot," "central device," and "hub."

Ring Topology

Traditional ring topologies consist of having all nodes wired to a single cable in a closed-loop format (see Figure 1-9).

Mesh Topology

A mesh topology has a connection to every other component in the network. This provides path redundancy because if one of the links goes down, there is still a path for the data to take to reach its final destination. A realistic use of the mesh topology is wiring multiple sites in a WAN together, rather than wiring multiple workstations together in a LAN (see Figure 1-9).

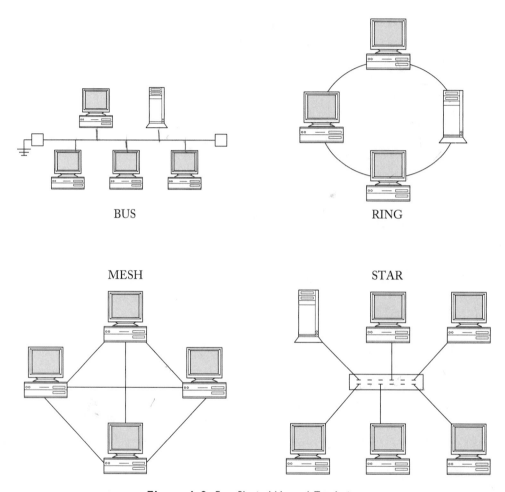

BUS   RING

MESH   STAR

Figure 1-9. *Four Physical Network Topologies*

Test Tip: Terms to look for on the test are "most connections," "redundancy," and "multiple paths."

Wireless Topology

Wireless topology consists of using devices called wireless access points (WAP) that wireless nodes can send signals to. WAPs are attached to the network cable so the signals can eventually make it to the network (see Figure 1-10).

• Signals can be interfered with by other devices operating at the same range of the radio spectrum.

Figure 1-10. *Wireless Topology*

Table 1.2 compares the advantages and disadvantages of the bus, star, ring, mesh, and wireless topologies.

TABLE 1-2. PHYSICAL TOPOLOGY COMPARISON

TOPOLOGY	ADVANTAGES	DISADVANTAGES
BUS	Easy to install Inexpensive	Difficult to reconfigure Difficult to expand Cable fault affects entire network Difficult to troubleshoot
STAR	Easy to troubleshoot Easy to reconfigure Easy to expand	Difficult to install Failure of the central node will affect entire network
RING	Easy to troubleshoot Easy to install Dual ring is fault tolerant	Failure of one node affects entire network Difficult to configure closed loop Failure of media in a single, closed loop ring will affect entire network
MESH	Fault tolerant, redundant paths Easy to troubleshoot	Expensive Difficult to install Difficult to reconfigure
WIRELESS	Easy to install Easy to reconfigure Installation is inexpensive	Unsecure signals Failure of a WAP brings network down Subject to interference from other devices operating at the same range of the radio spectrum (cordless phones and microwave ovens).

Hybrid Topology

A hybrid topology consists of having multiple topologies defined above, in the same network. Hybrid topologies often refer to large networks that often consist of multiple LANs. The Internet is an example of a hybrid network (see Figure 1-11).

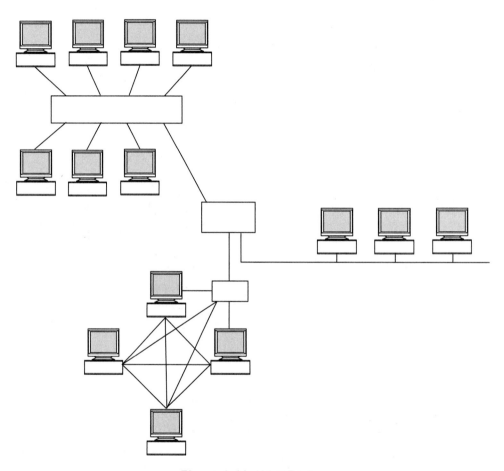

Figure 1-11. *Hybrid Topology*

LOGICAL TOPOLOGIES

A logical topology is the method data uses when traveling from one node to the next on a wire. There are two logical topologies to be concerned with: bus and ring.

Logical Bus Topology

The *logical bus topology* states that when data is placed on the network cable it will travel to all nodes connected to that segment. The bus topology offers a competitive environment for data to access the wire. Nodes attempt to transmit data with no priority. Whichever signal makes it on the wire first is the one that will be transmitted. There are several rules that are adhered to. In this topology, there is a fair amount of bandwidth that is consumed by *data collisions*. Data collisions occur when multiple computers attempt to transmit data at the same time in a network, and the two separate streams of data collide (see Figure 1-12).

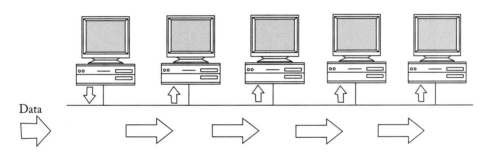

Figure 1-12. *Logical Bus Topology*

Logical Ring Topology

In the *logical ring topology*, a *frame* (term used to identify data sent from a node) called a token, is generated and placed on the network. The token travels around the ring from node to node, giving each station an opportunity to communicate. When a machine that needs to communicate receives the token, it appends the token with its data. The token and the data are then placed back on the wire and again sent from node to node until the token and the data reach the destination node. After the destination machine reads the data, it retransmits the token onto the wire. The token is passed around the ring to the original sending station, which will release the token for the next node to have the opportunity to transmit on the wire. In traditional logical ring topologies, only one token is allowed on the network at any given time. However, more recent versions of this technology allow for multiple tokens to be on the ring at once. Figure 1-13 shows data traveling in a logical ring topology.

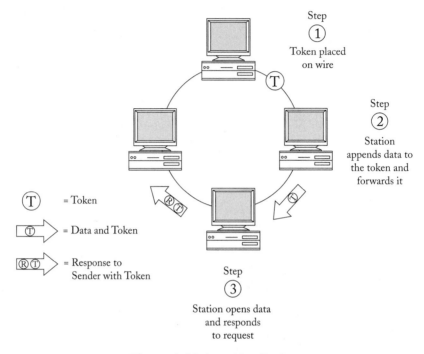

Figure 1-13. *Logical Ring Topology*

Networks combine the physical and logical topologies described above. For example, some networks use a physically-wired star and a logical bus topology to transmit the data. Hence, it is a logical bus running over a physical star (or a star-wired bus), as shown in Figure 1-14.

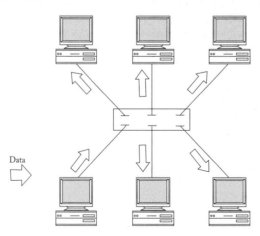

Figure 1-14. *Star-Wired Bus*

Another example includes a physically-wired bus and a logical bus together, as well as a star-wired ring. As stated earlier, traditional rings were wired with a single cable. However, current ring topologies are wired in a star format to prevent the complete failure of a ring if the single cable fails. Although the current ring topology is wired as a star, the components that connect each node to the network maintain the continuity of a ring (see Figure 1-15).

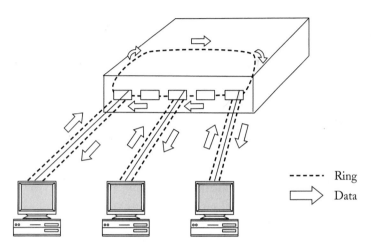

- - - - - Ring

⇒ Data

Figure 1-15. *Star-Wired Ring*

CHAPTER SUMMARY

This chapter focused on some topics that are key to the success of a Network+ candidate. Many subjects were covered; be sure to understand the topics covered in this chapter before going on to the next. Some of the key topics included network services, network types, and network topologies. Complete the Chapter One Knowledge Test before going on to the next chapter.

KNOWLEDGE TEST

Select one answer for each question unless otherwise directed in the question.

1. Which network is wired in an open loop format, with each node connected to the node next to it in a series?
   A. Bus
   B. Ring
   C. Star
   D. Mesh

2. You are asked to install a network for a company that has six computers. Security is not a concern at this point in time, however it may be in the future. What network computing model would you propose?
   A. Distributed processing (peer-to-peer)
   B. Server based
   C. Distributed processing (client/server)
   D. Centralized processing

3. Which networking topology has multiple connections per node?
   A. Bus
   B. Ring
   C. Star
   D. Mesh

4. In which computing model are all processing tasks done on one computer?
   A. Server based
   B. Distributed
   C. Cooperative
   D. Centralized

5. Which networking topology connects computers through multiple paths for redundancy?
   A. Bus
   B. Ring
   C. Star
   D. Mesh

6. Your company is going to rebuild its network. They would like it to be easy to troubleshoot, as well as scalable for the future. Which topology would you recommend?
   A. Bus
   B. Ring
   C. Star
   D. Mesh

7. In the exhibit there are four topologies shown. Write the letter of topology in the space shown.
   A. Bus   _____
   B. Ring   _____
   C. Star   _____
   D. Mesh   _____

8. In a peer-to-peer network, the number of nodes should be _____ or below.
   A. 10
   B. 15
   C. 20
   D. 25

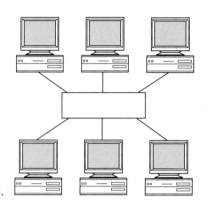

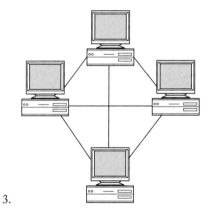

1.

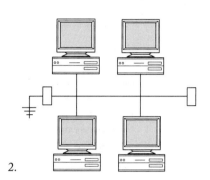

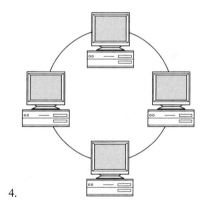

2.

3.

4.

Exhibit

9. What distributed computing model uses terminal services?
   A. Client/server
   B. Peer-to-peer
   C. Server based
   D. Front-end/back-end

10. What service allows computers to respond to requests from other nodes?
    A. Requester service
    B. Server service
    C. Client Service
    D. Responder service

11. What service allows users to authenticate to a network?
    A. Directory service
    B. Authenticator service
    C. E-mail service
    D. File service

12. If the users in your network cannot print to the network printer, which service on your server may be causing the problem?
    A. File service
    B. Directory service
    C. E-mail Service
    D. Print service

13. The company you work for has 100 nodes in a single building. What type of network does your company have?
    A. LAN
    B. CAN
    C. MAN
    D. WAN

14. What type of logical topology has the most data collisions?
    A. Logical ring
    B. Logical client/server
    C. Logical Bus
    D. Logical Star

15. What type of logical topology passes data from one node to the next in an orderly fashion?
    A. Logical ring
    B. Logical client/server
    C. Logical Bus
    D. Logical Star

16. You have users in different geographical locations that are supposed to be working on the same project together. What kind of network can you implement so they are logically located with one another.
    A. LAN
    B. VLAN
    C. MAN
    D. WAN

17. What is the physical layout of the components on a network called?
    A. Network type
    B. Logical topology
    C. Segment
    D. Physical topology

18. What service allows your computer to request data from another computer?
    A. Client
    B. Server
    C. Requester service
    D. The OS service

19. What controls how data is placed on the wire in a network?
    A. Network type
    B. Logical topology
    C. Segment
    D. Physical topology

20. What is a protocol?
    A. Rules that define communication standards.
    B. Designs that define communication standards.
    C. Rules that define design standards.
    D. Logical design of a network.

knowledge TEST

CHAPTER 2

Open Systems Interconnect (OSI) Reference Model and Network Devices

OBJECTIVES

At the end of this chapter you will be able to:

- Explain what the OSI Reference Model is.
- Explain what happens at each layer of the OSI Model.
- Describe the different types of network devices.
- Understand at what layer of the OSI Model network components operate.

INTRODUCTION

This chapter takes an in-depth look at the Open Systems Interconnect Reference Model, the OSI Model for short. An internetworking model is a conceptual framework that is normally used as a guideline when designing hardware or software used in the data communication process. Many standards are defined within the OSI Model. This chapter also takes a look at the hardware components that operate at each layer. Protocols also operate at different layers of the OSI Model, however protocols that operate at the different layers will be discussed in Chapter 3 and Chapter 4.

2.1 OPEN SYSTEMS INTERCONNECT (OSI) REFERENCE MODEL

In this section, a description of the internetworking model used most often in the networking industry is given. Network models act as blueprints for networking professionals and vendors to be used as developmental guides. Before discussing what the OSI Model is and how it facilitates network communication, it is important to understand that it is theoretical—it is not a physical component and cannot be seen nor touched. However, it does provide the blueprints of the current internetworking infrastructure.

The OSI Model is designed in a layered fashion with one layer built on top of the layer below it. Development of the OSI Model began in the late 1970s by the International Standards Organization (ISO) and consists of seven layers (see Figure 2-1).

7	Application	**A**ll	**A**way
6	Presentation	**P**eople	**P**izza
5	Session	**S**eem	**S**ausage
4	Transport	**T**o	**T**hrow
3	Network	**N**eed	**N**ot
2	Data-Link	**D**ata	**D**o
1	Physical	**P**rocessing	**P**lease

Figure 2-1. *Seven-Layered OSI Model with Tips to Remember It*

Having a layered model provides a logical process flow by defining tasks and roles at various levels of concept to accomplish communication. Layered models also enhance the ability to understand, learn, and teach the concepts within. They also allow for inter-operability between multiple vendors and standard makers.

Each layer has a different role to play in the communication process. When designing network devices and protocols, the vendor must decide at which layer of the OSI Model the component will fit best. Each layer of the OSI Model will be detailed in this chapter. However, before discussing each layer of the model, it is important to have an understanding of how each of the seven layers transfers data to the layers below it *(encapsulation)* and to the layers above it *(de-encapsulation)*.

ENCAPSULATION AND DE-ENCAPSULATION

Encapsulation and de-encapsulation are processes that data go through during network communication. Each layer in the OSI Model has a separate responsibility during the communications process. Before user data can be sent onto the wire, the sending or source device is responsible for encapsulating it. This process is invisible to the end user, and it consists of adding control and/or address information to the data at each layer. The information is added to the data in the form of *headers* and/or *trailers*. A header consists of information placed at the beginning of a data stream, while a trailer consists of information placed at the end of a data stream. When the data is taken off the wire, the receiving or destination device must de-encapsulate the data by stripping off the control and address information, layer by layer, before presenting it to the user. Encapsulation and de-encapsulation are further described below.

Encapsulation

Encapsulation facilitates communication between two networking components. For example, a user is attempting to access a file on a network file server using a file transfer protocol (FTP) application. The FTP request will act as the application data for this example and is considered a Protocol Data Unit (PDU), or simply "data" in the encapsulation process.

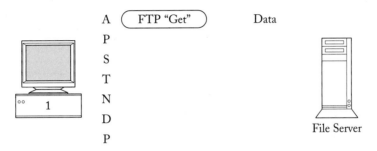

The FTP "GET" Command as Data

The FTP "GET" command, which is ultimately an application layer protocol command, is passed down to the presentation layer. The presentation layer will add information to the data stating what presentation layer protocol the user's computer is using.

A
P   (FTP "Get") P   Data
S
T
N
D
P

Data With Added Presentation Layer Information

The data will then be passed down to the session layer. The session layer will add control information.

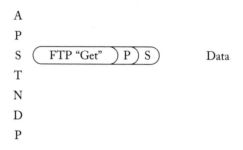

Data With Added Session Layer Information

Next, the data will be given to the transport layer. At this layer, the protocol responsible for delivery will encapsulate the data. The data has been a continuous stream until this point and did not undergo a physical change. In networking, the data stream cannot be continuous; it has to be broken down into chunks of data so all computers on the wire have a chance to communicate. If it is not broken down, communication would be next to impossible for any machine except the machine that is communicating at that exact moment. At the transport layer, the data stream is converted (or encapsulated) into *segments*.

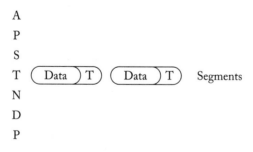

Segmented Data With Added Transport Layer Information

The segmented data is then passed down to the network layer, which encapsulates the segment into a *packet* or *datagram*.

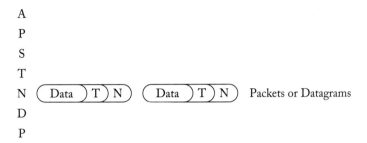

Pocketed Data with Added Network Layer Information

The data, now in the form of a packet, is passed down to the data-link layer. The data-link layer encapsulates the packet into a *frame* and then passes it down to the physical layer which transmits it across the wire as a series of bits (ones and zeroes).

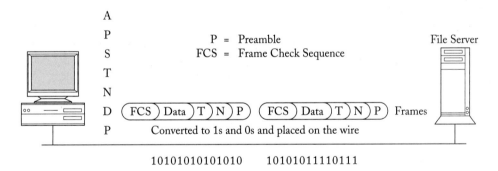

Framed Data with Added Data-Link Layer Information

De-Encapsulation

When the ones and zeroes reach the destination machine, they are de-encapsulated. The process of de-encapsulation is the exact opposite of the process of encapsulation. The control information that was added to the data is now stripped off at the same layer that the sending machine added it. The ones and zeroes enter at the physical layer and are handed up the OSI Model, each layer stripping the information its peer-layer added.

Test Tip: The PDU at each layer is: A, P, S = Data; T = segment; N = packet or datagram; D = frame; P = bits/1s and 0s.

Peer Layer Communication

Peer layer communication is the process of each of the seven OSI layers in one machine communicating with their peer OSI layers in another machine, for example data-link layer to data-link layer, network layer to network layer, etc. The only layer of the OSI Model that physically communicates with its peer layer is the physical layer because the two machines are connected to one another by physical layer components, such as the wire and connectors (see Figure 2-2).

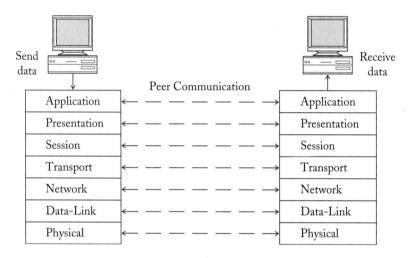

Figure 2-2. *OSI Peer-Layer Communication*

2.2 PHYSICAL LAYER (LAYER 1)

Now that encapsulation and de-encapsulation have been explained, we will examine each layer of the OSI Model. Each of the layers will be discussed based on the processes that take place at that layer and hardware that works at that layer. When vendors develop hardware or software for network communication, the product is normally designed to map to one or more layers of the OSI Model. The products that map to the lower layers of the model are not as intelligent as those that map to the higher layers.

Layer 1 of the OSI Model defines the electrical, mechanical, and functional specifications for activating and deactivating the physical connectivity between machines on the network. The physical layer does not guarantee that communication between machines on a network will be successful. However, it does guarantee that there is a path available for the ones and zeroes to travel over. To understand exactly how signals are sent and received, signaling standards are explained next.

SIGNAL AND WIRING STANDARDS

Signal Standards

Signaling methods for transmitting data are defined at the physical layer, specifically *broadband* and *baseband*.

- **Broadband** is an analog signaling method that uses multiple frequencies to send and receive data. Multiple broadband signals can reside on the same carrier (cable). Broadband signals are sent unidirectionally. However, more than one can reside on the cable at any time.

- **Baseband** is a signaling method that uses digital signals to send and receive data. In a baseband transmission, only one signal can be on the wire at a time. A single baseband signal consumes the entire cable. Once the signal is on the wire, it travels in both directions until it reaches its destination or is consumed by a terminator.

Wiring Standards

In addition to signal standards, the physical layer defines wiring standards for the physical topology of a network. The physical topologies are bus, star, ring, mesh, wireless, and hybrid. These were covered in Chapter 1.

ADDITIONAL PHYSICAL LAYER HARDWARE COMPONENTS

Many hardware components are mapped directly to one layer of the OSI Model, however there are instances where a component can map to several layers. The hardware components that map to the physical layer are considered the least intelligent (in terms of what they can do with data) and consist of transmission media and connectors, hubs, repeaters, Channel Service Unit/Data Service Unit (CSU/DSUs), transceivers, modems and mulitplexers.

Transmission Media

There are several types of transmission media and many connectors used to interconnect devices on a LAN. The transmission media discussed within consists of copper cable, fiber optic cable, and wireless technologies.

Copper

Copper transmission media consists of shielded or unshielded twisted pair and various coaxial cables.

Twisted Pair. Twisted pair cable consists of a two copper wires twisted together. There are normally several pairs of wire that make up a twisted pair cable. The core of each wire is made up of a solid wire or stranded copper wire.

• Shielded Twisted Pair (STP)

  STP has a metal sheath wrapped around the wires to prevent electromagnetic interference (EMI) or cross talk, which is the process of signals from one copper wire interfering with signals on a separate copper wire. STP is generally more difficult to install than unshielded twisted pair (UTP) because of its stiffness.

• Unshielded Twisted Pair (UTP)

  UTP is very common and consists of four pairs of copper wire twisted together, as seen in Figure 2-3. It is more prone to EMI than STP because it does not use the metal shield, and it is less expensive than STP (see Figure 2-4).

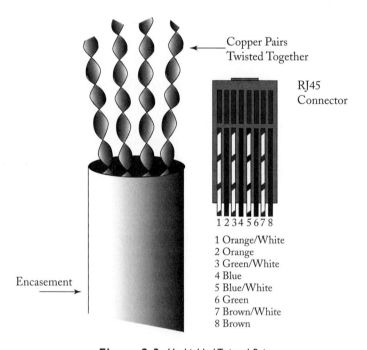

Copper Pairs
Twisted Together

RJ45
Connector

1 2 3 4 5 6 7 8

1 Orange/White
2 Orange
3 Green/White
4 Blue
5 Blue/White
6 Green
7 Brown/White
8 Brown

Encasement

Figure 2-3. *Unshielded Twisted Pair*

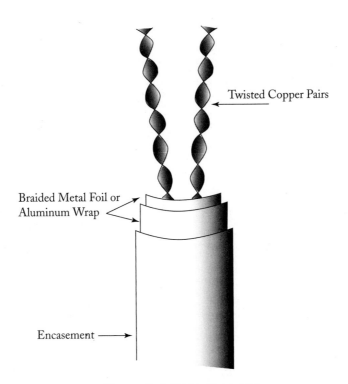

Twisted Copper Pairs

Braided Metal Foil or
Aluminum Wrap

Encasement

Figure 2-4. *Shielded Twisted Pair*

Twisted pair standards are identified based on several categories used today.

Category	Description
1	Voice only (UTP)
2	Four twisted pairs, 4 Mbps, Token Ring (UTP only)
3	Four twisted pairs, 10 Mbps, Ethernet
4	Four twisted pairs, 16 Mbps, Token Ring
5	Four twisted pairs, up to 100 Mbps, Ethernet, Fast Ethernet
5e	Four twisted pairs, up to 1000 Mbps, Gigabit Ethernet
6	Four twisted pairs, 155 Mbps, Fast Ethernet
6e	Four twisted pairs, used for 10GBase Standard, up to 10 Gbps
7	Four twisted pairs, 1000 Mbps, Gigabit Ethernet

The cable is terminated with an RJ-45 connector, which is similar to yet slightly larger than an RJ-11 telephone connector. A crimping tool is used to connect the RJ-45 to the UTP. Be sure to use matching cables and connectors. For example, if the cable has a stranded core, use stranded-core connectors. Once the crimping is done, use a cable tester to ensure it was done correctly (see Figure 2-5).

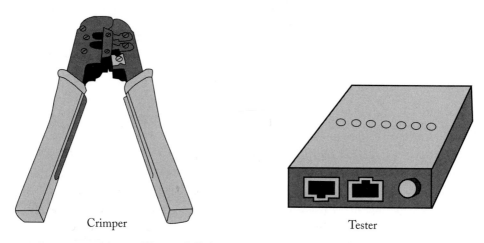

Crimper

Tester

Figure 2-5. *RJ-45 Crimper and Cable Tester*

Coaxial. Coax cable consists of a solid or stranded copper core protected by a plastic sheath, which is then surrounded by a braided or solid metal shield to prevent EMI and to provide ground. There are several types of coax cable used in networking. Each of them require resistance at both ends of the wire and ground at one end of the wire.

- RG58u

    RG58u can carry a signal for 185 meters, it is highly flexible, and transmits data at 10 Mbps. It is often referred to as Thinnet. Thinnet uses a British Naval Connector (BNC) and a T connector to make the connection between node and cable. This cable requires 50 ohms of resistance at both ends of the network to prevent *signal bounce*. Signal bounce occurs when a single signal continuously traverses the same cable segment, preventing other nodes from having access to the cable. Remember, only one baseband signal can be on the cable at any moment. By placing a terminator at both ends of the wire, the signal will be consumed when it reaches the end of the segment (see Figure 2-6).

- RG8 or RG11

    RG8 and RG11 are thicker than Thinnet, therefore they can carry a signal for longer distances, 500 meters to be precise. It is less flexible than Thinnet, transfers data at 10 Mbps, implemented as a network backbone, and referred to as

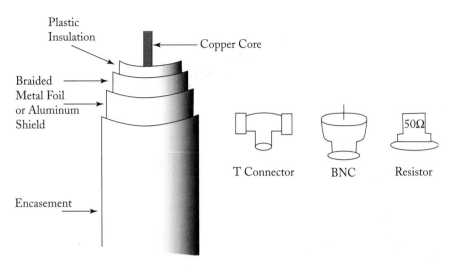

Figure 2-6. *Thinnet Coaxial Cable*

Thicknet. Nodes connect to a transceiver, which is a network component given its name because it is a transmitter and receiver of signals. Most network adapters have the transceiver built in to it, however the Thicknet standard uses an external transceiver that is known as a vampire tap or piercing tap. The network adapter connects to the transceiver through a fifteen-pin auxiliary unit interface, or AUI. The transceiver is then clamped onto the backbone itself. This cable requires 50 ohms of resistance at both ends of the network (see Figure 2-7).

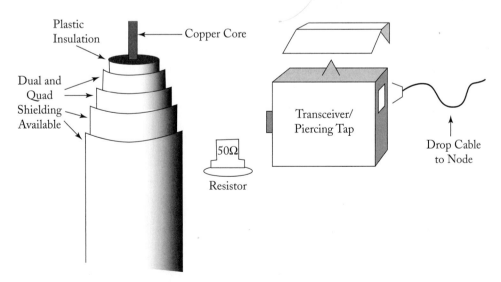

Figure 2-7. *Thicknet Coaxial Cable*

- RG59

    RG59 is thicker than Thinnet and thinner than Thicknet. This is the coax cable that carries cable television signals and is often used to provide Internet access to customers. RG59 use 75 ohms of resistance.

F-Type Connector. The F-Type connector is a common connector, used with coaxial cable. Its most popular use is for connecting televisions and VCRs to a cable television service provider's service. These connectors have recently also become popular with network technologies, simply due to the popular practice of connecting home networks to cable modems. Cable service providers have capitalized on the fact that their existing wired infrastructure can support data—and now even voice—over pre-existing cable. The F-Type connector connects to cable modems providing high-speed Internet service offered through the cable company's coaxial cable (see below).

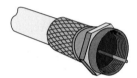

F-Type Connector

- RG62

    RG62 is used in ARCnet networks. This coax cable requires 93 ohms of resistance.

Fiber Optic

Fiber optic cable is made of a glass or plastic core with Kevlar® materials placed in the casing for protection. It can transmit data for greater lengths and has a much larger bandwidth than copper. It is immune to EMI because it uses light generated by laser to transmit a signal. There are two strands of fiber used in data transmission, one to send the data and one to receive. The two types of fiber optic cable are:

- Single-mode

    Single-mode uses a specific wavelength with a core diameter of 8 to 10 microns.

- Multimode

    Multimode uses multiple frequencies with a larger core. There are two types of connectors used with fiber optic cable: the SC connector (Subscriber Connector or Standard Connector), which is a push-pull connector, and the ST (Straight Tip) connector, which is a twist-on connector. Both connectors are seen in Figure 2-8, along with other connectors. There are additional fiber

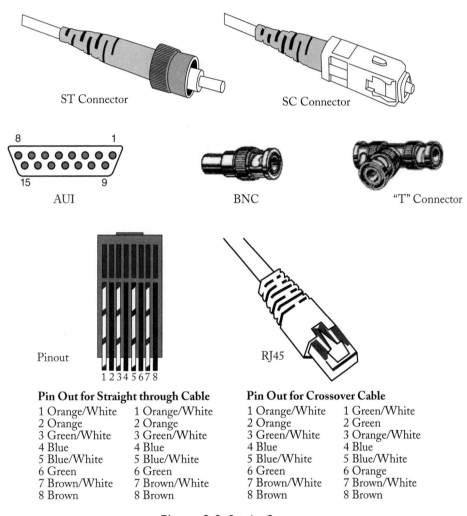

Pin Out for Straight through Cable

1 Orange/White	1 Orange/White
2 Orange	2 Orange
3 Green/White	3 Green/White
4 Blue	4 Blue
5 Blue/White	5 Blue/White
6 Green	6 Green
7 Brown/White	7 Brown/White
8 Brown	8 Brown

Pin Out for Crossover Cable

1 Orange/White	1 Green/White
2 Orange	2 Green
3 Green/White	3 Orange/White
4 Blue	4 Blue
5 Blue/White	5 Blue/White
6 Green	6 Orange
7 Brown/White	7 Brown/White
8 Brown	8 Brown

Figure 2-8. *Popular Connectors*

connectors. Those are the LC (Local Connector) and the MT-RJ (Mechanical Transfer-Registered Jack). Both of these are shown in Figure 2.8a.

 Test Tip: Understand which connectors go with each cable type: Twisted pair = RJ45; Coax = BNC; Fiber ST (twist) SC (push-pull) LC, MT-RJ.

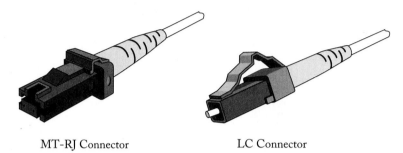

MT-RJ Connector   LC Connector

Figure 2-8a.

USB and IEEE 1394

There are two additional standards that have broken into the networking technologies market. They are Universal Serial Bus or USB and IEEE 1394 also known as Firewire.

USB. The USB technology has been around since 1996. However, over the past few years it has become more and more of a player in network communications. The USB standard allows consumers to connect peripherals to their PC allowing for additional hardware options "outside" of the system unit. For example, USB enabled devices include printers, jump drives, external hard drives, and digital cameras, to name a few. The importance of USB in the network market is through the ability to connect cable modems or external network adapters to the USB port of a PC. USB has a transfer rate of up to 12Mbps and is a Plug-and-Play standard.

IEEE 1394. The IEEE 1394 or Firewire (named after Apple's implementation of the standard) is similar to USB in principle: allowing additional peripherals to expand the capability of a computer. However, the IEEE 1394 implementation is much faster in terms of bandwidth than USB. The IEEE 1394 standard has a transfer rate of up to 400Mbps.

There are many devices that can connect through the use of IEEE 1394 and USB. Most computers built today can support these two types of connections. These two standards are even said to be the successor of the current parallel and serial ports of today's computers. See Figure 2.8b for an example of each connector.

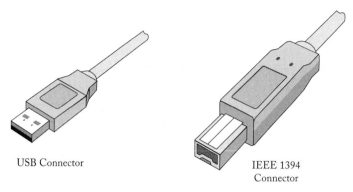

USB Connector   IEEE 1394
                                 Connector

Figure 2-8b.

Wireless Transmission

Wireless transmission includes technologies such as infrared, point-to-point laser, narrow band radio frequencies, and spread spectrum radio frequencies, which allows for secure transmission over multiple radio frequencies.

Infrared. Infrared uses light beams to transmit data between devices. Normal implementations provide a data rate of 10 Mbps. There are several types of infrared technologies.

- Line-of-sight. A clear path must exist between the devices
- Scattered infrared. Transmissions can bounce off of objects to reach their destination.
- Reflective. Optical transceivers are used to redirect the path of a signal.

Laser. Laser signals are sent in a point-to-point fashion where there is a clear line of sight between devices.

Narrow-Band Radio. Narrow-band radio consists of two devices that both tune a receiver to the same frequency. Signals can be carried a long distance, approximately 3 miles. However, the bandwidth available is below 5 Mbps.

Spread-Spectrum Radio. Spread-spectrum is similar to narrow-band radio, but offers more security because the sender and receiver must synchronize with one another before they can transmit. Spread-spectrum consists of two types of synchronization: frequency hopping and direct sequence.

- **Frequency hopping.** In spread-spectrum frequency hopping, the sender and the receiver consistently change both the frequency and the timing in which they transmit and receive. This can actually reduce the performance of the connection because it may take longer to synchronize.
- **Direct sequence.** In spread-spectrum direct sequence, the sender and receiver only synchronize the timing of the devices, which increases the data throughput between the two.

Wireless Interference

The range and speed of wireless networks can be affected by several variables. These include the type of antennae being used, interference, and environmental factors. Interference is often caused by other signals in the same proximity of the wireless devices. Some components that cause interference include microwave ovens, alarm systems, cordless phones, and two-way radios. Environmental factors that may affect wireless technologies include indoor components and outdoor components. The indoor components often affect short-range wireless networks such as 802.11. Indoor component factors include water fountains, water in pipes, concrete walls and pillars, and steel. Environmental factors that affect outdoor wireless connections include rain, snow, high humidity, extreme heat or cold, fog, and even high winds. Leaves and trees are often the cause of broken signals in long-range wireless connections such as microwave.

Repeaters and Hubs

Repeaters and *hubs* operate at the physical layer. Repeaters regenerate signals and retransmit them in an attempt to increase the distance of communication. Hubs act as a central point for connecting multiple nodes on a network. They come in two types: passive and active. A *passive hub* can only perform the role of wire management. It does not have any repeating capabilities and does not need power. Throughout this book the word "hub" implies "active hub" unless otherwise stated. *Active hubs* need power to operate. An active hub performs the role of a *multi-port repeater*. When a hub hears a signal on one of its ports, it regenerates the signal and repeats it to every port. Active hubs can send a signal significantly further than a passive hub (see Figure 2-9).

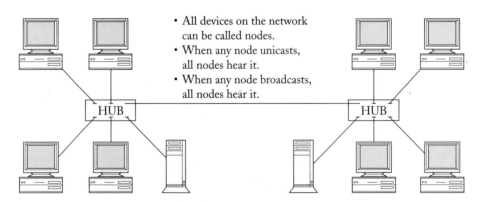

Figure 2-9. *Hub Network with the Same Collision Domain and Broadcast Domain*

A hub operates within a *collision domain* and a *broadcast domain*. A collision domain is a segment of the network where all devices compete for access to the wire, and all transmissions are forwarded to all cable segments of the network. In a broadcast domain, when one node on a segment broadcasts a signal, all nodes receive it. One broadcast domain can contain several collision domains, but one collision domain cannot span multiple broadcast domains.

CSU/DSU

CSU/DSU stands for channel service unit/data service unit. It converts a digital signal from the LAN media into a signal that is appropriate to traverse a WAN and vice versa.

Transceivers

Transceivers are components in the data communication process that may or may not be integrated into another component. The term transceiver refers to a device that can transmit and receive data. Network adapter boards/network interface cards (NIC) often have a transceiver built in. In some network implementations, transceivers can be separate devices that tap into the network and transmit and receive data on behalf of the node. In Figure 2-10, an example of a transceiver connecting to a Thicknet backbone is seen. This transceiver is often referred to as a piercing tap or a vampire tap.

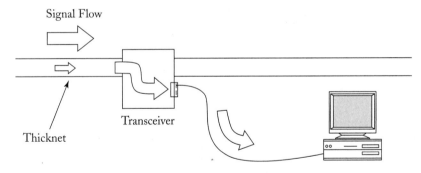

Figure 2-10. *Transceiver*

Modem

Modems allow for connectivity to networks through existing telephone wires using dialup services. Modems <u>mo</u>dulate digital signals into analog signals when sending data and <u>de</u>modulate analog signals into digital signals when receiving data.

Multiplexer

Multiplexers divide physical wires into logical channels. There are three types of multiplexers. *Time division multiplexer* divides baseband signals through timing. *Statistical time division* multiplexers, which use the same method as TDM but gives priority to urgent signals, and a *frequency division multiplexer* which divides up a broadband line to allow multiple signals to travel in multiple directions at one time.

 Test Tip: Physical layer = 1s and 0s, signaling, transmission media/connectors, hubs, repeaters, CSU/DSU, modems, multiplexers, and transceivers.

NOTE: When adding clients to an existing network, it is important to determine what type of media is being used and what type of connectors are needed. For example, if your network consists of a star and you would like to add another client, it is likely that you must use UTP and an RJ45 connector. The same is true for any other media. See below for other examples:

Existing network	Connector used
UTP	RJ45
Coaxial	BNC and T connector
Fiber	ST or SC

2.3 DATA-LINK LAYER (LAYER 2)

The data-link layer of the OSI Model is the second layer of the model. The data-link layer is divided into two sublayers. The logical link control sublayer (LLC) and the media access control (MAC) sublayer.

LOGICAL LINK CONTROL

The LLC sublayer describes how data will proceed from the second layer of the OSI Model to layers higher in the OSI Model. It does this by defining *service access points (SAP)* or *subnetwork access points (SNAP)*. SAPs and SNAPs act as pointers to upper-layer protocols and depend on the applications the system is running. The LLC sublayer is independent of the media being used.

MEDIA ACCESS CONTROL

The MAC sublayer of the data-link layer defines how ones and zeroes are placed on the network. It specifies the rules that all network adapter boards must follow when attempting to communicate. These specifications are known as media access methods, and there are primarily three types:

- **Contention:** Data is transmitted onto the wire on a first-come, first-serve basis.

- **Token passing:** Data is only transmitted when the transmitting device has control of the token circulating the network.

- **Polling:** Nodes transmit on the wire when polled by the centralized device.

The MAC sublayer of the data-link layer also defines physical addressing. Every network interface card (NIC) is given a unique address called a MAC address, also known as a *physical, data-link,* or *layer 2 address.* The MAC address is considered the physical address because it is physically burned into the NIC's read only memory (ROM). This address, defined by the IEEE, is 48 bits long and is represented with 12 hexadecimal digits. There are two sections of a MAC address. The first section of the number is the organization unit identifier (OUI). It consists of the first six hexadecimal digits and is assigned to companies that produce NICs. The second portion of the address consists of the remaining six hexadecimal digits and is assigned to the individual NIC by its manufacturer (see Figure 2-11).

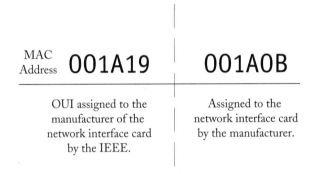

Figure 2-11. *Mac Address Showing Two Portions of Address*

Additional responsibilities of the MAC sublayer include line discipline, flow control, fragmentation, error control, error notification, and error detection.

LOGICAL TOPOLOGIES

Logical topologies, as defined in the previous chapter, operate within the data-link layer. To recap, a logical topology is the method data uses when traveling from one node to the next on a wire. The two logical topologies to be concerned with are the bus and ring.

PREAMBLE AND CYCLIC REDUNDANCY CHECK

Based on the protocol being used, the data-link layer may have additional responsibilities in the encapsulation process. Several popular protocol implementations add a set of ones and zeroes to the beginning of the PDU called a *preamble* and a trailer called a *field check sequence (FCS)*. Inside the FCS field of a frame there is a *cyclic redundancy check* (or *CRC*) that is used to verify the integrity of a frame.

Preamble

The preamble notifies all nodes that a frame is on the network destined for a specific node or a group of nodes. When a node reads its own MAC address in the destination field of the frame, it will process the frame and reply if necessary.

Cyclic Redundancy Check

The CRC, which is a component of the FCS field, is a mathematical algorithm run through every frame processed by the data-link layer. The CRC is specific to the lower-layer protocol that is being used on the network. For example, if your network is using Ethernet frames, all network interface cards will be configured to read and write CRCs that will be understandable by all Ethernet NICs in the network. Once the data-link layer receives a frame, it checks the CRC by running the exact mathematical algorithm that was run on the frame by the sending device. If the values of the two match, the frame is processed further. If the values do not match, the frame was either corrupt or not compatible with the receiving machine's lower-layer protocol and will be discarded. A request for a new frame may be issued.

DATA-LINK LAYER HARDWARE COMPONENTS

At the data-link layer of the OSI Model, there are three hardware components to be concerned with. First and foremost, the *network adapter board* or *network interface card (NIC)*. The NIC controls how data is placed on the wire, and this is directly related to the media access method discussed earlier. Therefore, the NIC operates at layer 2 of the OSI Model. It does, however, house the transciever for the cable and therefore has some physical layer characteristics.

Bridge

The next data-link layer device is the *bridge*. The bridge's main purpose is to physically divide an overpopulated network into sub-segments to free up bandwidth. Bridges create separate collision domains for each segment of wire that is attached to the bridge, but they still operate under one broadcast domain. Bridges do not filter out broadcast messages. Broadcast messages are forwarded to all segments attached to a bridge.

The reason why bridges operate at the data-link layer is because they filter data based on MAC addresses. There are three popular types of bridges in the networking industry: transparent or learning bridges, source routing bridges, and source-routing transparent bridges.

Transparent Bridge. Transparent bridges maintain a table sometimes called a MAC table, a forwarding table, or even a bridge table. This table records all addresses read in the source and destination portion of all frames that enter the bridge. When a bridge reads the source address of node 1 in a frame that came from segment A, it records the information and will now forward frames destined for node 1 to segment A (see Figure 2-12).

Step 1   Node 1 sends message to Node 3.
Step 2   All nodes and bridge hear it.
Step 3   Bridge opens the frame and reads the source and destination address; forwards to Port B.
           Source = Node 1
           Destination = Node 3
Step 4   Bridge learns Node 1 is connected to Port A, and adds an entry to its bridge table.

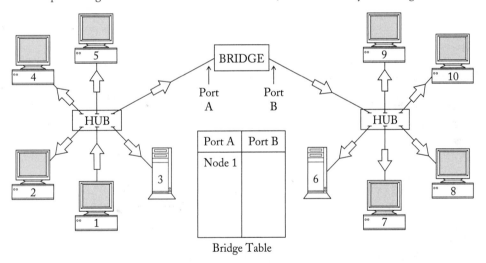

Figure 2-12. *Node 1 Sending Data to Node 3 in a Bridged Network*

If the source MAC address and destination MAC address of a frame are both located on the same segment of the bridged network, the bridge will not forward the frame to the other segment (see Figure 2-13).

Step 1   Node 1 sends message to Node 3.
Step 2   Nodes 2, 3, 4, 5 hear it.
Step 3   Port A opens message and reads the source and destination.
          Source = 1
          Destination = 3
Step 4   Bridge looks in table to determine if source and destination are on the same port. They are, so bridge does not forward the frame to Port B.

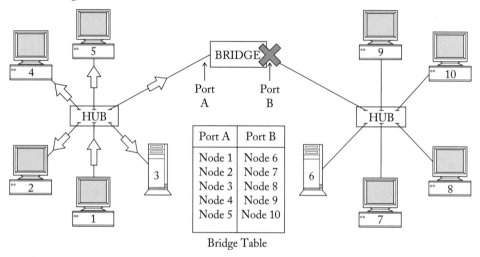

Figure 2-13. *Bridge Restricting Data Flow by Use of the Bridge Table*

Source Routing Bridge. Source routing bridges do not maintain a MAC table as the transparent bridge did. The responsibility of maintaining a list of nodes falls on the individual nodes in the network. Each node creates a table mapping where all other nodes are located. When a node sends data onto the network, the header of the frame identifies which segment the destination node is on. The bridge simply forwards the frame based on the destination address. This method of bridging is often used in Token Ring networks.

Source-Routing Transparent Bridge. This bridging method is used in hybrid networks that contain both of the other two bridges described previously.

Layer 2 Switch

Layer 2 switches use a technology similar to bridges. They filter packets using MAC addresses of nodes. They create multiple smaller collision domains but maintain one broadcast domain. Switches are a popular replacement for active hubs when trying to increase *throughput* in a network. Throughput on a network is defined as the actual data rate that is achieved throughout the network. For example, the bandwidth of a network may be 100 Mbps, but due to collisions the throughput could be reduced to 40 or 60 Mbps. Each switch interface (port) can be connected to a different node in the network. Collision domains are created at each switch interface. This dramatically reduces collisions between nodes connected to the switch. Nodes connected to the switch receive the full amount of bandwidth allocated to them. Switches provide full-duplex media access, which means the nodes can both send and receive data at the same time using the total bandwidth available of the media. Both switches and bridges must use the same frame type on all segments connected. Layer 2 switches are often used to create and manage VLANs. This allows you to have independent networks on a single device to control bandwidth.

 Test Tip: Data-link layer: 2 sublayers (MAC/LLC), logical topologies, CRC, MAC or physical addresses, NIC, Bridge, Switch, and VLANs.

2.4 NETWORK LAYER (LAYER 3)

The network layer of the OSI Model defines processes to transmit data between independent networks through the use and assignment of logical addressing.

NETWORK LAYER PACKETS

The packets that the network layer creates to fulfill its communication responsibilities conform to one of two general types, data or discovery. A *data packet* contains information being sent from one user on a network to another user on a separate network. These packets contain user information, such as upper-layer application data. Examples include data related to a user's e-mail or file transfers. The *discovery* or *update packet* is created by a router and sent to other routers to update information about what networks the router knows about or is connected to. The information in a discovery packet tells a router how to build its *routing table*. A routing table has entries for all known networks in an internetwork.

ROUTING TABLE

A routing table is created by the information exchanged between routers. When a router receives a packet that must be forwarded to another network, it examines its routing table to determine the best path to send the data. The best path is normally determined by the lowest cost route based on the *metric* of the entry in the routing table. The metric is determined by one or more variables. For example, the number of *hops* it will take to reach the destination network (a hop is the process of traveling through a router), line speed of the link, and time it will take to travel over the link to the destination router.

NETWORK ADDRESS

Routers send packets to their destination based on the best path available (lowest metric) in the routing table. To do this, the router must know where the packet's destination is. The network layer provides this information through addressing. However, the addresses used here are logical addresses. A logical address is sometimes referred to as a network, protocol, hierarchical, or layer 3 address. Network addresses are assigned automatically or by an administrator and are not permanent. Therefore, the characteristics of a network address and a MAC address are different. A logical address can be changed by an administrator, a MAC address cannot.

Logical addressing has two portions, one for the network ID and one for the host ID. The network layer is primarily concerned with the network ID portion of the address. That is why network addresses are recorded in routing tables. When the network layer of a user's PC is encapsulating the data sent from the transport layer, it adds the source and destination network IDs of the communicating hosts to the packet. When the packet reaches the router, the router examines the destination address and then compares it to its routing table to determine the best route to send the packet to its next hop on its way to the final destination.

NETWORK LAYER HARDWARE COMPONENTS

There are two primary hardware devices that operate at the network layer of the OSI Model: routers and layer 3 switches.

Routers

Routers have the functionality available to segment networks, yet a more accurate statement would be that routers connect separate, independent networks. Routers create separate broadcast domains because they do not forward broadcast messages by default. Since routers operate at the third layer of the OSI Model, they are not concerned with the protocol used at the data-link layer. Therefore, they can connect dissimilar layer 2 frame types. When a packet arrives at a router, the router de-encapsulates the packet up to the network layer. It then re-encapsulates the packet and forwards it out the destined interface. A packet can be received on the Ethernet interface and forwarded out of the Token Ring interface (see Figure 2-14).

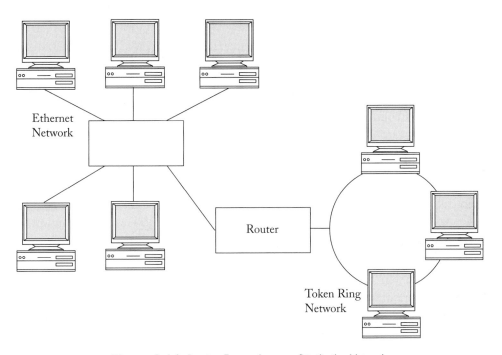

Figure 2-14. *Routing Frames between Dissilimilar Networks*

Layer 3 Switches

Layer 3 switches perform many of the same functions as routers. Their purpose is to connect separate, independent networks together. However, the means by which they calculate routes is slightly different than how traditional routers accomplish it. For example, routers are processor based and switches, in general, are not. Switches use application-specific integrated circuits (or ASICs), to determine the route a data packet should take. Because of the technology used to forward packets, switches can forward more packets per second (PPS) than routers. Switches have the capability of forwarding many more PPS than routers. Therefore, switches are a good, young technology with a great deal of promise.

 Test Tip: Network Layer: Logical/network/hierarchical addressing, routers, routing and layer 3 switches.

2.5 TRANSPORT LAYER (LAYER 4)

The transport layer of the OSI Model is primarily responsible for end-to-end session establishment between two stations. The logical connections created between two nodes can use connection-oriented or connectionless communication methods.

CONNECTION-ORIENTED AND CONNECTIONLESS COMMUNICATION

Connection-oriented and connectionless communication can happen at several layers of the OSI Model. It is often implemented by the protocol being used.

Connection-Oriented

Connection-oriented communication is the process of utilizing error correction procedures to provide reliable, guaranteed delivery of segments between peer transport layers. A connection-oriented session goes through three phases, session establishment, data transfer, and session disconnect. The first phase, session establishment, occurs when a sending node requests to set up a communication session with another node in the network. After the session has been established by the two nodes, the second phase begins. During the data transfer phase, the nodes transmit data and use control mechanisms to ensure data is not lost and communication is successful. The final phase consists of the two nodes agreeing to disconnect the session.

Connection-oriented communication consists of the following:

- Sequencing. Sequencing of segments at the transport layer allows the segments to be placed back into the correct order when they reach the peer transport layer. It also allows for the retransmission of data if a segment is lost during the communication process.

- Flow Control. Flow control provides several functions to the nodes of a connection-oriented session. The three basic methods of flow control used are:

    1. *Buffering*, which is the process of allocating memory to hold data as it comes into the device until it can be processed. Too much data can cause buffer overflow.

    2. *Congestion avoidance* is a technique normally used when a buffer is being overflowed. The receiving device will issue a source-quench packet to tell the sending device to send less data.

    3. *Windowing* is the process of the sending and receiving nodes, agreeing on a specified number of segments that can be transmitted in each transmission, throughout the connection-oriented session.

- Acknowledgements (ACK). An ACK is a portion of segment that confirms whether or not data has successfully made it to its destination (it is sent to the original source device by the original destination device). In a connection-oriented session, ACKs are sent confirming the receipt of every segment and are based on the sequence number of a segment. Since ACKs can consume a large part of a network's bandwidth, *windowing* is used to reduce the number of ACKs sent. Windowing is the process of the sending machine being able to forward an agreed-upon number of segments to the destination machine before receiving an ACK. For example, if PC1 and PC2 agree on a window size of three segments, PC1 would send PC2 three segments before PC2 would respond with one ACK (see Figure 2-15). If one of the three segments did not make it to PC2, it would either request retransmission of that single segment or the entire window of segments.

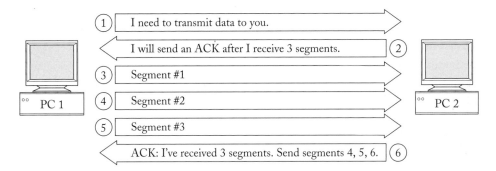

Figure 2-15. *PC's Communicating with the Use of Acks*

Connectionless

The primary difference between connection-oriented and connectionless communication is that connectionless communication does not establish a session before communication occurs. In connectionless communication, segments are sent to the destination machine with the hope that they make it there. This is a best-effort, non-guaranteed delivery method.

End users do not have the choice of using a connection-oriented or connectionless protocol; this is normally written into the code of the networked application being used. For example, if an end-user was transferring files, the application would, more often than not, be using a connection-oriented transport protocol and sending ACKs confirming whether or not the segments arrived. On the other hand, if the user was streaming a video over the World Wide Web, it would be useless to use a connection-oriented protocol because the time sensitivity involved with video streaming would not accommodate the transmission of ACKs.

HARDWARE AT THE TRANSPORT LAYER

At the transport layer, there is one primary hardware component to be aware of: the layer 4 switch.

Layer 4 Switch

Layer 4 switches are switches that can make forwarding and filtering decisions based on the source and destination address of the packet, as well as source and destination port. Ports are used to identify types of network applications being used. If a layer 4 switch is used to connect networks together, packets can be filtered based on the application's TCP or UDP port number (which will both be covered in Part II, Protocols, of this book).

 Test Tip: Transport layer. Connection-oriented or connectionless communication, end-to-end reliability, and end-to-end transport.

2.6 THE UPPER LAYERS (LAYER 5, 6, AND 7)

The upper three layers transmit and receive data to the transport layer as one single stream of data. The data can contain error correction information, specific formatting, and support for network applications. In this section, we will take a look at each of the upper three layers, first the session layer, then the presentation layer, and finally the application layer.

SESSION LAYER (LAYER 5)

The session layer of the OSI Model is responsible for establishing a session between two nodes. The session opened at this layer is available for communication that occurs between networked applications. This is in addition to the session established at the transport layer. The session layer offers three types of communication modes:

- Simplex. Provides one-way communication. For example, a television is a simplex communication standard.

- Half-duplex. Provides two-way communication, however only one device can communicate at a time. For example, walkie-talkies operate in half-duplex mode.

- Full-duplex. Provides two-way communication, and both entities can transmit and receive at the same time. For example, telephones operate in full-duplex mode.

 Test Tip: Session layer: Establishes host-to-host session.

PRESENTATION LAYER (LAYER 6)

The presentation layer of the OSI Model is responsible for presenting the data to the receiving machine in a readable format. The presentation layer deals with how the data will be read when it reaches the other machine. For example, some microprocessors read bits (ones and zeroes) from left to right, while others read them from right to left.

The presentation layer provides translation services for these nodes, ensuring that the data is properly formatted for the application layer protocol. Also at this layer, data compression, decompression, encryption, and decryption take place.

 Test Tip: Presentation layer: Presents/formats data.

APPLICATION LAYER (LAYER 7)

The application layer does not refer to applications such as word processing programs or spreadsheet programs; it is primarily involved with services and interfaces that support applications that require network resources. Such services include, but are not limited to, file transfer services, sending and receiving messages, database services, printing services, and networked application services. For example, a user is writing an e-mail message to another user. The process of writing the message in the application provided by a vendor is not part of the network transmission procedure. However, when the user clicks on the "Send Message" button, the message is handed to the application layer of the OSI Model to process it. There are many application layer protocols that will be covered in a later chapter.

 Test Tip: Application layer: Interface to the end user acts as the end point or the beginning of network communication.

MULTI-LAYERED COMPONENTS

In addition to the components already identified, there are two multi-layered components that must be mentioned: brouters and gateways.

Brouter

A brouter can operate at layer 2 working as a bridge and layer 3 as a router. It is primarily used in an internetwork that is operating with *non-routable* protocols as well as *routable* protocols. Non-routable protocols are broadcast based and are not forwarded by routers. They must be forwarded with a bridge. Routable protocols are forwarded by routers because they are not broadcast based.

Gateway

Gateways can operate at all seven layers of the OSI Model and come in the form of both hardware and software. The primary purpose of a gateway is to ensure that two dissimilar technologies (usually protocols) can communicate seamlessly.

2.7 PROTOCOLS AT THE LAYERS

Protocols can map directly to a single layer of the OSI Model, or they can combine functionality of multiple layers. Protocols are going to be covered in depth later in this book. For now, examine Table 2-1, which shows some of the protocols that map to the OSI Model. Many of these protocols will be elaborated on in future chapters.

TABLE 2-1   PROTOCOLS MAPPED TO THE OSI MODEL

A	SMTP SNMP DNS IMAP FTP TFTP POP HTTP	*Network Support Applications*
P	**Text:** ASCII EBCDIC HTML **Sound:** MIDI MPEG WAV **Graphic:** JPEG GIF TIFF Video: AVI QuickTime	*Presentation Standards*
S	NFS SQL RPC X Windows	*Session Services*
T	TCP UDP SPX	*Transport Protocols*
N	IP IPX ICMP ARP RARP	*Addressing and Routed Protocols*
D	ATM Frame Relay ISDN PPP SLIP Ethernet Token Ring ArcNet FDDI 802.3, 802.5	*Lower Layer and Routing Protocols*
P		

CHAPTER SUMMARY

This chapter covered the seven layers of the OSI Model. Many of the topics covered here were directly related to the OSI Model, such as the functions of each layer, the hardware devices that map to each layer, and standards for each layer. Physical addressing was covered, and logical addressing was introduced. Processes that take place at each layer were also explained. Protocols were shown mapping to the OSI Model. These protocols will be further explored in the next two chapters.

KNOWLEDGE TEST

1. What layers of the OSI Model does the NIC operate? (Choose two.)
   A. Network
   B. Session
   C. Physical
   D. Data Link
   E. Transport
   F. Application
   G. Presentation

2. Which component is used to connect multiple nodes to create a single network segment within a single collision domain?
   A. Hub
   B. Bridge
   C. Brouter
   D. Router

3. At which layer of the OSI Model does a switch that creates multiple collision domains yet a single broadcast domain work?
   A. Physical
   B. Data-link
   C. Network
   D. Transport

4. Which device forwards data to all hosts on a network (regardless of the destination) once the data is received?
   A. Gateway
   B. Router
   C. Switch
   D. Hub

5. What device would be used to connect two networks using different layer 2 standards?
   A. Hub
   B. Bridge
   C. Gateway
   D. Repeater

6. Which two network devices forward data based on the MAC address? (Choose two.)
   A. Bridge
   B. Hub
   C. Layer 3 switch
   D. Layer 2 switch
   E. AUI

7. You want to install two independent networks to control traffic in your network. Although the budget does not allow you to purchase a router, a layer 2 switch is priced within reason. What course of action must you take?
A. Buy the switch and configure it with two VLANs
B. Buy the router
C. Buy the switch and configure it as a router
D. Replace the switch with two hubs

8. Layer 2 switches create multiple collision domains. However, all devices attached to the switch, even if there are multiple VLANs, belong to the same _____.
A. Collision domain
B. Cable segment
C. Ethernet domain
D. Broadcast domain

9. Which devices operate at the data-link layer? (Choose all that apply.)
A. NIC
B. Router
C. Bridge
D. Switch
E. Hub
F. Brouter

10. You are a consultant working at a client's site. You notice that their entire site is connected together through hubs. You run some tests to determine what the throughput of the network is, and you realize they are losing bandwidth because of the hubs. What device can you use to replace the hubs and dramatically increase the throughput?
A. Router
B. Switch
C. Repeater
D. Gateway

11. If your internetwork consists of both routable and non-routable protocols on separate LANs, what device can you use to connect them together?
A. Switch
B. Router
C. Brouter
D. Gateway

12. Which layer of the OSI Model converts data into frames?
A. Physical
B. Data-link
C. Network
D. Transport
E. Session
F. Presentation
G. Application

13. Which layer of the OSI Model converts data into packets or datagrams?
    A. Physical
    B. Data-link
    C. Network
    D. Transport
    E. Session
    F. Presentation
    G. Application

14. Which layer of the OSI Model converts data into segments?
    A. Physical
    B. Data-link
    C. Network
    D. Transport
    E. Session
    F. Presentation
    G. Application

15. Which layer of the OSI Model deals with the electrical and mechanical functions of connecting two devices?
    A. Physical
    B. Data-link
    C. Network
    D. Transport
    E. Session
    F. Presentation
    G. Application

16. At which layer of the OSI Model is the data put into a readable format by an all-nodes communication process?
    A. Physical
    B. Data-link
    C. Network
    D. Transport
    E. Session
    F. Presentation
    G. Application

17. What is the transport layer of the OSI Model responsible for?
    A. Host-to-host session
    B. End-to-end reliability
    C. Network addressing
    D. Media access methods

18. What type of connector is used with Category 5 UTP?
    A. ST
    B. SC
    C. RJ45
    D. BNC

19. What type of connector is used with coaxial cable?
    A. ST
    B. SC
    C. RJ45
    D. BNC

20. What type of connectors are used with fiber optics? (Choose two.)
    A. ST (twist on)
    B. SC (push-pull or snap on)
    C. ST (push-pull or snap on)
    D. SC (twist on)

Project 802 and Layer 2 Protocols

OBJECTIVES

At the end of this chapter you will be able to:

- Describe the function of the IEEE's Project 802.
- Describe Ethernet and its functions.
- Describe Token Ring and its functions.
- Understand several layer 2 protocols.

INTRODUCTION

Chapter 3 takes a look at the Institute of Electrical and Electronics Engineers (IEEE) Project 802 standards, which primarily define layer 2 of the OSI Model. In this chapter you will learn how the Project 802 standards correlate to popular networking standards, such as Ethernet and Token Ring. Specifications and standards for these protocols will be explained.

3.1 PROJECT 802

In February of 1980, the IEEE decided to create a project model that would provide the basis for internetworking LANs and MANs. The IEEE LAN Standards Committee carried it out and labeled it Project 802 for the year (19<u>80</u>) and the month (2). The IEEE standardization proved to be invaluable to the networking community. The committee standardized some of the most popular protocols that were being used during that era, such as Ethernet. This standardization allowed vendors and organizations (in addition to those who created Ethernet) to develop and use a similar technology to Ethernet without having to pay additional money for it, which is often the case with proprietary technological solutions.

Not only did the IEEE standardize Ethernet, there were many standards developed based on the implementation of several vendors' networking advances. Some of the 802 standards are almost identical to those of the companies that developed the technology and some are not. Here is a list of some of the current IEEE committees working on the development of IEEE standardization:

- 802—Defines the LAN/MAN Standards Committee (LMSC)
- 802.1—Internetworking
- 802.2—Logical Link Control
- 802.3—Ethernet
- 802.4—Token Bus
- 802.5—Token Ring
- 802.6—Metropolitan Area Networks
- 802.7—Broadband Technical Advisory Group (TAG)
- 802.8—Fiber Optic Technical Advisory Group (TAG)
- 802.9—Isochronous LANs
- 802.10—Standards for Interoperable LAN/MAN Security (SILS)
- 802.11—Wireless Local Area Networks (WLAN)
- 802.12—Demand Priority
- 802.15—Wireless Personal Area Networks (WPAN)
- 802.16—Broadband Wireless Access Standards For Wireless Metropolitan Area Networks (WMAN)
- 802.17—Resilient Packet Ring Working Group (RPRWG)
- 802.18—Radio Regulatory Technical Advisory Group (TAG)

The IEEE continues to develop and improve upon networking standards and has a very large voice in the internetworking community. Some of the IEEE standards that are discussed within are 802.3 and Ethernet, 802.5 and Token Ring, 802.4 and ARCNet, 802.2, 802.11, and several more.

3.2 802.3 AND ETHERNET

Ethernet is a layer 1 and 2 media access method that organizes data into frames before sending it onto the wire in a network. It was developed by Digital, Intel, and Xerox in the 1970s. It was later standardized by the IEEE as 802.3. Both Ethernet and 802.3 define the physical as well as the data-link layer standards to follow when using it in a network. Because the Ethernet and 802.3 standards are so similar, the terms will be used interchangeably throughout this text.

Test Tip: 802.3 = Ethernet, 802.5 = Token Ring, and 802.11 = Wireless.

ETHERNET/802.3 STANDARDS

Ethernet standards are described at two layers of the OSI Model: the data-link layer, and the physical layer. At the data-link layer, Ethernet standards describe the size and description of the frame used, as well as the media access method used to transfer it to the wire. At the physical layer, standards include the signaling method used, the physical topology, and the type of hardware used to transfer the data from one point to another.

Data-Link Layer

The data-link layer defines the method by which the nodes access the wire. This is referred to as the media access method, of which there are three media access methods used to allow nodes on a network to transmit data onto the wire. They are: polling, token passing, and contention. Ethernet is based on a logical bus topology and uses the contention method. In a logical bus topology, only one signal can be on the wire at a time, and stations have to contend for the wire so many data collisions occur. When data collisions occur, neither signal is sent successfully. *The Carrier Sense Multiple Access with Collision Detection (CSMA/CD)* access method was created to address this problem. CSMA/CD is used by Ethernet to assist in data transmission. CSMA/CD allows a node to sense the carrier (wire) to determine whether or not there is a signal already on the wire. If the wire is occupied by another signal, the node will continuously sense the wire until the wire is free. Once the wire is free, the node will transmit its signal (see Figure 3-1).

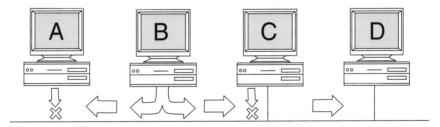

- Node B is sending data
- Nodes A and C must wait until the dataline
  is free before transmitting

Figure 3-1. *Logical Bus Topology*

Half-Duplex versus Full-Duplex

Ethernet can transmit data in half-duplex mode or full-duplex mode. Remember that half-duplex means only one station can transmit at a time, and full-duplex means both stations can transmit at the same time. Ethernet NICs normally have an auto-detect feature that allows the board to determine whether or not it is in half- or full-duplex mode. If either station is in half-duplex mode, both stations will have to communicate in half-duplex mode (see Figure 3-2).

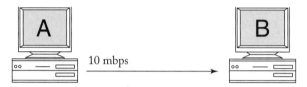

- Node A can send data to node B at 10 Mbps.
- Node B must wait until Node A has finished transmitting.
- Node B can then transmit to Node A, and Node A will wait until Node B has finished.

Figure 3-2. *Ethernet in Half-Duplex Mode*

When two nodes have a direct connection between them (which will occur when nodes are directly connected to a layer 2 switch) it will be possible to communicate in full-duplex mode. Nodes connected to a hub rather than a switch will be using half-duplex. This is because a hub does not create a direct connection between nodes. In half-duplex mode, the network is using only a percentage of the bandwidth due to collisions. The amount of collisions that occur will vary depending on the number of nodes on the network segment. In some environments, the bandwidth can be reduced by sixty to seventy percent. If a full-duplex connection is negotiated between two end nodes, one hundred percent of the bandwidth is used. In full-duplex mode, the collision detection circuit of CSMA/CD is disabled, and two separate circuits of cable are used to send and receive data (see Figure 3-3).

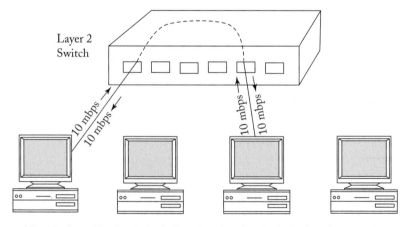

- All nodes have 10 mbps in both directions (sending/recieving) at the same time.

Figure 3-3. *Ethernet in Full-Duplex Mode*

Physical Layer Standards

At the physical layer, signaling methods, physical topologies, and the physical components are described.

Signaling Method. Ethernet uses a baseband signaling method when sending data on the network. Baseband is a digital transmission that consumes the entire bandwidth of the line that it is placed on.

Physical Topologies. In an Ethernet network, one of several different physical topologies can be used. Ethernet standards support the star topology, the bus topology, and the wireless topology.

Identifying Ethernet Standards

The Ethernet standards are based on the 802.x standard. For example, 802.3 is based on the first version of Ethernet, and the physical layer standards consist of 10Base2, 10Base5, 10BaseT, and 10BaseF. On the other hand, 802.3u is based on Fast Ethernet, and that supports and entirely different set of standards such as 100BaseTX and 100Base4 to name a few. Several standards are listed here.

802.3 and Ethernet LANs transmit data over a copper of fiber optic cable. The following standards transmit 10 megabits per second in a baseband transmission. The standards are written as 10Base2, 5, T, or F. The first number is the Mbps, the base means baseband, and the last identifier is the length of the cable or the type of cable used.

10Base2 (Thinnet or Thin Ethernet). 10Base2 uses RG58u coaxial cable, T-connectors, and BNCs to connect nodes together in a node-to-node, physical bus topology. In a coaxial network, each end of the wire must have a resistor, called a terminator, on it to prevent signal bounce. Signal bounce occurs when there is no resistor to terminate a signal on a coaxial cable. Ethernet networks use a 50 ohm resistor (see Figure 3-4).

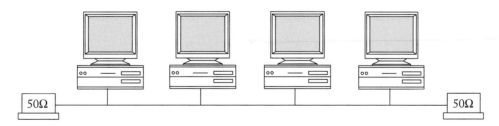

Figure 3-4. *Ethernet Network with Resistors*

It is also important to have one end of the cable grounded. Although the metal shield in a coax cable provides ground, the level of ground for the entire network will be uneven unless one of the ends is grounded to the chassis of a PC. This is a simple procedure, and in an Ethernet LAN it usually consists of having a resistor with a ground chain as shown in Figure 3-5.

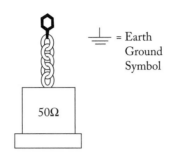

= Earth Ground Symbol

Figure 3-5. *Resistor with Ground Chain*

10Base2 follows the 5-4-3 rule, which states that the network can have five cable segments of 185 meters each, separated by four repeaters, with three of those cable segments being populated. The unpopulated cable segments are used only to gain distance (see Figure 3-6).

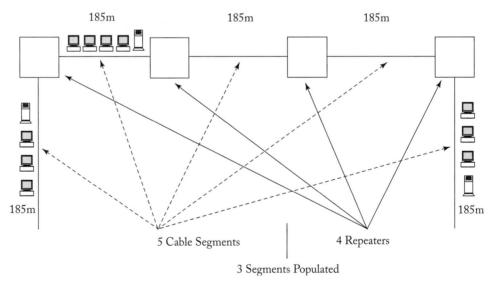

Figure 3-6. *The 5-4-3 Rule*

The 5-4-3 rule is based on the attenuation of an electrical signal. The strength of an electrical signal in a cable is similar to the pressure of water in a garden hose. The longer the hose, the less pressure the flowing water will have.

10Base5 (Thicknet or Thick Ethernet). 10base5 is often implemented as a network backbone with RG8 or RG11 coaxial cable. Each cable segment can be 500 meters in length with 100 transceivers per segment. The total number of nodes in a 10Base5 network cannot exceed 1024. The physical topology is a bus, and it also is governed by the 5-4-3 rule. To connect a node to the wire, an Auxiliary Unit Interface (AUI) is used from the node to a transceiver. The transceiver is attached directly to the wire (see Figure 3-7).

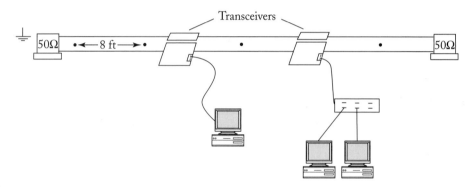

Figure 3-7. *Bus Network*

A transceiver is often referred to as a vampire tap because of its role in the network. A vampire tap has a piercing device located on it. Once the vampire tap is applied to the wire, it pierces the outer casing and touches the copper core allowing signals to flow through it (see Figure 3-8).

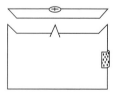

Figure 3-8. *Vampire Tap*

The vampire tap is connected to the network nodes via an AUI (or auxiliary unit interface) as seen here.

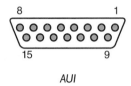

AUI

There must be at least 8 feet between each vampire tap in a 10Base5 network. In most Thicknet implementations, the vampire tap will carry signals to another type or device, such as a hybrid hub. This allows more than one node to be connected to a single vampire tap (see Figure 3-9).

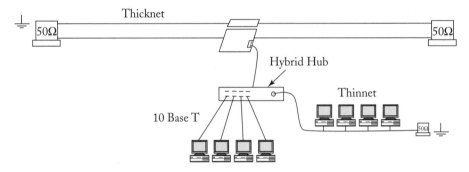

Figure 3-9. *Thicknet Network to Thinnet and 10BaseT*

As with 10Base2 networks, 10Base5 networks must use 50 ohms of resistance at each end of the wire, and one end of the wire must be grounded.

 Test Tip: If shown a diagram of a 10Base2 or 10Base5 network, ensure there are terminators at both ends of the wire and that one end is grounded.

10BaseT. 10BaseT uses Category 3 unshielded twisted pair (UTP) or better (i.e., Cat 5). It only uses two of the four pairs of wire for transmission. In a 10BaseT network, each cable segment can be no longer that 100 meters, and it is prone to the 5-4 rule which states that there can be five cable runs connected by four repeaters. Each connection is in a point-to-point fashion ending at a central device. Therefore, it uses a physical star topology. The media connector between the NIC and the cable is an RJ-45, seen here.

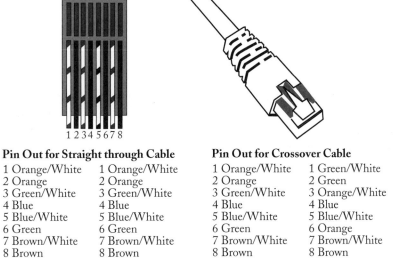

Pin Out for Straight through Cable

1 Orange/White	1 Orange/White
2 Orange	2 Orange
3 Green/White	3 Green/White
4 Blue	4 Blue
5 Blue/White	5 Blue/White
6 Green	6 Green
7 Brown/White	7 Brown/White
8 Brown	8 Brown

Pin Out for Crossover Cable

1 Orange/White	1 Green/White
2 Orange	2 Green
3 Green/White	3 Orange/White
4 Blue	4 Blue
5 Blue/White	5 Blue/White
6 Green	6 Orange
7 Brown/White	7 Brown/White
8 Brown	8 Brown

NOTE: Hold the Clip Side of the Connector Down, Count Left to Right to Number Wires.

RJ-45 Connector

In a true 10BaseT, the UTP normally runs through the walls of a building, to a punch-down block, then to a patch panel and, finally, to a hub or a layer 2 switch (see Figure 3-10).

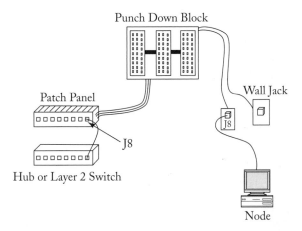

Figure 3-10. *10BaseT in a Building*

Be sure not to exceed 100 meters of cable without a repeater since the attenuation of the signal may adversely affect the data transmissions.

 Test Tip: If given a question that shows or discusses lengths of cable, be sure to add the distance to the next repeater since it cannot exceed 100 meters for any network using UTP.

10BaseFL. 10BaseFL uses multimode or single-mode fiber optic cable with a maximum distance of 2000 meters.

802.3u and Fast Ethernet

802.3u defines fast Ethernet LAN standards that operate over copper or fiber optics with a 100 Mbps baseband signal.

100BaseTX. 100BaseTX uses two pairs of wire within the category 5 UTP. Each cable segment can be no more than 100 meters. Each connection is point-to-point connecting to a central device such as a hub or a switch. The physical topology is a star, and the wiring of this network is similar to the 10BaseT.

100BaseT4. 100BaseT4 uses four pairs of wire within the category 3 UTP. Each cable segment can be no more than 100 meters. Each connection is point-to-point connecting to a central device such as a hub or a switch. The physical topology is a star, and the wiring of this network is similar to the 10BaseT.

100BaseFX. 100BaseFX uses multimode fiber which can transmit for 1 kilometer, or single-mode fiber optic cable which can carry a signal for 2 kilometers. To connect a node to the cable, an ST connector is used. When configuring 100BaseFX, there will be two cables and two connectors for each device. Since light travels in only one direction, every fiber device has an in and an out connector. Be sure to connect the correct end of the cable to the correct port. The topology used here is point-to-point, and in most networks the fiber is used to connect centralized devices together to provide a high-speed backbone (see Figure 3-11). 100BaseFX can be used to provide high-speed connections to the desktop as well.

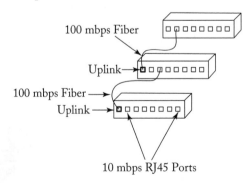

Figure 3-11. *100BaseFX as a Backbone*

802.3z, 802.3ab and Gigabit Ethernet

802.3z and 802.3ab standardized gigabit Ethernet, which transmits data at 1000 Mbps with a baseband transmission over copper or fiber optic cable.

1000BaseCX. This standard was designed for very short distances over shielded copper cable. It will only carry a signal for 25 meters.

1000BaseSX. This standard will carry a signal for 550 meters and is used for short backbone connections. It uses fiber optic multimode cable.

1000BaseLX. This standard will carry signal for 5 kilometers and is used for longer backbone connections than 1000BaseSX. It uses fiber optic single-mode cable.

1000BaseT (802.3ab). 1000BaseT uses four pairs of category 5 UTP. Each cable run is limited to 100 meters. Physical topology is a star with each cable ending at a central device.

10GBaseSR. 10GBaseSR supports 10Gbps over short distances. The distance is based on the type of cable. The three lengths supported are 26 meters, 82 meters, or 300 meters, depending upon the type of multi-mode fiber cable being used.

10GBaseLR. 10GBaseLR can support 10Gbps for 10km over single-mode fiber.

10GBaseER. 10GBaseER can support 10Gbps for 40km over single-mode fiber.

3.3 802.5 AND TOKEN RING

Token Ring was developed as an IBM standard and later standardized as 802.5 by the IEEE.

802.5 ACCESS METHOD

Nodes in an 802.5 network use the token passing access method to gain access to the wire. This method ensures that nodes will have a chance to access the wire, and it dramatically reduces the amount of collisions on a network. When a node has control of the token, which is created by the first node on the Token Ring network, it can transmit. When done, the transmitting node releases the token, and the downstream neighbor will then have the opportunity for transmission. In a Token Ring network, the first node on the wire becomes the *active monitor*. The active monitor is responsible for creating the token and passing it to the next node on line. The active monitor also removes any duplicate tokens that may be on the network.

Token Ring networks also include a process called *beaconing*, which is an alarm process initiated if one of the nodes is not forwarding frames correctly. Since all frames are passed in the same direction on a Token Ring network, all nodes expect to receive frames from the same node. This is called the upstream neighbor. If a node does not receive an expected frame from its upstream neighbor, it will issue an alarm.

This alarm is the beacon, which will alert the active monitor that the beaconing node's upstream neighbor is not operational (see Figure 3-12).

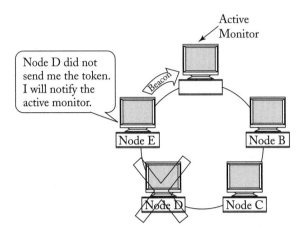

Figure 3-12. *Beaconing Token Ring Node*

The stations in the network (the active monitor) can attempt to bring the node on line, however manual intervention may not be unavoidable.

PHYSICAL TOPOLOGY

Although Token Ring uses a logical ring to transmit data, it is wired as a star through a device called a *multi-station access unit,* or *MSAU.* The MSAU actually contains the ring within it, and when a node connects to the MSAU it opens a relay circuit allowing data to flow down to the newly-connected node. MSAUs are intelligent devices and can monitor the status of the nodes connected to it (see Figure 3-13).

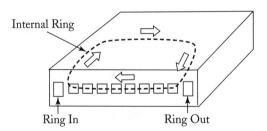

• All ports have a relay within it. If there is no cable connected to a port the port is bypassed.

Figure 3-13. *Token Ring MSAU*

In a Token Ring network, all nodes are repeaters. Each frame received by each node is de-encapsulated to the destination field of the frame. If the node opening the frame is not the destination node, the frame is re-encapsulated and sent to the next node in the ring as a fresh signal. When the frame finally reaches the destination node, it is read and then the token is sent back to the sending node, denoting the fact that the data was or was not read successfully. Once the originating node receives the token again, it releases it and the next node in the ring is allowed to transmit data.

The failure of one node in a Token Ring network can disrupt the entire ring. Therefore, MSAUs have the capability of closing a relay if they detect an error. An MSAU can be connected together in a Ring In/Ring Out fashion (see Figure 3-14).

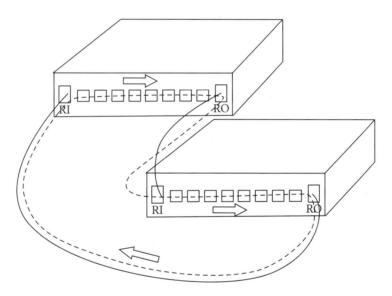

Figure 3-14. *Token Ring MSAUs*

A total of thirty-three MSAUs, each supporting eight nodes, can be connected together based on IBM standards. MSAUs are connected together using patch cables (see Figure 3-15).

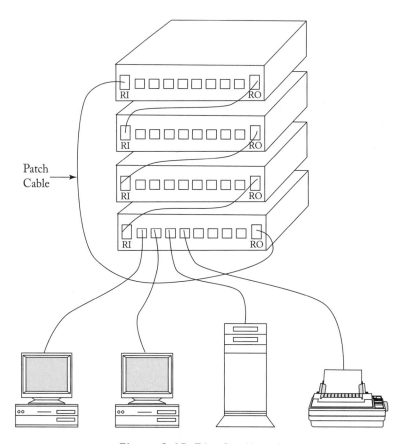

Figure 3-15. *Token Ring Network*

Test Tip: Multi-Station Access Units are sometimes referred to as MSAU as well as MAU. Be aware of these acronyms.

IBM Cabling Standards and Speed

IBM cabling standards are used for Token Ring networks. Primarily, they are wired with IBM type 1 shielded twisted pair or IBM type 3 UTP. If the network is using UTP, it is limited to 72 nodes. If the media is STP, the Token Ring network can have as many as 260 nodes in it. Other vendors offer Token Ring equipment; the standards implemented in the Token Ring network will be based on the vendor's limitations.

Token Ring supports 4 or 16 Mbps, and you should never put a 4 Mbps network adapter in a network that is using 16 Mbps. Since Token Ring network adapters are repeaters, if a signal is regenerated at 4 Mbps in a 16 Mbps network, your network will suffer substantially. Token Ring and Ethernet are layer 2 standards and cannot be in the same network without a translation device, such as a gateway or a router.

 Test Tip: If you put a 4 Mbps Token Ring NIC in a 16 Mbps Token Ring network, you will have extreme problems.

FIBER DISTRIBUTED DATA INTERFACE (FDDI)

FDDI has not been given a Project 802 standardization, however it uses a very similar technology to those described in the 802.5 standard. FDDI is a high-speed LAN standard implemented over fiber optic cable, which uses a token passing access method. FDDI token passing is much more advanced and more conducive to high-speed data transmission. Remember, in a Token Ring network only one token was on the network, and only one node could take control of the token to transmit. When the transmitting node received the token back from the destination device, it released the token to the downstream neighbor to transmit. FDDI allows each node to release a new token after each transmission, which results in multiple tokens on the wire at any given time.

Physical Topology

The physical topology used by FDDI is the ring topology. However, it uses a counter-rotating fiber ring for fault tolerance (see Figure 3-16).

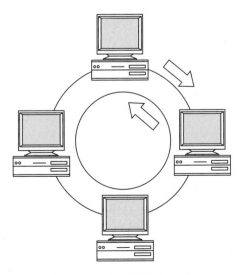

Figure 3-16. *FDDI Network*

A FDDI network has Class A nodes and Class B nodes in the network. The Class A nodes are those that are connected to both fiber rings through a wire concentrator. The Class B nodes are only connected to the primary fiber ring (see Figure 3-17).

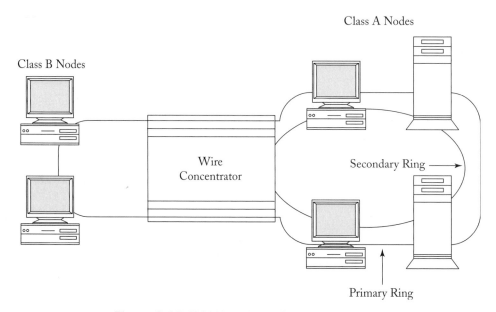

Figure 3-17. *FDDI Network with Class A and Class B Nodes*

If the primary fiber ring goes down, the Class A nodes will continue to send and receive data. The Class B nodes, however, will not have access to the network. The idea behind this is to keep the critical nodes in the network attached to both rings.

The FDDI data rate is 100 Mbps. The maximum distance of the two fiber rings combined is 200 kilometers. Each ring can be 100 kilometers in length with up to 1000 nodes connected to it. The distance between the nodes can be as far as 2 kilometers. The FDDI standard has the potential to act as a backbone for LANs, CANs and MANs due to the distances that can be reached.

There is also an FDDI implementation over copper cable called copper distributed data interface (CDDI). CDDI can be configured with STP or voice-grade UTP. In a CDDI implementation, it is not uncommon to use an FDDI backbone with copper to the desktop. Of course the copper cable runs are limited between 50 and 100 meters. Using a combination of CDDI and FDDI could result in additional hardware costs.

3.4 WIRELESS 802 STANDARDS

Wireless networking has come to the forefront of the internetworking community. The IEEE has four working groups developing wireless standards: the 802.11 working group is developing wireless LANs; the 802.15 group is developing wireless personal area networks (PAN); the 802.16 group is working on wireless MANs; and the 802.18 group monitors and participates in the first three groups mentioned. 802.11, 802.15, and 802.16 are discussed within.

802.11

802.11b was developed to standardize the development of wireless LAN technology, which is becoming increasingly popular. It provides between 5.5 Mbps, 11 Mbps, and 54 Mbps of bandwidth.

Physical Topology

Nodes use wireless network adapters that send signals to wireless access points (WAP) (see Figure 3-18).

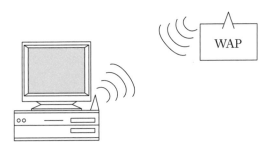

Figure 3-18. *Wireless Network*

WAPs can forward signals to other WAPs, or they can bring the signal to the backbone cable of a destination network (see Figure 3-19).

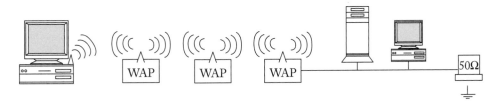

Figure 3-19. *Wireless Network with WAPs*

802.11 works at the 2.4 Ghz range of the radio spectrum. This happens to be the same range that most cordless phones operate at. 802.11a is a wireless standard that specifies the 5 Ghz range of the radio spectrum.

The access method is CSMA with collision avoidance (CSMA/CA). *CSMA/CA* is similar to CSMA/CD, however, nodes inform other nodes of their intention to transmit before they actually do. CSMA/CA is also used by Apple's LocalTalk network standard.

802.15

802.15 is the IEEE working group that is developing the wireless personal area network (WPAN) standard. A personal area network consists of devices that are within a person's operating space (POS). POS consists of an area 10 meters around a person, and the PAN devices can be held or worn by the person. The 802.15 standard identifies and investigates the need for low-power, low-complexity devices that are used within a person's POS. This standard has also been called "Bluetooth," and the devices include cell phones and PDAs among other hand-held devices.

The 802.15 Committee has several task groups working within it on multiple wireless technologies. Here is a list of the task groups:

- Task Group 1 works with the WPAN/Bluetooth Technology.
- Task Group 2 works on the coexistence of WPANs with 802.11-based wireless LANs.
- Task Group 3 is developing high data rate (up to 20 Mbps) WPANs.
- Task Group 4 develops low data rate (20 Kbps to 250 Kbps) WPANs.

Physical Topology. Connections between devices can be point-to-point or point-to-multipoint. The distance between transmitting devices can be up to 10 meters. The WPAN/Bluetooth standard operates at the 2.45 GHz range of the radio spectrum. It can transmit data at 1 Mbps (2 Mbps in a future release).

3.5 ADDITIONAL 802 STANDARDS

There are additional Project 802 standards. Not all of them will be covered here, however we will discuss the popular standards such as 802.2, 802.4, and 802.12.

802.2

802.2 is the IEEE standard that defines the logical division of the data-link layer of the OSI Model. 802.2 focuses on the Logical Link Control sublayer of the data-link layer of the OSI Reference Model. It provides the higher layers of the OSI Model with a consistent view of the lower layers. The LLC sublayer provides connection-oriented or connectionless service as well as flow control and upper-layer protocol flexibility. It masks the physical media from the layers above it allowing multiple standards to transmit data onto the media. The LLC also defines service access points (SAP) that allow data to travel to higher layers of the OSI Model. The MAC sublayer is defined by the layer 2 protocol being used, such as Ethernet or Token Ring.

802.4 AND ARCNET

ARCNet was proposed to the IEEE by General Motors. 802.4 standardized the ARCNet Token Bus Network Model. It uses the logical ring technology with a physical bus. The nodes pass a token from node to node in the LAN (see Figure 3-20).

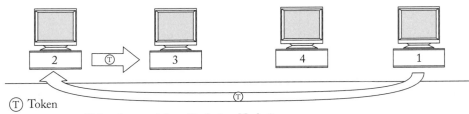

ⓣ Token

• Token is passed from Node 1 to Node 2
• When 2 has finished transmitting, it passes the token to node 3

Figure 3-20. *Token Bus*

ARCNet uses coaxial cable to connect stations together through passive hubs. The coax is RG-69, and it uses a 90 ohm resistor. ARCNet networks are not very popular in the internetworking community today.

802.12 100VG–ANYLAN

100VG-AnyLAN was proposed to the IEEE by Hewlett Packard and standardized as 802.12. 802.12 was originally developed to be able to forward both Ethernet and Token Ring frames on the same physical network without requiring the use of a router or gateway. It uses the demand priority access method, which grants nodes access to the network based on the priority of the data being sent by the node. This standard uses the hubs to control access to the wire, again based on the priority of the data sent. Once the hub allows a node to communicate, the node sends a unicast to the destination device thereby reducing broadcasts.

Physical Topology

The physical topology for 802.12 is a star but the network designer must take into consideration the fact that every device connected to the network must be 802.12 compatible, including NICs and hubs. Because of these hardware limitations, an 802.12 network can become costly. The transmission speed for 802.12 is 100 Mbps. It can be run over copper cable or fiber optic. The demand priority access method allows the parent hub control which node on the child hub can transmit data based on priority. There are only two priority levels: high and low. 802.12 hubs linked together build a hierarchical structure.

CHAPTER SUMMARY

Chapter 3 focused on layer 2 standards of the OSI Model. It described the specifications for the multiple Ethernet and 802.3 standards. Token Ring and 802.5 were also discussed, in addition to FDDI. Other layer 2 standards were also explained, such as 802.2, 802.4, 802.11 and 802.12. One of the key concepts to remember when dealing with layer 2 technologies is that you cannot mix and match layer 2 standards within the same LAN. Therefore, choosing the right layer 2 standard is an important decision to make when implementing a network. Before proceeding to the next chapter, complete the Knowledge Test in Chapter 3.

KNOWLEDGE TEST

1. Which connector should you use in 10BASE2?
   A. RJ-45
   B. ST
   C. BNC
   D. RJ-11

2. Which network transmission medium uses 10 Mbps and has a distance limitation of 100 meters?
   A. 10BaseF
   B. 10Base5
   C. 10Base2
   D. 10BaseT

3. There are several technologies that use a logical ring topology. Which IEEE specification maps to these?
   A. 802.2
   B. 802.11
   C. 802.3
   D. 802.12
   E. 802.5

4. What connector is shown in the figure?
   A. RJ 45 connector
   B. BNC connector
   C. AUI connector
   D. STC connector

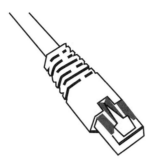

Exhibit

5. What cable is used in a 100BaseT network?
   A. RG58u
   B. RG62
   C. Cat 5
   D. Cat 3

6. Choose the three connectors that can be used in an 802.3 network.
   A. ST
   B. SCSI
   C. BNC
   D. RJ-45
   E. MIC

7. What transmission media is used to connect nodes to a 100BaseFX switch?
   A. Cat 3
   B. Cat 5
   C. Coax
   D. Fiber

8. You are supporting a Token Ring network. You have to increase the number of nodes on the network, so you add another MSAU. What do you have to ensure is properly configured for the ring to continue to operate?
   A. Ensure a bridge is used to connect the additional MSAU.
   B. Ensure the ring in is connected to the ring out of another MSAU and vice versa.
   C. Install the active monitor.
   D. Ensure the ring in port is connected to ring in port on another MSAU.

9. Which 802.3 standard uses a transceiver or vampire tap to connect nodes to the network?
   A. 10BaseT
   B. 100BaseTX
   C. 10Base2
   D. 10Base5

10. How many pairs of wire are used in a 10BaseT network cable?
    A. One
    B. Two
    C. Three
    D. Four

11. You are hired to set up a network printer for a company. You run a cable from the wall jack to a hub. You then run another cable from the hub to the printer. The network is a 100BaseT network. You connect a laptop to the printer locally and print a couple test pages to ensure it works. Users on the network, however, seem to be having a problem accessing the printer on the network. What do you think the problem may stem from?
    A. The printer is incompatible.
    B. All of the connectors used are RJ-45.
    C. The cable length is greater than 100 meters.
    D. The printer needs a vampire tap to connect to the backbone.

12. The building you are working in is wired with Category 3 UTP. All of the workstations have 10BaseT NICs installed in them. Your boss wants the entire network to be faster. What can you do to increase the speed of the network to at least 100 Mbps? (Choose two.)
    A. Rewire the entire building with Category 5 UTP or better.
    B. Install 100BaseTX NICs in all the workstations.
    C. Implement a Token Ring network.
    D. Replace all of the hubs with layer 2 switches.

13. The connection from your computer to the first hub is 103 meters. You cannot connect to the server in the network. You assume this is because the cable run is too long. What can you do to correct the problem?
    A. Replace the NIC.
    B. Use better cable.
    C. Add a repeater closer to the node.
    D. Put a 100BaseFX NIC in your machine.

14. What type of connector is in the figure?
    A. RJ-45
    B. ST
    C. SC
    D. BNC
    E. AUI

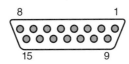

Exhibit

15. Which cable type is most susceptible to crosstalk?
    A. STP
    B. UTP
    C. Coaxial 1
    D. Fiber optic

16. If the NIC being used has an AUI, how can it be connected to the network?
    A. With an RJ-45
    B. With a BNS
    C. With a T connector
    D. Through a transceiver

17. What is the distance limitation of a 10Base2 cable segment?
    A. 100 Meter
    B. 185 Meters
    C. 500 Meters
    D. 1000 Meters

18. Choose two 802 standards that use token passing as their media access method?
    A. 802.3
    B. 802.3ab
    C. 802.4
    D. 802.5
    E. 802.12

19. What 802 standard uses CSMA/CD?
    A. 802.3
    B. 802.4
    C. 802.5
    D. 802.12

20. What do 802.11 and AppleTalk have in common?
    A. They both use CSMA/CD as their media access method.
    B. They both use token passing as their media access method.
    C. They both use CSMA/CA as their media access method.
    D. They both use polling as their media access method.

CHAPTER 4

Network Protocols

OBJECTIVES

At the end of this chapter you will be able to:

- Differentiate between routable and non-routable protocols.

- Explain what a protocol suite is.

- Understand the Transmission Control Protocol/Internet Protocol (TCP/IP) protocol suite.

- Explain what protocols operate within the TCP/IP suite.

- Explain the Internetwork Packet Exchange/Sequenced Packet Exchange (IPX/SPX) protocol suite.

- Understand several protocols.

INTRODUCTION

In Chapter 4, several *protocol suites* will be discussed. A protocol suite is a group of protocols that work together to provide communication. There are several protocol suites that are popular in the networking industry. For the Network+ exam you will have to become extremely familiar with the TCP/IP protocol suite of which much of this chapter focuses on. You will learn the history of the suite, how the suite is further developed, as well as what protocols work within the suite. Novell's proprietary IPX/SPX suite will also be discussed, along with several other protocols. First we will begin with a discussion about routable and non-routable protocols.

4.1 ROUTABLE VERSUS NON-ROUTABLE PROTOCOLS

Protocols come in two general categories: routable and non-routable. A *routable protocol* is a protocol that can traverse a router without any additional router configuration. A *non-routable protocol* is a protocol that cannot cross through a router by default. Most non-routable protocols are broadcast based. This means that when they are to communicate with hosts on a network, they send a broadcast to all directly-attached nodes, and the node that the message is destined for responds. Protocols send messages in one of three methods: broadcast, which goes to all nodes; unicast, which goes to a single node; and multicast, which goes to a specific group of nodes. Since routers filter out broadcasts, the non-routable protocols are filtered at the router. For a router to forward broadcasts it must follow the specifications noted in RFC 1542.

Routable protocols are more popular in large internetworks simply because they can transport data from one end of an internetwork to the other end, without saturating the communication lines with broadcast messages. They often have many configurable options and can sometimes require additional support. Non-routable protocols are popular in small networks because they do not have many configurable options, often requiring little or no support. Non-routable protocols are best suited for networks that consist of one cable segment and do not have any routers in it. This chapter focuses on routable protocols first, then non-routable protocols.

4.2 TCP/IP

Transmission Control Protocol/Internet Protocol (or TCP/IP as most refer to it) is the most popular protocol suite or protocol stack in the world. The term protocol stack is interchangeable with the term protocol suite. TCP/IP is the universal transport protocol of the Internet. It is supported by documents called Request For Comments, which are available to the public. RFCs go through several stages before they become a standard. For example, an RFC is first considered a draft, then it becomes a proposed standard and, if it is accepted, it finally becomes an approved standard. Each TCP/IP standard is recorded in an RFC by number and increased incrementally. For example, the first RFC written about TCP/IP is RFC 1. Currently, there are several thousand RFCs. RFCs and TCP/IP standards are maintained by the IETF, which stands for the Internet Engineering Task Force. The IETF grew out of the Internet Architecture Board (IAB) when the Internet became too large for a single organization (the IAB) to maintain. The IAB is still active, however it has spawned the Internet Society, the Internet Research Task Force, and the IETF. There is a list of popular RFCs at the end of this chapter that may be of use.

HISTORY OF TCP/IP

The roots of the TCP/IP protocol suite actually go further back than the current seven-layered OSI Model used today. In the 1970s, the Defense Advanced Research Projects Agency (DARPA) had a set of protocols created to forward data in a packet-switched network. The protocol had four layers (see Figure 4-1). The Department of Defense (DoD) protocol suite evolved into the TCP/IP suite used today.

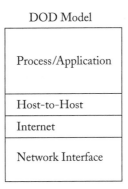

DOD Model

Process/Application
Host-to-Host
Internet
Network Interface

Figure 4-1. *The DOD Model*

THE TCP/IP MODEL AND THE OSI MODEL

The TCP/IP model consists of four layers. The layers of the TCP/IP suite do not directly correspond with the layers of the OSI Model (see Figure 4-2).

OSI Model	TCP/IP Protocol Suite	DOD Model
Application	Application	Process/Application
Presentation		
Session		
Transport	Transport	Host-to-Host
Network	Internet	Internet
Data-Link	Network Access	Network
Physical		

Figure 4-2. *The OSI Model, TCP/IP Model and the DOD Model*

Several protocols operate at each layer of the model. Although the suite is named after two protocols (TCP and IP), there are many more that make up the suite. Each layer's protocols will be explained here, beginning with the lowest layer and working up to the upper-most layer.

Test Tip: A simple way to remember the four layers is to use the acronym ATIN. Application, Transport, Internet, Network Interface.

NETWORK ACCESS LAYER

The network access layer of the TCP/IP model is closely related to the lower two layers of the OSI Model. The standards that are covered in the network interface layer include wiring standards such as 10BaseT, 10Base2, etc. Protocols that map to the first layer of the TCP/IP suite include Ethernet (IEEE 802.3), Token Ring (IEEE 802.5), and all other data-link layer standards, such as 802.4, ATM, frame relay, PPP, ISDN, X.25, and HDLC. The MAC and LLC sublayers of the OSI Model are also included in the network interface layer. Remember, the MAC sublayer describes how data transfers onto wire. The LLC sublayer defines SAPs for data to travel to the layers higher in the suite.

INTERNET LAYER

The internet layer maps to layer 3, the network layer, of the OSI Model. Routing and network addressing occur at this layer. There are several protocols that operate at this layer in the TCP/IP model. Some of these are the *Internet Protocol (IP)*, the *Internet Control Message Protocol (ICMP)*, the *Address Resolution Protocol (ARP)*, and the *Reverse Address Resolution Protocol (RARP)*.

Internet Protocol (IP)

IP is the protocol that deals with the delivery (and routing) of packets or datagrams. It is a connectionless, unreliable protocol that receives its error correction from upper-layer protocols. IP is responsible for the fragmentation and reassembly of packets. For example, the following figure shows how a router fragments a packet. Router A receives a packet from an interface that is connected to a network using a frame size of approximately 4202 bytes. The destination node is located on a line that can only handle frames that are 1500 bytes. Because the frame exceeds the maximum transmission unit (or MTU) of the destination line, the router, using IP, must fragment the larger frame before placing it on the destination network. IP will reassemble the packet at the final destination.

During this process the same IP header is placed on each packet that was derived from the original packet. Only the data within the packet is being split up. The IP header contains the destination and source IP addresses of a packet. IP uses a hierarchical addressing scheme, rather than a flat addressing scheme which is used for physical (MAC) addressing. Hierarchical addressing consists of a logical grouping of addresses that share a commonality. All nodes using IP addresses on the same network share the same network number but have different node numbers. With a flat addressing scheme, every address is different with no relation to each other. IP addressing is covered in Chapter 5.

Internet Control Message Protocol (ICMP)

ICMP is the protocol that sends error and control messages between networked devices. The protocol sends several types of messages. Five of the most popular are:

- Echo request: Message requesting ICMP at a receiving node to send a reply to test connectivity.

- Echo reply: Reply to an echo request.

- Destination unreachable: Message sent stating that a router is unable to deliver a packet.

- Time exceeded: Message sent stating that a specific packet has exceeded its hop limit.

- Source quench: A receiving node will send an ICMP message to a node that is sending data too fast for its memory buffers and processor to handle (a form of flow control).

To see ICMP in action, use the PING or tracert utility. ICMP is the protocol that sends the replies when using these commands. Both of these utilities are very useful and test the network connections to the second layer of the TCP/IP suite.

Address Resolution Protocol (ARP)

The ARP protocol performs address resolution so nodes can successfully communicate in a TCP/IP network. When two nodes communicate, they are using the physical addresses of one another to send data back and forth. However, when TCP/IP is implemented in a network, the nodes prefer to utilize IP addresses to communicate. ARP allows nodes to use IP addresses by resolving IP addresses into MAC addresses. For example, a source node attempts to contact a destination node. In most cases, the source node will send an ARP request to determine the MAC address of the destination node. The destination node will respond with its MAC address, which allows them to continue communicating (see Figure 4-3).

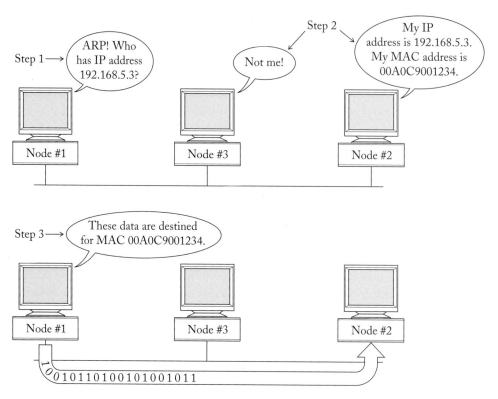

Figure 4-3. *Example of ARP*

Once each node knows the MAC address of the other node, the MAC address is placed into the ARP cache of the node. The ARP cache will maintain the entry for a specified amount of time, normally two minutes. After two minutes, the entry will be removed if the node does not use it again. If the node needs to send data to the destination node again, it will first look to its ARP cache to determine if the MAC address is there. If it is, the source node does not have to send an ARP request again. If the ARP entry is used again before the initial two minutes expire, the entry will remain in the ARP cache for an additional time limit, normally eight minutes.

ARP requests are broadcasts and, as already discussed, broadcasts are filtered out by routers. This is interesting because all nodes in the TCP/IP network must know the MAC address of the node they are communicating with. In a single LAN without routers, each node can send an ARP request for another node and receive an ARP response. In an internetwork, the process is slightly different. When a node sends an

ARP request for a node on a different cable segment with a different network address, the default gateway will respond. The default gateway is usually a router or a proxy server in the network. If this is the case, when a source node sends an ARP request for a node on a separate network, the router will respond with an ARP response. The source now talks directly with the router. The router is responsible for sending an ARP request on the destination network and waiting for an ARP response. The source node must now trust the router to successfully transfer the data to the final destination. MAC addresses are unique to all network interface cards. They are twelve hexadecimal digits long and look like this:

00A0C1 BE2F10

The first six digits are called the organizational unit identifier (OUI). They are given to the manufacturer of the NIC by the IEEE. The second six digits are given to the NIC by the manufacturer.

Reverse Address Resolution Protocol (RARP)

RARP operates similar to ARP, but it is the reverse process. RARP allows for MAC-to-IP address resolution. It is possible to utilize diskless workstations with a RARP server. When a diskless workstation boots up, the only address it knows is its MAC address. During the boot process it will send a RARP request to receive an IP address. When a RARP server hears the RARP broadcast it will respond with an IP address. After it receives it, it can then request an operating system from the RARP server. The dynamic host configuration protocol (DHCP) and the bootstrap protocol (BOOTP) are similar to RARP.

Internet Group Management Protocol (IGMP)

IGMP maintains the list of nodes that are intended to receive multicast packets. A multicast packet is one that is destined for a specified group of nodes. IGMP and multicasts are often used for system settings that require a specified number of servers or routers to communicate with each other.

Network Time Protocol (NTP)

NTP allows for time synchronization of nodes on a network. If servers that have an Internet connection implement NTP, they can synchronize their real-time clocks with the Coordinated Universal Time, previously known as Greenwich Mean Time.

IP Version 6

IP is undergoing a revision. At the time of this writing, IP version 4 is being used. The version on the horizon is IPv6, also known as IP Next Generation (or IPNG). It is already included as part of IP support in many vendor products. IPv6 is covered in RFC 2460, which overwrites RFC 1883. It was designed as an evolutionary improvement to IP version 4. Ipv6 was developed to work either independently of or with IPv4 nodes; the two protocols are completely compatible with one another. IPv6 is scheduled to become the primary IP used between the years 2005 and 2015.

There have been several improvements to the protocol in this revision. The most obvious is that IP addresses are lengthened from 32 bits to 128 bits. Examples of the address will be examined in the next chapter. This larger addressing scheme plans for considerable future growth of the Internet and solves the problem associated with the depletion of IPv4 addresses.

Another enhancement to the protocol is the standard creation of the "anycast." Anycasts occur when one host transmits to the nearest host of multiple hosts. This is similar to multicasts but only communicates with the first available node of the group. IPv6 will still support both unicasts (one node to one node communication), multicasts (one node to a group of registered nodes), and broadcasts (one node to all nodes).

Other enhancements include an extension to the header that is examined only at the destination, which will speed up overall network performance. The header extensions will support authentication, data integrity, and confidentiality. Furthermore, some of the IPv4 header fields have been removed or made optional to lessen the overhead on the packet. Finally, packets can be identified as belonging to a particular "flow" of data. This is a quality-of-service measure that will significantly improve real-time applications, such as video streaming.

TRANSPORT LAYER

The transport layer of the TCP/IP model maps directly to the transport layer of the OSI Model. It does, however, contain some session layer functionality. There are two protocols that operate at this layer, one offering connection-oriented communication, and one offering connectionless communication. The connection-oriented protocol is the *Transmission Control Protocol (TCP)*. The connectionless protocol is the *User Datagram Protocol (UDP)*.

Transmission Control Protocol (TCP)

TCP meets the connection-oriented standards of the transport layer because it has several features that include:

- Sequencing—TCP sequences its segments as they are sent to the Internet layer of the TCP/IP suite. Remember, during encapsulation the transport layer converts data into segments. These segments are numbered and then forwarded. Sequencing takes place because IP sends packets of the same stream in different directions on the way to the final destination. The packets are reassembled once they reach the final destination. However, it is a connectionless process so TCP has to check the sequence numbers of the segments to ensure they all made it to the destination. If one is missing, TCP will request it be retransmitted.

- Acknowledgements—TCP segments are acknowledged by the destination machine. ACK segments are sent back to the sending node, reassuring that a segment was received. The ACK segment specifies which segment the receiving node should receive next by increasing the sequence number it is acknowledging receipt of by one. For example, if Node A sends a segment with a sequence number of 1 to Node B, Node B's ACK will request segment number 2 from Node A.

- Sliding Windows—Sliding windows allow two nodes using TCP to agree upon the number of segments received before an ACK must be sent. For example, Node A and Node B can agree on a window size of eight. Once Node B receives the eighth segment, an ACK requesting segments nine through sixteen will be sent from Node B to Node A. This cuts down on meaningless traffic and bandwidth usage.

- Flow control—If a node using TCP becomes overloaded with data, it can reduce the sliding window size to zero, thereby preventing the sending node from forwarding any data. Once its buffers are free it will reset its window size, and communication will occur once again.

TCP uses a *three-way handshake* to establish a session. The three-way handshake consists of a series of segments sent as session requests and acknowledgments between nodes. It is used to determine whether or not a session can be established. If so, a session between the nodes called a *virtual circuit* is established. The following is an example of a three-way handshake. When PC A would like to establish a session with file server 1, it sends one segment requesting a session. This is the first handshake. File Server 1 will respond with an acknowledgement to the first handshake and will then request to establish a session with PC A. PC A will then send an acknowledgement back to File Server 1 confirming that it received the last segment and that a session has been established (see Figure 4-4). When a session between two nodes is closed correctly, a three-way handshake will occur, again ending the session.

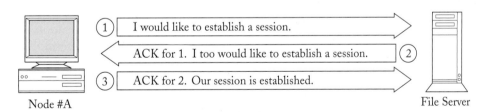

Figure 4-4. *Three-Way Handshake*

Test Tip: TCP is associated with the following terms: connection-oriented, reliable, guaranteed delivery.

User Datagram Protocol (UDP)

UDP is a connectionless protocol that operates at the transport layer. UDP does not offer sequencing, acknowledgements, windowing, flow control, or the three-way handshake. Because UDP does not offer any of these features, it adds much less header information, reducing the overhead on the network's bandwidth. UDP is used for application layer protocols that do not require a connection-oriented transport. Application layer protocols that do not require a connection-oriented transport normally have error correction mechanisms built in to the protocol.

Test Tip: UDP is associated with the following terms: unreliable, connectionless, non-guaranteed delivery.

Sockets and Ports

When two nodes using TCP/IP communicate, there must be a means for the sending node's transport protocol to tell the receiving node's transport protocol where to deliver the application layer data. TCP/IP uses a socket to create the connection and a port to deliver the application layer data.

Sockets. A *socket* is a combination of the destination node's IP address, transport protocol (TCP or UDP), and port number. A socket is equivalent to a virtual pipe, which is established to give the sending node the ability to reliably send data.

Ports. A *port* represents the address assigned to the application layer protocol, in the TCP/IP suite, that is ultimately responsible for receiving data. When a node receives data, it must travel up the protocol stack. The data receives directions from the LLC of the data-link layer on how to go up the stack. However, once the data makes it as high as the transport layer, the transport protocol must know which application layer protocol to give the data to. Both TCP and UDP use port numbers to determine the application layer protocol that the data is destined for. Ports are represented by a value between 0-65534. This information is placed in the header of the TCP or UDP segment during encapsulation and must be read during de-encapsulation.

Although there are tens of thousands of ports, only 0-1023 are used on a regular basis. These port numbers are considered well-known port numbers. Ports 1024 and above are either randomly-assigned ports or privately-registered ports (for vendor specific applications). Table 4.1 lists popular, well-known ports and the respective application layer protocols that use them.

TABLE 4-1   PORT NUMBERS FOR POPULAR APPLICATION LAYER PROTOCOLS

Protocol		TCP Port	UDP Port
FTP	Program	20	
	Data	21	
Telnet		23	
SMTP		25	
DNS		53	53
TFTP			69
SNMP			161
RIP			520

In some cases, port numbers are shared by both TCP and UDP. However, in most implementations the application layer protocol only uses a TCP or UDP port. In the Windows 2000 operating system, there is a file called Services. This file lists the well-known ports that the operating system will be aware of after boot up. To see the file, simply navigate to the System32/Drivers/etc directory and open the file using Notepad. TCP and UDP are also given port numbers, considered protocol numbers. TCP uses port 6 and UDP uses port 17. These ports are used to identify the destination of the data coming from the Internet layer in an IP packet going to the transport layer. They are identified in the IP header's protocol field.

Ports are always identified in TCP/IP communication. The default ports are normally written into the application that is being used. For example, if using a web browser to navigate to a web site, port 80 is assumed because the web site is going to be requested via HTTP. It is possible to use a port number other than 80 in this instance. For a computer to host a web site it must be using a web service. Microsoft's web service is called Internet Information Server (or IIS). When managing web sites with IIS it is possible to change the default port from 80 to another port number, for example 12001. When a user attempts to access the web site, she will find a web page unavailable error message if she does not properly identify the port. To identify the proper port, simply add a colon and then the port number to the end of the URL, as seen below:

http://www.delmarlearning.com:12001

APPLICATION LAYER

The application layer of the TCP/IP model is responsible for interfacing between the transport layer and the end-user's application. It is not the end-user's application, but it provides the end-user's application with the ability to operate in a networked environment. It is the equivalent to the application, presentation, and session layer of the OSI Model. This means that protocols developed for the application layer of the TCP/IP model have presentation and session layer code written into them. Application layer protocols are assigned port numbers. There are many application layer protocols. Some of the popular protocols are described herein:

- File Transfer Protocol (FTP)—Transfers files between two nodes. TCP port 20 for data and TCP port 21 for control.

- Secure Copy Protocol (SCP)—A remote copy protocol used with Secure Shell (SSH) that allows users at remote locations to copy data from one host or server to another. SSH provides the authentication and encryption; therefore, SCP works over port 22.

- Secure Shell (SSH)—SSH is a Unix-based protocol and command line interface that operates over TCP port 22 and UDP port 22. It is used to securely access a remote computer. SSH utilizes RSA public key cryptography as well as digital certificates between the client and the server. The IETF has proposed a set of standards for SSH2, which is the latest version.

- Telnet—Terminal emulation that provides remote connection services. It is often used to connect to routers remotely for configuration over a TCP/IP LAN connection. Telnet transfers data in clear text. TCP port 23 is used by Telnet.

- Simple Message Transfer Protocol (SMTP)—E-mail sending protocol. SMTP uses TCP port 25.

- Trivial File Transfer Protocol (TFTP)—A smaller version of FTP used to transfer files between hosts. This protocol is often used to store router configurations over the network. TFTP uses UDP port 69.

- Domain Name System (DNS)—Provides domain name resolution. The domain name system is used on the Internet to translate computer host names (also known as fully-qualified domain names, or FQDNs) into IP addresses. TCP port 53 is used for zone transfers, and UDP port 53 is used for name resolution.

- Dynamic Host Configuration Protocol (DHCP)—DHCP provides a service that allows for nodes on a network to automatically receive an IP address during their initial boot sequence. DHCP is based on the BOOTP protocol. Both DHCP and BOOTP use UDP port 67 for the server and UDP port 68 for the client.

- Bootstrap Protocol (BOOTP)—Allows diskless workstations to determine their IP address while booting up with an operating system assigned by a remote server. BOOTP uses UDP port 67 for the server and UDP port 68 for the client.

- Hyper Text Transfer Protocol (HTTP)—Used to transfer web pages often consisting of text, image, video, and multimedia files over a network between a client and a server. There are also secure versions of HTTP, such as HTTPS, to allow for the encryption and de-encryption of web page requests. HTTPS is based on the secure sockets layer (SSL) security protocol. It uses port 443. HTTP uses port 80.

- Post Office Protocol and Internet Messaging Access Protocol (POP3/IMAP4)—Both are electronic mail-receiving protocols. POP3 uses TCP port 110 and IMAP4 uses TCP port 143.

- Secure File Transfer Protocol (SFTP)—SFTP is a protocol similar to FTP that runs over an SSH or SSH2 tunnel. Since the protocol runs through an SSH or SSH2 tunnel the data within an encrypted tunnel is considered to be secure. SFTP operates over TCP port 115.

- Network News Transfer Protocol (NNTP)—Allows a newsgroup reader to subscribe to, post articles to, and retrieve articles from newsgroups. A newsgroup is a form of network discussion group in which users from all over the world can participate. TCP port 119 is used for NNTP.

- Simple Network Management Protocol (SNMP)—SNMP is a remote management protocol that monitors network components. It uses UDP port 161.

- Network File System (NFS)—Allows clients to access resources on remote servers through the mapping of virtual drives. NFS uses UDP port 2049.

- Network Time Protocol (NTP)—Although NTP is discussed at the Internet layer, it is given a port number for data to travel to. NTP uses UDP port 123.

- Lightweight Directory Access Protocol (LDAP)—LDAP is a set of protocols for accessing information directories. LDAP is based on the X.500 standard, which is the ITU's standard for directory access. LDAP utilizes TCP port 389.

- X-Windows—A method of remotely controlling the GUI of another machine. There are two components: the X server and the X client. It was developed and copyrighted by the Massachusetts Institute of Technology (MIT). X-Windows uses TCP as its primary transport protocol.

- Line Printer Request (LPR)—A network printer protocol that allows for IP printing in a network. LPR operates on port 515.

 Test Tip: Be aware of port numbers and their protocols.

4.3 IPX/SPX

The Internetwork Packet Exchange/Sequenced Packet Exchange (IPX/SPX) protocol is a proprietary protocol that was developed by Novell and is used by the NetWare network operating system. Although NetWare 5.0 has gone to TCP/IP as its native protocol, earlier versions of NetWare still retain a fair share of the networking industry.

THE PROTOCOL SUITE

IPX/SPX is a scaleable protocol, which means it can work well in large internetworks. IPX/SPX is similar to the TCP/IP suite in terms of design and how it maps to the OSI Model. It also uses a hierarchical addressing scheme with the combination of host and network addresses similar to TCP/IP addressing. In terms of the actual functionality of the protocol, it is quite different from the TCP/IP suite.

The IPX/SPX protocol suite maps to the OSI Model with a four-layered model (see Figure 4-5). Notice the differences in the two models. When comparing the TCP/IP

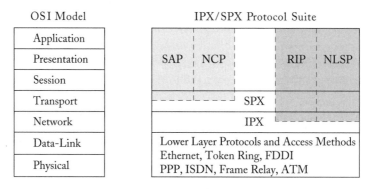

Figure 4-5. *IPX/SPX Suite with the OSI Model*

suite to the OSI Model, it did not map directly to the OSI Model either. In Figure 4-6, the TCP/IP suite and the IPX/SPX suite of protocols are compared.

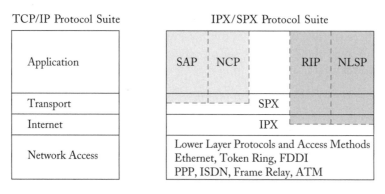

Figure 4-6. *IPX/SPX Suite with the TCP/IP Suite*

When comparing the IPX/SPX model to the TCP/IP model it is possible to make correlations between the protocols. For example, the SPX portion of the IPX/SPX protocol suite maps to the TCP portion of the TCP/IP protocol suite. Like TCP/IP, more than two protocols make up the suite. The basic protocols in the IPX/SPX suite include: IPX, SPX, Netware Core Protocols (NCP), RIP for IPX/SPX, and the Service Advertising Protocol (SAP).

INTERNETWORK PACKET EXCHANGE (IPX)

IPX works at layer 3 of the OSI Model and is the routed protocol of the IPX/SPX suite. IPX is a connectionless protocol and does not utilize acknowledgements. The IPX header controls the network layer addressing. IPX uses *sockets* to establish virtual connections with upper-layer protocols, which are similar to TCP/IP ports.

SEQUENCED PACKET EXCHANGE (SPX)

SPX operates at layer 4 of the OSI Model. It is the primary transport protocol of the IPX/SPX suite and uses sequence numbers and acknowledgements to guarantee delivery. SPX provides connection-oriented communication.

 Test Tip: IPX is equivalent to IP. SPX is equivalent to TCP.

NETWARE CORE PROTOCOLS (NCP)

NCP are the upper-layer protocols that allow for the ability to access files over the network and print in a networked environment. NCP also handles security functions on the network.

IPX ROUTING INFORMATION PROTOCOL (IPX RIP)

IPX RIP allows for the routing of information between networks.

NETWARE LINK SERVICES PROTOCOL (NLSP)

NLSP is Novell's link-state routing protocol.

SERVICE ADVERTISING PROTOCOL (SAP)

SAP is an important feature of the IPX/SPX suite. It is used by servers to advertise the services available to other nodes in the IPX Internetwork. Such services include, but are not limited to, file, print, time synchronization, and directory services. Each server stores a list of services they know about in a SAP table.

4.4 ADDITIONAL ROUTABLE PROTOCOLS

Listed below are additional routable protocols to include NwLink, XNS, AppleTalk, SNA, and OSI.

NWLINK

Although IPX/SPX was designed for Novell NetWare, Microsoft has created its own version of IPX/SPX so its operating systems can interconnect with Novell's in a mixed-networking environment. The NWLINK protocol utilizes the same configuration settings used with IPX/SPX.

XEROX NETWORK SYSTEM (XNS)

Developed by Xerox, this protocol was popular for Ethernet LANs in the 1980s. XNS uses a five-layered model, identified by layers 0 through 4. Although once popular, it has largely been replaced by TCP/IP Networks.

APPLETALK

Introduced in 1984, AppleTalk is a proprietary protocol suite used in Apple networks. AppleTalk is a broadcast-based protocol that organizes nodes into logical groups called zones. Nodes can be up to 1000 feet apart, and the protocol transmits data at 230 Kbps. The AppleTalk suite does include other protocols that work at layers that map to the OSIRM. For example, the AppleTalk filing protocol (AFP) is an application-layer protocol used to transfer files. The AppleTalk Transaction Protocol (ATP) and the Routing Table Maintenance Protocol are transport-layer protocols. The network-layer protocol of the AppleTalk suite is the Datagram Delivery Protocol (DDP). It provides best-effort delivery for packets. Finally, one of the data-link protocols is the LocalTalk Link Access Protocol, or LLAP.

Apple's latest operating system, Mac OS X, utilizes TCP/IP as its primary protocol suite. However, when connecting to older versions of the OS, you may be required to utilize a gateway protocol that can translate between AppleTalk and IP. Apple's version of this gateway is AppleTalk-over-IP, and it does do the conversion needed to allow for file sharing among different versions of the Mac OS.

SYSTEMS NETWORK ARCHITECTURE (SNA)

SNA is the most widely-used mainframe protocol suite. It is traditionally a hierarchical, centralized protocol, which are normally non-routable. However, it is now moving to a peer-to-peer distributed processing model through the use of Advanced Peer-to-Peer Networking/Communications, or APPN/APPC. The technology behind APPN and APPC is allowing SNA end nodes to communicate with other end nodes bypassing the centralized processor. APPN/APPC is a fully-routable implementation of SNA.

OPEN SYSTEMS INTERCONNECT (OSI)

The OSI protocol suite is one that maps directly to the OSI Model. It includes protocols that work at each layer of the model. It was designed to provide full networking functionality. It did not, however, become popular in North America and did not generate enough support to be the premiere internetworking protocol, as TCP/IP did.

4.5 NON-ROUTABLE PROTOCOLS

Non-routable protocols are protocols that cannot be passed over routers in the router's default configuration. There are several non-routable protocols to discuss. However, because of their limited use in large internetworks, not much of this book will be dedicated to them. There are several non-routable protocols that may be encountered in the networking industry. The most popular of the few is NetBEUI, which originally came from IBM's NetBIOS standard.

NETBIOS

Before discussing NetBEUI, a short explanation of the NetBIOS standard is in order. It provides the services available for applications and programs to communicate seamlessly with the underlying network components. NetBIOS is a session-layer protocol that allows for nodes on the same LAN to communicate with one another through its interface. NetBIOS works with several protocols providing session-layer support. It was at one time integrated with the NetBEUI protocol. However, it can work independently of NetBEUI, supporting both TCP/IP and IPX/SPX.

NETBIOS EXTENDED USER INTERFACE (NETBEUI)

It is important to understand NetBEUI because for many years it was integrated into Microsoft's operating systems. Although NetBEUI was developed by IBM, it is most popular for its integration with Windows NT. NetBEUI is a small, fast, non-configurable protocol that works best with peer-to-peer networks. NetBEUI uses NETBIOS names rather than addresses for all nodes to be uniquely identified on the network. NetBEUI networks should not exceed 200 nodes. NetBEUI was designed as the transport mechanism for the NetBIOS standard described above.

LOCAL ACCESS TRANSPORT (LAT)

LAT is a non-routable protocol that is implemented in a mainframe environment. It was developed by the Digital Equipment Corporation and was used in DECnet environments. LAT was designed to reside on one LAN without a protocol field that specifies network addresses. Therefore, it is non-routable.

DATA LINK CONTROL (DLC)

DLC was originally designed as a client-to-mainframe protocol. However, current implementations of DLC are primarily related to connecting printers to networks.

CHAPTER SUMMARY

Chapter 4 prepared you for many questions you will see on the Network+ exam. Understanding protocols is very important in the internetworking industry. In this chapter, you learned about the two most popular protocol suites, TCP/IP and IPX/SPX. Although IPX/SPX is being phased out of many networks, you may run into a network using it in the future. You were also shown the difference between routable and non-routable protocols and given many examples of both. Be sure to complete the Knowledge Test before going on to the next chapter.

KNOWLEDGE TEST

Choose one answer for each question unless otherwise stated in the question.

1. What transport protocol does TFTP utilize?
   A. IP
   B. TCP
   C. UDP
   D. SPX

2. What secure protocol is based on SSL?
   A. PPTP
   B. IPSec
   C. IPTP
   D. HTTPS

3. Choose the protocol that is used to troubleshoot a TCP/IP network.
   A. NNTP
   B. SMTP
   C. IMAP
   D. SNMP

4. What transport protocol does Telnet utilize?
   A. TCP
   B. UDP
   C. SPX
   D. IP

5. Match the application layer protocols to their respective port numbers.

HTTP	21
SMTP	80
POP3	23
FTP	110
Telnet	25

6. It is possible to block ports with some network devices. This ensures hackers cannot gain access to your network through well-known ports. If your company uses a firewall to block ports 75 through 100, which service may be affected?
   A. FTP
   B. NTP
   C. HTTP
   D. SMTP

7. What port number does SNMP utilize?
   A. TCP 169
   B. UDP 169
   C. TCP 161
   D. UDP 161

8. Which TCP/IP port number identifies NTP?
   A. UDP 123
   B. TCP 123
   C. UDP 121
   D. TCP 121

9. What are some of the characteristics of NetBEUI? (Choose all that apply.)
   A. Large amount of overhead
   B. Small, fast protocol
   C. Difficult to administer
   D. Self-configurable
   E. Uses names to uniquely identify nodes on a network.
   F. Addresses are based on MAC address

10. If you have a mixed network with a few Macintosh computers in it, what protocol do you have to ensure the network printer is compatible with for the Macs to be able to print?
    A. TCP/IP
    B. NetBEUI
    C. DLC
    D. AppleTalk

11. What protocol in the TCP/IP suite maps IP addresses to MAC addresses?
    A. ARP
    B. ASP
    C. AARP
    D. ARAP

12. What application layer protocol does AppleTalk use to transfer files.
    A. RCP
    B. ARP
    C. AFS
    D. AFP

13. The TCP/IP application layer maps to which three OSI layers?
    A. Physical, data-link, network
    B. Network, transport, session
    C. Session, presentation, application
    D. Transport, session, presentation

14. Which protocol sends Echo Request, Echo Reply, and Destination Unreachable messages?
    A. ICMP
    B. IMCP
    C. IMSP
    D. ISMP
    E. IP

15. What port would be used if the following command was typed in a web browser: Ftp.delmarlearning.com
    A. 23
    B. 25
    C. 21
    D. 80

16. You install a network device that prevents hackers from accessing the internal network. Your users can no longer gain access to their POP3 e-mail accounts. What is most likely causing the problem?
    A. You have already been hacked and it is too late.
    B. The SMTP service is no longer working.
    C. Port 161 is being blocked, therefore POP3 mail cannot make it to the nodes.
    D. Port 110 is being blocked, therefore POP3 mail cannot make it to the nodes.

17. What protocols use the MAC address to uniquely identify nodes on the network? (Choose two.)
    A. IPX/SPX
    B. AppleTalk
    C. TCP/IP
    D. NWLink

18. If you have a Microsoft computer in a Novell NetWare 4.11 network, what protocol must be loaded on the Microsoft workstation?
    A. IPX/SPX
    B. NWLink
    C. TCP/IP
    D. DLC

19. Most e-mail programs utilize what two protocols? (Choose two.)
    A. IMAP
    B. SNMP
    C. POP3
    D. SMTP

20. Which of the following protocols have mechanisms in place to request data be resent if it is corrupted or lost during transmission? (Choose all that apply.)
    A. IP
    B. ICMP
    C. TCP
    D. UDP
    E. IPX
    F. SPX

knowledge TEST

CHAPTER 5

Network Addressing

OBJECTIVES

At the end of this chapter you will be able to:

- Understand how to address a TCP/IP network.
- Understand how to subnet addresses in a TCP/IP network.
- Describe CIDR and how it is used.
- Recognize IP version 6 addresses.
- Explain how IPX/SPX addressing is configured.

INTRODUCTION

In any network, there is always a need to uniquely define each node. Similarly, in an inter-network there is always a need to uniquely address the networks from one another. TCP/IP has a hierarchical addressing scheme that allows for unique network addresses each with unique host addresses available on it. In this chapter you will learn how to design and address a TCP/IP internetwork with IP version 4. IP version 6 addressing will also be described. You will also learn about addressing an IPX/SPX network.

5.1 IP ADDRESS REGISTRATION

TCP/IP is the universal language of the Internet. Every node on the public Internet must have a unique address from every other node on the Internet. The authority that monitors and maintains the records of IP address assignment is the Internet Corporation for Assigned Names and Numbers (ICANN). If a company or an individual wishes to connect to the Internet, there are several ways they can do this. One method would be to contact ICANN and submit a request for registration of an IP address or an entire range of IP addresses. Another method is to connect through an Internet service provider, which usually charges a monthly fee. Not all companies, however, need to have a public Internet address for all computers in the local network. In other words, it is possible to have a private TCP/IP network without a registered IP address. If this is the case, Internet connections will be impossible until a unique registered address is sourced (see Figure 5-1).

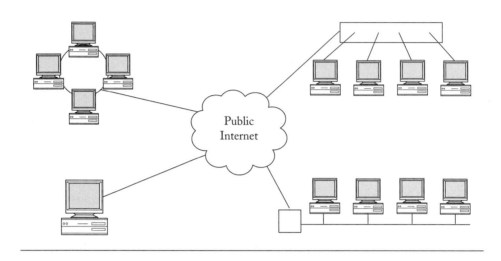

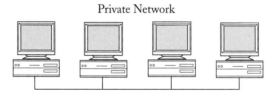

Figure 5-1. *Private Network and Public Internet*

Registration of IP addresses is not a requirement for a network to use the TCP/IP protocol suite as the primary protocol. Many companies, however, prefer to have registered IP addresses so other users in the world can access their network as well as their web servers, which often contain support and technical information, company information, and product information and availability with the ability to purchase products online. Also, if a company requires their core workforce use the Internet for daily activities, it may also be beneficial to request an IP address from ICANN. This will reduce the monthly cost associated with having to lease the service from an ISP, especially if multiple locations are involved.

5.2 IP ADDRESSING

In the TCP/IP protocol suite, addressing occurs at two levels, the network interface layer which deals with physical (MAC) address, and the Internet layer which deals with logical (hierarchical) addressing. IP is currently in its fourth version (IPV4). The next version to be released is IP version 6, or IPV6. IPV6 is due to be released between the years 2005 and 2015. Therefore, it is important to concentrate on learning IPV4 addressing techniques. A prerequisite to learning how to address an IP network is converting decimal numbers to binary and binary numbers to decimal. Before learning how to address a network, a binary refresher is in order.

BINARY-TO-DECIMAL CONVERSION

An IP address is 32 bits long divided into 4 *octets*. It is considered a dotted decimal notation. For example, 192.19.43.29 is an IP address that has 4 octets, each separated by a dot. The word octet means a group of eight. In this context it is referring to 8 *bits*, also known as a *byte*. The term bit is a derivative of the term **b**inary dig**it**. A bit is used to signal data in computers. Although the IP address above is 192.19.43.29, when a computer processes the number it reads:

11000000.00010011.00101011.00011101

This is because computers only know two states, electrical voltage ON and electrical voltage OFF. The ON state is equivalent to a one, or an electrical signal that is above or below electrical ground (i.e., +5/−5 volts). The OFF state is equivalent to a zero, or an electrical ground (i.e., 0 volts). To further understand what a computer sees when an address is typed with the decimal notation, a discussion on binary-to-decimal conversions is necessary.

The decimal numbering system has ten possible digits to choose from (0,1,2,3,4,5,6,7,8,9) and is known as base 10. The binary numbering system has two, 1 and 0, and is known as base 2. For example the decimal numbers **9 7 3** represent a total value of 973 when grouped together. It is easy to figure this out because placeholders are assumed for each digit. For example, in the ones column there is a 3, so it has a value of 3. In the tens column there is a 7, so it has a value of 70, and in the hundreds column there is a 9, therefore representing 900. When added together from left to right, a value of 973 is reached. The placeholders are part of the base 10 system, so each placeholder has a value equivalent to ten times (10x) the holder before it. For example, start with the ones column x 10 = 10; the tens column x 10 = 100; the hundreds column x 10 = 1,000; the thousands column x 10 = 10,000, etc. See the example below:

etc | 1,000,000s | 100,000s | 10,000s | 1,000s | 100s | 10s | 1s

9 | 7 | 3

The number in the example above is nine hundred seventy-three. If the numbers 9, 7, and 3 are placed under the chart beginning with the 3 in the ones column, the 7 in the tens column and the 9 in the hundreds column, the value is 900 + 70 + 3 = 973.

As stated, binary is a base 2 system and works in a similar fashion. However, all of the placeholders are powers of two rather than ten. For example, 1 x 2 = 2, 2 x 2 = 4, 4 x 2 = 8, 8 x 2 = 16, etc. IP addressing uses octets so the number of bits in a single octet cannot exceed eight. See the following.

128s | 64s | 32s | 16s | 8s | 4s | 2s | 1s

If the number 11001010 needed to be converted into decimal, it could be placed into its respective placeholders, and where there is a one (1) add it where there is a zero (0) ignore it. See the following.

128| 64 | 32 | 16 | 8 | 4 | 2 | 1

1 | 1 | 0 | 0 | 1 | 1 | 0 | 1 | 0

128 + 64 + 0 + 0 + 8 + 0 + 2 + 0 = 202

The highest value possible in an octet is 255; this is a combination of all binary ones and is seen below.

128| 64 | 32 | 16 | 8 | 4 | 2 | 1

1 | 1 | 1 | 1 | 1 | 1 | 1 | 1

128 + 64 + 32 + 16 + 8 + 4 + 2 + 1 = 255

There are, however, 256 possible combinations within an octet. The 256th combination is all zeroes. Since the highest decimal value is 255, each octet can only have a value between 0 to 255. When examining an octet in binary, the bit to the right (which is under the 1 decimal placeholder) is considered the low-end bit. The bit to the left, which is under the 128 decimal placeholder, is considered the high-end bit. If unsure of the answer when converting binary numbers to decimal, remember that the only instance the number will be an odd integer is if the 1 bit is on.

DECIMAL-TO-BINARY CONVERSION

To convert a decimal number to binary, simply divide the decimal number by the values of the base 2 placeholders starting with 128 and working down to 1. If the decimal number can be divided by the base 2 placeholder, that placeholder receives a value of 1, and, if not, it receives a value of 0. See below to convert the number 233 into binary.

128 | 64 | 32 | 16 | 8 | 4 | 2 | 1

233 divided by 128 = 1 with a remainder of 105

105 divided by 64 = 1 with a remainder of 41

41 divided by 32 = 1 with a remainder of 9

9 divided by 16 = 0 with a remainder of 9

9 divided by 8 = 1 with a remainder of 1

1 divided by 4 = 0 with a remainder of 1

1 divided by 2 = 0 with a remainder of 1

1 divided by 1 = 1 with a remainder of 0

128| 64 | 32 | 16 | 8 | 4 | 2 | 1

233 = 1 | 1 | 1 | 0 | 1 | 0 | 0 | 1

 Test Tip: The Network+ exam may not ask you to convert binary to decimal, however it is a foundational skill.

5.3 IP ADDRESS CLASSES

When using IP to address a network, there are two methods that can be used: classful IP addressing and classless IP addressing. Classful addressing has been used for many years and is still used today, mostly in small companies. Classless addressing, on the other hand, is currently the preferred method of addressing a network. Due to its simplicity, classful addressing is a good way to begin learning about IP addresses. Hence, that is where this lesson will begin.

There are five IP address classes: class A, class B, class C, class D, and class E. The address classes are based on the value of the first octet (see Table 5-1). To break it down further, the address class is based on the first few bits of the first octet in an IP address. In IP addressing class A addresses, use the first octet for networks and the last three octets for hosts. Class B addresses use the first two octets for networks and two octets for hosts. Class C addresses use three octets for networks and the last octet for hosts. To see possible combinations and total networks and hosts available for each class of addresses, refer to Table 5-1. Class D and E addresses are considered special addresses and are not assigned to hosts on a regular basis.

TABLE 5-1 IP ADDRESS CLASSES

Class	First Octet	Network #s	Networks Available	Hosts per Network
A	1–127	1–126.0.0.0	126	16,777,214
B	128–191	128–191.1–254.0.0	16,384	65,534
C	192–223	192–223.1–255.1–254.0	2,097,152	254
D	224–239	NA	NA	NA
E	240–255	NA	NA	NA

Address Structure   First octet in binary
* Class A   NNN.HHH.HHH.HHH   00000001†
  Class B   NNN.NNN.HHH.HHH   10000000
  Class C   NNN.NNN.NNN.HHH   11000000

*NNN = Network portion of address
 HHH = Host portion of address
†Underlined bits in the first octet will always be set to the valve shown
 NA = Not applicable

NETWORKS AND HOSTS

IP addresses are divided into two parts, the network and the host. The network and host method of addressing can be compared to the addressing of a street with houses on it. The network address is equivalent to the street name, and the host addresses are equivalent to the houses on the street (see Figure 5-2).

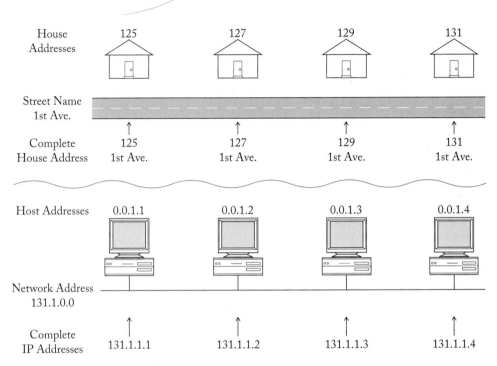

Figure 5-2. *Network (Street) and Host (House) Address Assignment*

Although a node normally has a MAC address assigned to it already, IP has to assign an address to it as well. Then during communication, the IP node address is resolved down to the MAC address using the address resolution protocol, or ARP. All nodes on the same network must have the same address in the network portion of the IP address. Each host portion of the IP address must be unique on that network.

There is a limited number of IP addresses allocated for networks and a limited number of hosts that can be on those networks based on what address class the network falls into. If a network address is 15.0.0.0, this is a class A address. A class A address can have 16,777,214 hosts. This is because three octets are dedicated to hosts. Since each octet has eight binary digits within it, there are twenty-four binary bits available for hosts. Two (2) to the 24th power equals 16,777,216, minus 2 for all ones (1s) and all zeroes (0s), and the total amount of hosts available is 16,777,214 (all 1s and all 0s are illegal addresses and is explained in the **Special IP addresses** section). So, in this example there are over 16,000,000 hosts available. See possible hosts in Table 5.2.

TABLE 5-2   EXAMPLES OF HOST ADDRESSES FOR THE 15.0.0.0 NETWORK

15.0.0.1–15.0.0.254
15.0.1.0–15.0.255.254
15.1.0.0–15.255.255.254

Test Tip: Questions may show a complete IP address and subnet mask and ask what is the host address and what is the network address.

SUBNET MASKS

When an IP address is assigned to a node, the node only reads a series of 32 bits. It has no way to distinguish between the host portion of the address and the network portion of the address without an additional entry. The *subnet mask* is the entry that is responsible for telling the computer which part of the IP address is allocated for networks and which is allocated for hosts. The subnet mask must be assigned to the node at the same time that the IP address is assigned. It is a series of ones starting from left to right with no breaks in it.

In classful addressing, each IP address class has a default subnet mask. Since we only use class A, class B, and class C for IP address assignment, that is what we will concentrate on. The default subnet mask for a class A network is 255.0.0.0. This subnet mask uses 8 bits, and in binary it looks like:

　　　11111111.00000000.00000000.00000000

The class B default subnet mask is 255.255.0.0 and looks like this in binary:

　　　11111111.11111111.00000000.00000000

The class C default subnet mask is 255.255.255.0, and in binary is represented as:

　　　11111111.11111111.11111111.00000000

When assigning an IP address and a subnet mask, it is easy to look at it all in binary to determine which portion of the address is assigned for the network and which portion is assigned for hosts. For example, the decimal IP address assignment and subnet mask would look like this:

IP address 163.100.1.50

Subnet mask 255.255.0.0

In binary it looks like this:

IP address 10100011.01100100.**00000001.00110010** (host in bold)

Subnet mask **11111111.11111111**.00000000.00000000

In the binary example, notice that where the ones (1s) stop in the subnet mask, the host addresses begin in the IP address. In the previous example, there are 16 bits used in the subnet mask. Cisco routers represent the subnet mask and the IP address in one statement like this:

IP address and subnet mask 163.100.1.50/16

The /16 means that there are 16 bits used, counting from left to right forming the subnet mask. So if all bits were on (set to 1) in both octets that would give us a subnet mask of 255.255.0.0 because the highest value we can have in each octet is 255.

 Test Tip: The Network+ exam is troubleshooting oriented. One style of question that is used is to show a diagram of a network. The IP addresses for nodes will be listed in the diagram. The question will say "Why is host A having problems connecting to server or Internet?" Your first step in these style questions should be to verify all IP addresses are on the same network.

SPECIAL IP ADDRESSES

There are several special IP addresses. For example, class D addresses are pre-assigned multicast addresses. A multicast is when a group of nodes are sent data but not the entire network. Another series of special IP addresses consists of the class E address range. Class E addresses are used for experimental purposes and should not be a concern when addressing a network. In addition to the class D and E addresses, there are more special addresses. For example, 127.0.0.1, is considered the loopback address. It is used in conjunction with the PING command. PING tests the TCP/IP connection between two nodes using ICMP. If you PING the address 127.0.0.1, it will self test the node's TCP/IP configuration that the PING command was generated from.

Another special address is 255.255.255.255. This is an "all networks" broadcast address and will send data to all nodes on all networks. There is also a "directed broadcast," which consists of all ones (1s) in the host portion. An example of a directed broadcast would look like this: 15.255.255.255. Notice the first octet contains the number 15, which is a class A address. The next three octets, which are 255.255.255, are directing a broadcast message to all nodes on the 15.0.0.0 network. By default, routers filter "all networks broadcasts" but will forward "directed broadcasts."

All bits ON or OFF in either the network or host portion of an IP address is not to be used to address a node. For example, it is not possible to assign a host with this address:

197.9.15.0.

This is a valid IP address, however it is a class C address and in the last octet (the host octet for class C) is a zero. This represents the network the host is on. Using the same example, the following address is illegal for host addressing as well because it will be misconstrued as a directed broadcast:

192.9.15.255

So, the valid range of host addresses for this example would be:

192.9.15.1—192.9.15.254

There are also three private networks to be aware of. The backbone routers of the public Internet filter packets that contain the private network addresses located in Table 5-3. However, private IP addresses can be used by companies that plan on using IP on their private network without registering their IP address with the Internet authorities. These addresses and more are identified in Table 5-3 with additional special addresses.

TABLE 5-3   SPECIAL IP ADDRESSES

Class D	223–239
Class E	240–255
All Networks Broadcast	255.255.255.255
Directed Broadcast	131.1.255.255 (example)
Default Route	0.0.0.0
Loopback Address	127.0.0.0
This Network Only	131.1.0.0 (example)
Private Network	10.0.0.0
Private Network	172.16–31.0.0
Private Network	192.168.1–255.0

All binary 1s or 0s in the host portion of the address is illegal.
All binary 1s or 0s in the network portion of the address is illegal.

5.4 IP SUBNETTING

One of the drawbacks of classful IP addressing is that when one company is given a class A address, they have only one network address with over 16,000,000 hosts. That is very wasteful. If a company registered a class B address, they would have one network available with over 65,000 hosts. Since the Internet grew in popularity and IP addresses were being depleted, the Internet authorities began conserving addresses. One means of conserving addresses was to subnet one network address into several network addresses by manipulating the subnet mask. When using this method, a host octet can be split up and used for both hosts and networks. It then becomes a VLSM, or variable length subnet mask. Another method of conserving IP addresses is Classless Interdomain Routing (CIDR). The same rules that apply to classful addressing do not apply to CIDR.

Here is an example of how a class B address could be manipulated to have several networks with less than 65,000 hosts per network. Company X applies for and receives a class B address. They are given the following address:

> 150.16.0.0/16

The network administrator realizes that they need more than one network. They need five networks, and the Internet authority turns down their request for four more network addresses. Company X must now generate five networks out of the single address they were issued. They can do this by utilizing the third octet as a network octet rather than a host octet. If Company X uses all 8 bits of the third octet for networks rather than hosts, their subnet mask would become 255.255.255.0. In binary the IP address and the subnet mask would look like this:

> IP address 10010110.00010000.00000000.00000000

> Subnet mask 11111111.11111111.11111111.00000000

Remember, where the ones stop in a subnet mask, the hosts begin in the IP address. Therefore the fourth octet in the IP address is reserved for hosts. Based on this subnet mask, the network administrator for Company X will have 254 legal network combinations with a possible 254 hosts on each network. The address is represented as

150.16.0.0/24. Table 5.4 shows examples of the network and host address combinations available to Company X.

TABLE 5-4   COMPANY X'S NETWORK AND HOST COMBINATIONS

Networks	Hosts
150.16.1.0	150.16.1.1 – 150.16.1.254
150.16.2.0	150.16.2.1 – 150.16.2.254
150.16.3.0	150.16.3.1 – 150.16.3.254
150.16.4.0	150.16.4.1 – 150.16.4.254
150.16.5.0	150.16.5.1 – 150.16.5.254
150.16.6.0	150.16.6.1 – 150.16.6.254
150.16.7.0	150.16.7.1 – 150.16.7.254
150.16.8.0	150.16.8.1 – 150.16.8.254
150.16.9.0	150.16.9.1 – 150.16.9.254
150.16.10.0	150.16.10.1 – 150.16.10.254

Networks will increase by 1 up to 254. 255 is an illegal network address.

Hosts will increase from 1 to 254 on each network. 255 is an illegal host address.

Subnet 150.16.1.0 and Hosts in Binary

Network ID	Subnet	Hosts	
10010110.00010000	.00000001	.00000001	
10010110.00010000	.00000001	.00000010	
10010110.00010000	.00000001	.00000011	
11111111.11111111	.11111111	.00000000	**Subnet Mask**

In IP address subnetting, it is not mandatory to utilize an entire octet for networks. It is possible to borrow half of an octet or only a couple of bits. If Company X only needs five additional networks, it is not necessary to utilize all 8 bits of the third octet for networks. For example, what would happen if Company X required more than 254 hosts on each of the five networks? Using subnetting we can accommodate both of those requests. Refer to Table 5-5 and Table 5-6 throughout the example.

TABLE 5-5   BINARY CONVERSION CHART WITH SUBNET MASKS AND NUMBER OF NETWORKS

Binary to Decimal Conversion	128	64	32	16	8	4	2	1
Subnet Mask	128	192	224	240	248	252	254	255
Number of Networks Needed	NA	2	6	14	30	62	126	254
Possible Combinations of 1s and 0s	2	4	8	16	32	64	128	256

NA = Not applicable

TABLE 5-6   POWERS OF 2 CHART –2 FOR SPECIAL ADDRESSES

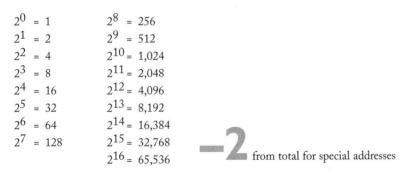

$2^0 = 1$ $2^8 = 256$
$2^1 = 2$ $2^9 = 512$
$2^2 = 4$ $2^{10} = 1,024$
$2^3 = 8$ $2^{11} = 2,048$
$2^4 = 16$ $2^{12} = 4,096$
$2^5 = 32$ $2^{13} = 8,192$
$2^6 = 64$ $2^{14} = 16,384$
$2^7 = 128$ $2^{15} = 32,768$
                 $2^{16} = 65,536$

–2 from total for special addresses

In the example, if Company X needs five networks we can determine what their subnet mask will be in several ways. First, take the number of networks that are needed (five), round up to the next higher number that is in the "Number of Networks" column (see Table 5-5). Follow the column up to the "Subnet Mask" row and that is the value that must be placed in Company X's third subnet mask octet. The subnet mask that will allow Company X to have at least five networks is 255.255.224.0. Once the subnet mask is determined, it is time to determine what the networks will be numbered. The networks will begin with the number 32 because this is the low-end bit in the subnet mask. The networks will increment by 32 for a total of six legal networks (see Table 5-7).

TABLE 5-7   EXAMPLE OF COMPANY X'S NETWORKS IN BINARY AND DECIMAL

	Networks in Decimal	Networks in Binary
	150.16.32.0	10010010.00010000.00100000.00000000
	150.16.64.0	10010010.00010000.01000000.00000000
	150.16.96.0	10010010.00010000.01100000.00000000
	150.16.128.0	10010010.00010000.10000000.00000000
	150.16.160.0	10010010.00010000.10100000.00000000
	150.16.192.0	10010010.00010000.11000000.00000000
Subnet Mask	255.255.224.0	11111111.11111111.1110000.00000000

224 is an illegal network address because it contains all 1s and will be considered a broadcast. All network IDs fall within the same 3 bits of the third octet in the subnet mask.

Subnetting using Table 5-5 works well but is not ideal for every situation. The next method is more accurate with fewer steps. In this example Table 5-6 will come in handy. Company X still needs five networks. To determine what the subnet mask will be, look to Table 5-6 and determine 2 to the power of which number, minus 2 will equal five networks. Remember, all ones and all zeroes are not valid network addresses so it is important to subtract 2 from the value. Two to the 3rd power will allow for eight networks minus 2 (all 1s and all 0s), which equals six networks. Since it is 2^3, that means 3 bits out of the third octet will be used for the subnet mask. Once the first three bits of the third octet are converted to decimal, the value will be 224. The subnet mask would be 255.255.224.0.

In the example, Company X needed 300 hosts per network. To determine whether or not the administrator can accommodate that number, just look at the number of bits set to zero (0) in the subnet mask and determine their power. See below.

IP Address   10010110.00010000.00000000.00000000

Subnetted mask 11111111.11111111.11100000.00000000

In this example, the decimal subnet mask is 255.255.224.0, which leaves a total of thirteen remaining zeros (0s). Two (2) to the 13th power is 8192, subtract 2 which allows for 8190 hosts per network. Table 5-8 shows the host and network addresses for Company X.

TABLE 5-8   COMPANY X'S NETWORK AND HOST IDS

Networks in Decimal	Hosts in Decimal
150.16.32.0	150.16.32.1 − 150.16.63.254
150.16.64.0	150.16.64.1 − 150.16.95.254
150.16.96.0	150.16.96.1 − 150.16.127.254
150.16.128.0	150.16.128.1 − 150.16.159.254
150.16.160.0	150.16.160.1 − 150.16.191.254
150.16.192.0	150.16.192.1 − 150.16.223.254

Examination of the 32 Subnet

Networks and Hosts for the 32 Subnet

Example 1

In this example, each host ID is in a different octet than the network ID.

Networks	Hosts
10010010.00010000.001	00000.00000001
150.16.32	.1
10010010.00010000.001	00000.00000010
150.16.32	.2
10010010.00010000.001	00000.00000011
150.16.32	.3
10010010.00010000.001	00000.00000100
150.16.32	.4
10010010.00010000.001	00000.00000101
150.16.32	.5
10010010.00010000.001	00000.00000110
150.16.32	.6

Example 2

In this example, the networks and hosts are in the same octet. The network ID is 32. The host ID is added to the network ID to give a decimal number higher than 32 because they share the same octet. In binary you can clearly see the distinction between the network and host IDs.

Networks	Hosts		
10010010.00010000.001	00001.00000001		
150.16.32	+ 1.1	=	150.16.33.1
10010010.00010000.001	00001.00000010		
150.16.32	+ 1.2	=	150.16.33.2
10010010.00010000.001	**11110.11111110**		
150.16.32	+ 31. 254	=	150.16.63.254

Subnet Mask   11111111.11111111.111   00000.00000000

There are additional benefits to subnetting a network. They include reducing network traffic and optimizing your bandwidth. Subnetting also provides a method to simplify administration since you can only have a certain number of hosts per network. With all of the benefits there are also disadvantages as well. For example, although subnetting can conserve addresses as a whole, it is also wasteful when connecting an internetwork together because each link needs an entire network address. This includes point-to-point links between source and destination routers. Therefore, the only two addresses used in this network are the two router interfaces.

 Test Tip: Subnetting is an important skill. Practice looking at an IP address and subnet mask to determine what portion of the address is network and what portion is host.

ASSIGNING IP ADDRESSES

In most operations, there are two ways to assigning hosts with IP addresses on the network: manually (or statically) and dynamically. The manual allocation of addresses consists of the administrator going to each node in the network and configuring its IP address. The dynamic allocation consists of using a service such as the *Dynamic Host Configuration Protocol (DHCP)*, which dynamically assigns addresses to hosts. This reduces the administrative effort by a large margin. A mechanism availabe in Windows networks, APIPA is another tool utilized to obtain IP addresses. APIPA stands for Automatic Private IP Addressing. It provides IP addresses (from a predefined range) to Windows DHCP clients that attempt to get an IP address from a DHCP server which, for some reason or other, is not available. For example, if a client boots up and sends a request to obtain an address, yet a DHCP server cannot provide the address, APIPA will assign an address from the following IP address range:

169.254.0.1–169.254.255.254. Subnet mask 255.255.0.0.

This is an internal service-generated IP address; if your existing network is utilizing an address range other than this, the client will not be able to connect to other machines in the network. Although APIPA is a useful service, it works best in home networks where DHCP servers are not commonplace.

There are at least three values in the TCP/IP properties page of the workstation that must be configured. The three values consist of the IP address, the subnet mask, and the default gateway. IP addresses and masks have already been discussed, the default gateway, however, has not. The default gateway is not a mandatory parameter but, if the workstation is to access the Internet or another private network, the default gateway is required. When a node attempts to communicate with another node it sends the message to the local network. If the destination node is not on the local network, the data will be sent to the default gateway. The default gateway, which is normally the router in the network, will then forward the message on to the next network that will transfer the data one hop closer to its destination.

CLASSLESS INTERDOMAIN ROUTING (CIDR)

This chapter began with a discussion of classful IP addressing. In a classful IP address there was a default subnet mask for each address class. Using CIDR, there are no IP class boundaries placed on the addressing scheme. CIDR uses an IP prefix (shown earlier) that designates how many bits are used in a subnet mask. For example:

180.6.16.0/20

The above address shows an IP address with 20 bits from left to right being used for the subnet mask. By looking at this, can you tell what the IP network address is? It is 18.6.16.0 because using this scheme the third octet is the octet that was divided up. Four bits of the third octet were used for the subnet mask. Therefore, networks will increment by 16 in this internetwork, for example, 16, 32, 48, etc.

CIDR was not designed to prevent the depletion of IP addresses. It was implemented to slow down the large-scale address allocation issues associated with the fact that there was no IP address class available for mid-size companies. Class B addresses, which support over 65,000 nodes, were being assigned to companies that did not need to support that many hosts. The second reason for CIDR was to reduce the number of entries in routing tables since they were becoming overwhelmed with many sub-netted network entries. CIDR was aimed at both of these issues and subsequently slowed down the depletion of IPv4 addresses in conjunction with the explosion of network address translation (NAT) software. NAT allows companies to only require one public IP address for thousands of nodes to connect to the Internet. NAT will be covered in a future chapter. CIDR is covered in RFCs 1517-1520.

IP VERSION 6 (IPV6) ADDRESSING

IPv6 is the protocol that will supercede IPv4 sometime in the future. IPv6 has extended the addressing scheme of IPv4 from 32 bits to 128 bits. This is quite a large jump in the numbers of IP addresses that will become available. IPv6 addresses will be expressed in hexadecimal, with colons as separators. Here is an example of an IPv6 address:

ffff:ffff:ffff:ffff:ffff:ffff:ffff:ffff

This is only an example address. IPv6 will use three types of addresses once it is released. The first type of address will be the unicast address. The unicast address will be assigned to one host in a network as single IPv4 addresses are assigned now. The next type of address is the multicast address. Again, multicasting in IPv6 is similar to multicasting in IPv4. A group of registered nodes are assigned a multicast address, and when a multicast packet arrives, all of the registered nodes will receive the packet. The last type of address is an enhancement to the IPv6 addressing scheme. It is called the anycast. The anycast acts similar to a multicast address. Several registered nodes will have the anycast address, and packets destined for that address will be received by at least one of the nodes.

5.5 IPX ADDRESSING

IPX addresses are not required to be registered as public TCP/IP addresses are. However, Novell recommends that if an IPX network must be globally unique from all others, it can be registered with Novell. If your network is using IPX/SPX as its primary protocol, it is still possible to connect to the Internet. To accomplish this, the internal side of the router is configured on the IPX network established, and the far side of the router will have an IP address (see Figure 5-3).

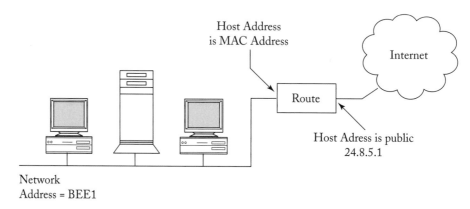

Figure 5-3. *IPX Network Connected to the Internet*

IPX addressing uses a network and node hierarchical concept like the TCP/IP addressing scheme. However, IPX/SPX uses a different means of developing and representing the network and host addresses. IPX uses an 80 bit (or 10 byte) hierarchical addressing scheme, represented in hexadecimal notation (Base 16). The host number part of the IPX address is the 48 bit (or 6 byte) MAC address of the network adapter board. Therefore, there is no need to develop a scheme to design an IPX host number. A benefit to using the MAC address as the host address is that it allows the IPX/SPX protocol to drop the ARP protocol used in the TCP/IP suite, saving bandwidth and processor utilization.

Even though it is not necessary to define host addresses for IPX/SPX hosts, it is important to develop the network numbers for your IPX networks. The network number of an IPX network can be up to 32 bits (or 4 bytes) long and is represented by one to eight hexadecimal digits. Each hexadecimal digit represents 4 bits. For example, the hexadecimal digit of 0x5 (0x is not part of the number, it is a hexadecimal notification) would be represented as 0101 in binary, which is 4 bits long. See below to view other hex values:

Hexadecimal digit	Binary value
1	0001
2	0010
3	0011
4	0100
5	0101
6	0110
7	0111
8	1000
9	1001
A	1010
B	1011
C	1100
D	1101
E	1110
F	1111

A typical network address may be represented like this: 00BEE1. The leading zeroes in an IPX network address do not need to be represented. So, given the address above it is likely that it would be represented as BEE1. Another example would be a network address of 5D. With the leading zeroes included it would look like this: 0000005D.

When dealing with IPX addressing, the MAC address of a network adapter may be divided into three sections to take on a different appearance. So the address 00A0C0.00ACB1, becomes 00a0.c000.acb1. Using the network numbers above, our network and node combinations become BEE1.00A0.C000.acb1 and 5D.00A0.C000.acb1 respectively. There are a total of twenty hexadecimal digits (including the two leading 0s) in each address. Each digit represents 4 bits. Four multiplied by 20 equals 80.

IPX addressing consists of two more parameters: *internal network address* and *socket number*. Internal network addresses are 8 hexadecimal digits (32 bits) long. They are there as a system process so the server can internally route data to the proper upper-layer service. It is a system address and is created during the installation of the NetWare server. The second parameter described is the socket number. A socket number represents the service (upper-layer protocol) in which the data is to be routed to. For example, SPX, NCP, SAP or RIP. Sockets are equivalent to ports in the TCP/IP suite. Sockets are 16 bits long and consist of four hexadecimal digits.

CHAPTER SUMMARY

Chapter 5 covered several protocol addressing concepts. It is important to understand how a network is addressed. When working as a network administrator, the network will already be configured with addresses. However, being able to look at an IP address of a node to determine whether or not it is on the correct network is a very useful troubleshooting skill. Not only were IP addresses covered in this chapter, but there was also a section on how to convert binary to decimal and vice versa. Again, this may seem like a technique that is not used often but once you become familiar with the conversion you will be able to determine the number of bits required for any number of networks or hosts you may need in the future. IPX addressing was also discussed in this chapter.

KNOWLEDGE TEST

1. There are two types of IP networks: public and private. What are some of the characteristics of a private IP network? (Choose all that apply.)
   A. Private addresses are represented on the Internet.
   B. Private hosts are directly accessible from the Internet.
   C. Private host addresses are visible only on the LAN.
   D. Private addresses are not exposed to the Internet.

2. Which protocols are responsible for network layer addressing? (Choose two.)
   A. LocalTalk
   B. IPX
   C. SPX
   D. DLC
   E. IP

3. You are statically configuring IP addresses in a network. As soon as you place the address into a workstation you receive a phone call stating that another user lost his connection. What do you think the problem could be?
   A. The complaining user's NIC overheated.
   B. The hub the user is connected to went down.
   C. Duplicate MAC addresses have been assigned.
   D. Duplicate IP addresses have been given out.

4. When data is sent to a different network than the network it is currently on, where does the data go?
   A. The bridge.
   B. The upstream neighbor.
   C. The packet is given to the default gateway.
   D. The layer 4 switch handles it.

5. When would a network address need to be registered with Internet authorities?
   A. When setting up a public IPX network.
   B. When setting up a private IP network.
   C. When setting up a private IPX network.
   D. When setting up a public IP network.

6. Choose the correct statements about IP addresses. (Choose all that apply.)
   A. For a node to communicate with a node on a separate subnet, a default gateway (router) is needed.
   B. All hosts in an IP subnet must have a different address.
   C. Routing between nodes on different subnets is transparent to the users.
   D. All networks in an internetwork must have a unique network address.
   E. All hosts in an internetwork must have a unique host address.

7. What IP classes can be used to address hosts in an IP network? (Choose all that apply.)
   A. Class A
   B. Class B
   C. Class C
   D. Class D
   E. Class E

8. What is the purpose of having a default gateway in an IP network?
   A. It resolves IP addresses into MAC addresses.
   B. It forwards packets to destination networks.
   C. There is no purpose of having a default gateway.
   D. It is a DHCP server.

9. What is a valid host IP address for a computer located on network 209.41.87.0/24?
   A. 209.42.87.100
   B. 209.41.86.100
   C. 208.41.87.1
   D. 209.41.87.9

10. What is the host (only) address for the computer with the IP address 10.18.7.2/24?
   A. 10.18.7.0
   B. 0.0.0.2
   C. 10.18.7.2
   D. 255.255.255.0

11. What is the network (only) address for the computer with the IP address 150.8.65.9/19?
    A. 150.8.16.0
    B. 150.8.32.0
    C. 150.8.64.0
    D. 150.8.128.0

12. Your network is using the IP network address of 19.15.3.0/24. Your default gateway is using the first available address on the network. Your host is using the second available address in the range. What parameters would you place in the host to ensure they had the correct settings?
    A. Host address: 19.15.3.1—Mask: 255.255.255.0—Gateway 19.15.3.1
    B. Host address: 19.15.3.2—Mask: 255.255.255.0—Gateway 19.15.3.2
    C. Host address: 19.15.3.2—Mask: 255.255.0.0—Gateway 19.15.3.1
    D. Host address: 19.15.3.2—Mask: 255.255.255.0—Gateway 19.15.3.1

13. If your network address has 9 bits left over for hosts, how many valid host IDs can you have?
    A. 512
    B. 510
    C. 256
    D. 254

14. You have an IP address of 165.100.32.35/27. What are the valid host addresses for the network?
    A. 165.100.32.32—165.100.32.47
    B. 165.100.32.33—165.100.32.47
    C. 165.100.32.33—165.100.32.63
    D. 165.100.32.32—165.100.32.63

15. You have an IP address of 165.100.32.0/ 19. What are the valid host addresses for the network?
    A. 165.100.17.1—165.100.63.254
    B. 165.100.32.1—165.100.63.254
    C. 165.100.32.1—165.100.95.254
    D. 165.100.33.1—165.100.96.254

16. The /18 in the IP address 131.1.71.0/18 means?
    A. There are 18 bits reserved for the subnet mask.
    B. There are 18 bits reserved for hosts.
    C. There are 18 network addresses available.
    D. There are 18 host addresses available.

17. What statements are true about the IP address 85.1.66.245/20?
    A. The subnet mask is 255.255.224.0.
    B. The subnet mask is 255.255.240.0.
    C. The host address is 0.0.2.245.
    D. The network address is 85.1.0.0.
    E. The host address is 0.0.0.245.
    F. The network address is 85.1.64.0.

18. Which IP address class allows for the most network addresses and the least amount of host addresses?
    A. Class A
    B. Class B
    C. Class C
    D. Class D
    E. Class E

19. The binary value of 197 is?
    A. 11000101
    B. 11001001
    C. 11011011
    D. 11100001

20. The decimal value of 11100010.10000111.00010101.10100101 is?
    A. 226.137.21.165
    B. 220.141.15.165
    C. 228.238.41.155
    D. 226.135.21.165

knowledge TEST

Routing and WAN Protocols

OBJECTIVES

At the end of this chapter you will be able to:

- Explain the difference between routed and routing protocols.

- Define the categories of routing protocols.

- Describe routing algorithms.

- Understand several routing protocols.

- Understand WAN encapsulation and WAN terminology.

- List and explain WAN protocols and standards.

INTRODUCTION

This chapter focuses on how routing protocols and WAN protocols compliment an internetwork. The chapter begins with an overview of routing and then describes what the difference is between routing protocols and routed protocols. Then, several routing protocols, including RIP for IP, RIP for IPX and OSPF are described. The chapter then covers the information needed to understand Wide Area Networking. You will learn about leased lines, circuit-switched connections, and packet-switched connections. Some of the specific technologies that are covered include, but are certainly not limited to, ISDN, Frame Relay, and ATM.

6.1 AN OVERVIEW OF ROUTING

Routing, in computer networking terms, is the process of sending data packets from one network to another. The separate networks may belong to a small private Internetwork, or they may be members of the global Internet. Routers know where to send data packets because they maintain a table called a *routing table*. A routing table lists known networks and routes (paths) available to those networks. A routing table can be built by one of two methods; statically or dynamically. Statically building a routing table consists of an administrator logging into the router and adding an entry for every network in the internetwork. Dynamically building a table is done by a routing protocol that is configured on the router. There are advantages and disadvantages to both. For example, statically configuring routes provides for more security, however there is a high administrative overhead and the possibility for human error. Dynamically configured tables are less secure and have high processor overhead but they are much easier to manage.

 Test Tip: Static routing often results in high administrative overhead, whereas dynamic routing results in high processor overhead.

When building tables dynamically, the routers operate based on a set of rules. The rules are known as *routing algorithms*. A routing algorithm defines how a router learns about the Internetwork, how it builds its routing table, and how it communicates with other routers. *Routing protocols* implement routing algorithms and provide the communications mechanism. In this section, routing protocols and algorithms are described.

ROUTED VERSUS ROUTING PROTOCOLS

A *routed protocol* is a protocol, such as IP, that can be routed by a router. Routed protocols encapsulate packets of data and send them to their destination via the router's interfaces. The *routing protocol* enables the routing process by learning routes and preparing routing tables to be sent to other routers in the Internetwork. Therefore, each router is aware of all of the networks in the internetwork and can subsequently route data in the correct direction when it arrives at the router.

Routing Protocols

There are two major types of routing protocols which are further broken down into routing protocol classes. Routing protocol classes refer to the protocols that actually implement the routing algorithms. The two major types of routing protocols are *Interior Gateway Protocols (IGP)* and *Exterior Gateway Protocols (EGP)*. Most interior gateway protocols are used within an *autonomous system*. An *autonomous system (AS)* is a grouping of networks given an administrative number by the Internet Corporation for Assigned Names and Numbers (ICANN) (see Figure 6-1).

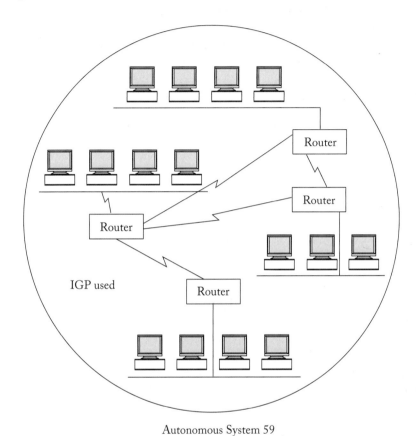

Autonomous System 59

Figure 6-1. *Autonomous System*

 Test Tip: The Network+ exam may refer to ICANN as IANA. They are the same organization. ICANN grew out of IANA.

All networks with the same autonomous system number are normally under the same technical management domain. It is possible to operate within a private AS, which would not be assigned a number by ICANN and would not be part of the public Internet. As a matter of fact, ICANN has set aside a range of AS numbers that are used for private autonomous systems. The AS numbers within that range are filtered by Internet backbone routers. The process is similar to the filtering of private IP addresses on the public Internet. There are 65,535 autonomous systems. The range of private AS numbers is between 64,512 and 65,535. Examples of interior gateway protocols are *Routing Information Protocol (RIP)* and *Open Shortest Path First (OSPF)*.

Exterior gateway protocols, such as the *Border Gateway Protocol (BGP) version 4* or the *Exterior Gateway Protocol (EGP)*, which has largely been replaced by BGPv4, are used to connect autonomous systems together through a border router. It is considered a border router because it resides on the logical border of an autonomous system (see Figure 6-2). Be sure not to confuse BGP with EGP, since BGP is the replacement protocol for EGP.

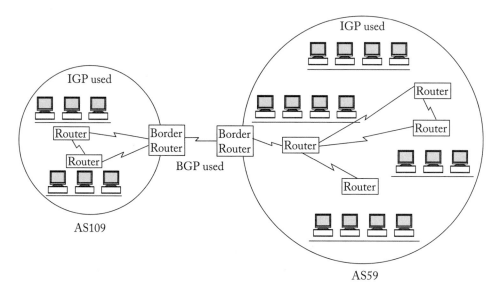

Figure 6-2. *Two Autonomous Systems Connected with BGP*

 Test Tip: BGP is the routing protocol that connects the many autonomous systems of the Internet together.

6.2 ROUTING ALGORITHMS

Routing protocols must have rules that specify how information will be passed on to other routers in the internetwork. These rules are defined by routing algorithms. Therefore, the routing protocols implement the routing algorithms used in the internetwork. There are primarily two routing algorithms used by interior gateway protocols and one routing algorithm used by exterior gateway protocols. The algorithms used by IGPs are *distance-vector routing* and *link-state routing*. The exterior gateway protocols, primarily BGP, use the *best path algorithm*, also known as *path vector routing*, which is not to be confused with other algorithms. Each routing protocol is associated with a type of routing algorithm as seen below:

- Distance-vector routing = RIP
- Link-state routing = OSPF
- Path-vector routing = BGP

ROUTING ALGORITHM RULES

Some of the rules defined by routing algorithms are metrics, convergence, and route selection. These rules must be understood before learning how to configure the protocols.

Metrics

Routers examine their routing table when they need to forward packets to a destination network. The routing table maintains a listing of all networks and known routes or paths to the networks. Each network is associated with a *metric* that will determine the *cost* of the network path. Normally, routers will send the data to the next router with the lowest cost in the routing table. There are several different metrics routers use to determine the cost. Some of the more common metrics are described herein:

- Hop count. The number of routers the packet must pass through to reach its destination.
- Tick count. Timing mechanism to determine how long it will take the packet to go from one router to the next. A tick is approximately 55 milliseconds.
- Cost. An arbitrary value assigned by an administrator that can be based on monetary cost, bandwidth, or other calculation.
- Bandwidth. Data capacity of the line.
- Delay. Timing mechanism.
- Reliability. Reliability of the line.
- Maximum Transmission Unit (MTU). Defines the size of the packets allowed on all links in the path.
- Load. This value is based on the routing traffic of an interface.

Convergence

Convergence is the process of all routers updating neighboring routers (also known as *adjacencies*) with their current routing information. When all routers know about all networks in an internetwork, the internetwork is fully converged. The time it takes to converge with adjacent routers is one means of evaluating a routing algorithm. Therefore, the less time it takes to converge, the more efficient the algorithm. Each algorithm converges in a slightly different manner.

Route Selection

Routing algorithms determine how a router will build its routing table by selecting and placing the best path to a destination network in its active routing table. Route selection also involves forwarding data out of the correct interface to send the data to the destination network. Each routing algorithm uses a predefined method of route selection. Only one route should be maintained in the routing table per destination network. It will normally be the route with the lowest cost. Each algorithm has a mechanism in place to determine this. As routers receive updates from neighbor routers, each update is examined, and the best path to the destination networks are placed in and maintained by the routing table.

IMPLEMENTING ROUTING ALGORITHMS THROUGH ROUTING PROTOCOLS

Each routing algorithm handles the rules previously discussed differently. In this section we will describe the individual routing algorithms, as well as the protocols that operate within the guidelines of the algorithms. Specifically, the distance vector algorithm will be discussed with the RIP for IP and RIP for IPX. A general overview of the link-state algorithm will be given.

Distance-Vector Routing Algorithm

The distance-vector routing algorithm is also known as the Bellman-Ford algorithm. It builds its routing tables on the distance and vector (direction) of destination networks. One of the metrics used in the distance-vector algorithm is the hop count. When a network is two routers away from the current router, it is two hops away. Therefore, if the only metric being used is the hop count, then the metric in the sending router's routing table for this situation would be 2.

In a distance-vector based internetwork, the routers initially seed their own routing tables by adding their directly-connected networks (as configured) to the route table. The initial routing tables that are sent out to other routers are small, but many exchanges are made as the routers converge. This method of convergence causes a great deal of congestion on the network links but this is the only way that distance-vector routers converge. Distance-vector routing has a slow convergence time because each router only sends updates every 30 seconds.

Distance-vector algorithms use second-hand information when creating their routing tables. All of the routes that are learned through update packets are based on information given by other routers in the internetwork. Therefore, if one router is giving out inaccurate route information, all other routers in the internetwork are prone to using it. See Figure 6-3 for an example.

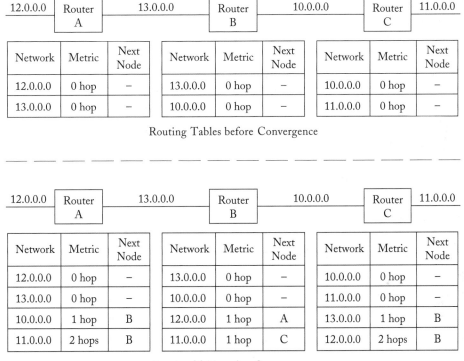

Figure 6-3. *Convergence with the Distance Vector Algorithm*

In the figure, Router B is directly connected to network 13.0.0.0 and network 10.0.0.0. Router C is directly connected to network 10.0.0.0 and 11.0.0.0. Router B will learn about network 11.0.0.0 from Router C during convergence. If the information in Router C's routing table is inaccurate, then Router B's routing table will be inaccurate as well. When Router B converges with Router A, Router A's routing table will also be inaccurate.

When Router A sends data to Router C, it bases its metric on the metric given to it by Router B. Since Router B says network 11.0.0.0 is one hop away, Router A assumes network 11.0.0.0 must be 2 hops away. When the topology of a network using the distance-vector algorithm changes, convergence must take place again. However, distance-vector protocols do not send the changes immediately. They hold them until it is time to send the next update packet, which occurs every 30 or 90 seconds. Changes flow through the network iteratively until convergence is achieved. Each adjacent router will examine the route table, and if there are any differences between its current table and the new table, the router will update its table and then forward the updated table to its neighbors.

Problems in a distance-vector algorithm-based internetwork may occur because of the slow convergence time of the algorithm. *Routing loops* are one of the problems encountered and are the process of routers in an internetwork becoming caught in a loop of sending falsely advertised routes to one another.

In the following example, there are four networks and three fully-converged routers.

| 15.0.0.0 | Router A | 20.0.0.0 | Router B | 145.10.0.0 | Router C | 35.0.0.0 |

Network	Metric	Next Node
15.0.0.0	0 hop	–
20.0.0.0	0 hop	–
145.10.0.0	1 hop	B
35.0.0.0	2 hops	B

Network	Metric	Next Node
20.0.0.0	0 hop	–
145.10.0.0	0 hop	–
15.0.0.0	1 hop	A
35.0.0.0	1 hop	C

Network	Metric	Next Node
145.10.0.0	0 hop	–
35.0.0.0	0 hop	–
20.0.0.0	1 hop	B
15.0.0.0	2 hops	B

Converged Network

Network 35.0.0.0 goes down. The only router that knows about the problem is Router C, which advertises the route as down.

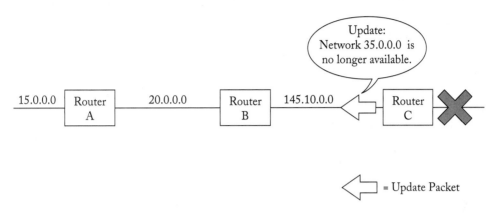

35.0.0.0 Network Advertised as No Longer Available

Before Router A receives the new information, it advertises 35.0.0.0 as 2 hops away. Router B will update its own table (which is currently accurate) with the inaccurate information learned from Router A. Router B will assume that the information is valid and will place the cost in its own routing table, adding a metric of 1 hop to it. Now Router B believes network 35.0.0.0 is 3 hops away and will advertise it is such. When Router A receives this update it will assume Router B learned a new route to network 35.0.0.0 and will increment its hop count to 4. Router A will advertise this route, and Router B increments the value of the cost to 5. This loop will continue until a mechanism is in place to stop it.

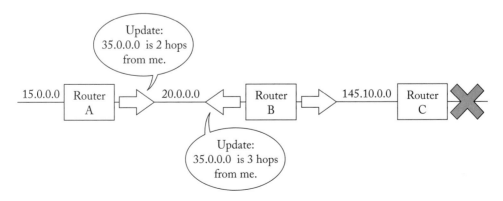

Routing Loop Occurs from False Information Advertised by Router A

This continuous looping is called *count to infinity*. There are several mechanisms in place to keep it to a minimum. The four methods of avoiding the count to infinity follow:

1. **Defining a maximum hop count.** The *maximum hop count* for the RIP distance-vector algorithm is 15. Anything above 15 hops is considered unreachable. With the maximum hop count in place, routing loops can still occur, but they will never loop more than fifteen times.

2. **Split horizon.** *Split horizon* does not allow any router to advertise information about a route on the interface that the information was learned from. In the previous example, Router A would have never sent the wrong information back to Router B because Router A learned about the 35.0.0.0 network from Router B.

3. **Route poisoning (poison reverse).** *Route poisoning* is the process of advertising the downed route with an infinite cost such as 16 for RIP. If route poisoning were used in the example above when the 35.0.0.0 network was taken off line, Router C would have changed its metric to the 35.0.0.0 network to 16, which is unreachable. The update would have been sent to Router B and subsequently to Router A.

4. **Holddown timers.** A *holddown timer* is a timer set in a router that begins counting after a router receives an update packet. After the router receives an update packet, the holddown timer will not allow the router to accept any route changes until the timer expires, unless the change has a better metric to a specified route.

The two distance vector protocols that are covered on the Network+ exam are the routing information protocol (RIP) for IP and RIP for IPX.

RIP for IP. The RIP distance-vector protocol has a maximum hop count of 15, therefore any routes learned with a metric of 16 are unreachable. Due to this limitation, RIP cannot be used in large internetworks. RIP routers forward their entire routing table to neighbor routers every 30 seconds. Although this may seem to take up an excessive amount of bandwidth, RIP routing tables are normally very small. The problem with sending updates every 30 seconds is that convergence for a RIP router takes a long time. For example, in an internetwork that is connected by eight routers it could take up to four minutes for the entire internetwork to be aware of a route table update. Each of the eight routers would take thirty seconds to propagate the change. This can be an extremely long time, especially if the route change is for the worse, i.e., a failed network.

There are two versions of RIP: RIPv1 and RIPv2. RIPv1 uses classful addressing and does not include the subnet mask in route table updates. RIPv2 is a classless routing protocol and includes the subnet mask in route table updates.

RIP for IPX. IPX RIP is similar to the IP version of RIP only IPX RIP uses 2 metrics in its determination of the cost to a network. IPX RIP first uses the tick count, which is a metric based on the number of ticks it will take for a packet to reach its destination. A tick is 1/18 of a second.

Link-State Routing Algorithm

Link-state routing algorithms operate differently from distance-vector algorithms and are more complex than distance-vector algorithms and more efficient when dealing with larger internetworks. Link-state routing handles route selection, convergence, and route metrics differently from distance-vector routing. In an internetwork, routers send updates to other routers when changes to the database occur, rather than at a predefined time limit. To communicate with one another, the routers make use of multicasting data to specific multicast addresses. Therefore, the only recipients of the data are the routers that are a part of that multicast address.

Link-state algorithms overcome many of the shortcomings of distance-vector algorithms. Some of the differences between link-state routing and distance-vector routing are addressed here:

- Link-state routing maintains the topology of the entire network in a separate database.

- Link-state algorithms use first-hand information about routes to send data.

- Link-state algorithms only forward updates or changes to the routing tables after the initial convergence.

- Link-state algorithms can use classless IP addressing because the subnet mask is forwarded with routing table updates.

- Link-state algorithm routing metrics are more complex, which require more processor overhead on the router.

- Link-state algorithms have a faster convergence time.

- Link-state algorithms are not prone to the count-to-infinity.

IP uses the Open Shortest Path First (OSPF) routing protocol. The IPX/SPX equivalent to OSPF is NetWare Link Services Protocol. The operations of these protocols are slightly different, but for the most part they both utilize at least two databases. One database is used for routing, and one maintains the topological view of the entire network.

6.3 WIDE AREA NETWORKING (WAN)

Before discussing the protocols used to transmit data, a brief discussion about wide area network terminology and the three primary connection types is in order.

WAN TERMINOLOGY

Wide area networks are used to connect multiple local area networks to one another so an organization can maintain a seamless integration of data between sites. To accomplish this, companies usually look to WAN service providers to provide low-cost data transmission from one LAN to another. To lease these services from a service provider, there are some terms to be aware of. They are:

- **Customer Premises Equipment (CPE).** These are the devices owned or leased by the subscriber. CPE is located at the customer's premises.

- **Demarc or Demarcation.** This is the point where the responsibility of the data changes hands. The subscriber turns the responsibility of the data and equipment over to the service provider or vice versa.

- **Local Loop.** The cable run that connects the subscriber to the central office, also known as the last mile.

- **Central Office (CO).** This is the service provider's switching facility that receives the subscriber's data before forwarding it to its ultimate destination. The CO is often referred to as the point of presence (POP).

- **Toll Network.** This is the service provider's collection of switches, cable, and links that are often represented as a cloud. The mechanisms that are in the WAN provider's cloud are not discussed in this chapter.

 Test Tip: A subscriber normally has a router connected to a CSU/DSU that interfaces with the provider's local loop. The CSU/DSU is normally the provider's equipment.

Figure 6-4 shows how these components of a WAN are designed.

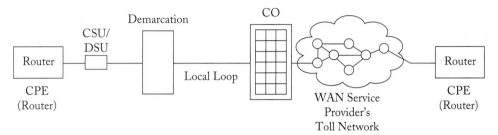

Figure 6-4. *Components of a WAN*

- **Local Exchange Carrier (LEC).** LEC is often the local telephone service provider.

- **Local Access Transport Area (LATA).** The geographic area serviced by a local exchange carrier.

- **Inter-Exchange Carrier (IXC).** An IXC provides the service between LATAs. In other words, it is the long distance service provider that handles calls from one LATA to another LATA.

 Test Tip: In many operations the LEC or provider will normally interface directly with the company subscribing to their service.

Although it seems that the roles of the service provider are clearly defined, current regulations allow local service providers to offer long distance service and long distance providers to offer local service, which gives the organization many options when looking for a WAN service provider.

WAN CONNECTION TYPES

A WAN connection type is comprised of the components (such as wire, switches, and routers often referred to as a cloud) that the service provider uses to forward data from one subscriber's location to another subscriber's location. There are three WAN connection types to be aware of. They are leased (dedicated) lines, packet-switched connections, and circuit-switched connections. All three of these technologies are described within.

Leased Lines

Leased lines (or dedicated connections) are typically used if an organization needs a guaranteed connection that is always available and not shared with other subscribers. Leased lines are considered point-to-point connections. When leasing a line from a provider, there is normally a monthly fee associated with the service and different types of lines that can be purchased. This is usually based on the amount of bandwidth that is required. Leased lines are based on the *digital stream* or *DS standard.*

The Digital Stream (DS) Standard. There are several levels of the DS standard, and each level is multiplexed or aggregated into the layer above it. For example, DS0 is a 64 Kbps channel. DS1 is comprised of 24 DS0 lines, which equal 1.544 Mbps. The term "T1" is often used to describe the DS1 standard. The DS3 standard is 44.732 Mbps. It is often referred to as "T3." The DS3 line speed is made up of 672 DS0 channels, and the North American DS 4 standard has 4032 DS0 channels. The bandwidth of a DS4 line is 274.176 Mbps.

The North American T carrier standards support the bandwidths listed here:

T Carrier Service	Bandwidth
T1	1.544 Mbps
T2	6.312 Mbps (not offered to public)
T3	44.736 Mbps
T4	274.176 Mbps

E carrier service is offered in Europe. The bandwidths available are listed here.

E Carrier Service	Bandwidth
E1	2.048 Mbps
E2	8.448 Mbps
E3	34.368 Mbps
E4	139.264 Mbps
E5	565.148 Mbps

J carrier service is offered in Japan. The available bandwidths include a J1 carrier that supports 2.048 Mbps and a J3 carrier service.

Fractional Service. One of the benefits of leasing these circuits is that it is possible to lease only a portion of the circuit. For example, if 1.544 Mbps (the capacity of a T1) is too much bandwidth and 64 Kbps (DS0) is not enough bandwidth, it is possible to lease a fraction of the T1 line, for example 512 Kbps. This is considered a fractionalized T1, and the bandwidth is available in blocks of 64 Kbps.

Circuit-Switched Connections

Circuit-switched connections are used on a per-connection basis and are normally implemented in a dial-up modem or ISDN environment where the connection is only made available when data needs to be transmitted. Circuit switching works best for organizations that only need periodic WAN connectivity.

Packet-Switched Connections

Packet switching was originally developed and used as a method for transmitting United States military voice communications in the early 1960s. The idea driving the development of packet switching was simple: if there was a nuclear catastrophe and a communications switching facility was destroyed, communications may seize. Because of this, developers designed packet switching, which breaks up a single message into multiple packets before sending them to their destination. Using this method, each individual packet could take a different route to reach its destination, bypassing any destroyed communications facility. The transmission of packets via different routes also made it difficult to tap voice communication wires. Eventually, when all packets made it to the destination, they would be reordered and read by the destination device.

 Test Tip: The three primary WAN connection types are leased lines, circuit switched or packet switched.

WAN ENCAPSULATION

WAN protocols encapsulate data at layer 2 of the OSI Model before forwarding the data out of the interface of a router. There are several WAN protocols that provide encapsulation for data transport. The Network+ exam focuses on the Point-to-Point Protocol (PPP), Frame Relay, and Asynchronous Transfer Mode, or ATM.

Point-to-Point Protocol (PPP)

PPP encapsulation is an industry standard and can be implemented between Cisco and non-Cisco devices. It can be used for router-to-router connections or for hosts to dial into networks over asynchronous telephone lines. PPP works over synchronous lines, asynchronous lines, and ISDN lines. PPP does support authentication between devices. In this section, PPP features and how to configure PPP will be described. Some of the features of PPP include:

- Authentication, using the password authentication protocol (PAP), which uses a two-way handshake and the challenge handshake authentication protocol (CHAP), which uses a three-way handshake.

- Compression, using the Stacker or Predictor compression protocol.

- Error detection, using the Quality and Magic Number protocol.

- Multilink, which divides up the networking load over multiple links using the Multilink Protocol.

Serial Line Internet Protocol (SLIP)

SLIP is the predecessor of the Point-to-Point Protocol. SLIP is used to dial from one computer to another. It has been replaced by the much more functional protocol PPP. A SLIP server would allow a client to dial in to it and get access to the Internet.

However, SLIP does not support many of the features that PPP supports. SLIP does not support dynamic IP address allocation or authentication.

Integrated Services Digital Network (ISDN)

ISDN is a wide area connection standard that is offered by existing telephone service providers and implemented over existing telephone lines. It typically uses PPP to encapsulate network-layer protocols to traverse the WAN. ISDN requires specialized equipment to access the ISDN network.

ISDN Features. ISDN is used to send voice, video, and data over a digital line using a dial-up method. However, it is not a traditional dial-up line since it dials into an ISDN service provider and offers higher rates of speed when compared to traditional dial-up technology. ISDN uses PPP as its encapsulation protocol in addition to ISDN protocols. An ISDN connection may require additional hardware. In this section, ISDN hardware components, protocols, and reference points will be described.

ISDN HARDWARE COMPONENTS. To connect to an ISDN network, certain hardware components are needed. ISDN terminology represents these connections as listed here:

- **Terminal End Point 1 (TE1).** A TE1 is a component such as a PC or a router with an ISDN adapter installed in it.

- **Terminal End Point 2 (TE2).** A TE2 is a component within the ISDN network that does not have an integrated ISDN adapter in it. These components often need an additional hardware component, such as an external ISDN adapter, which is considered a terminal adapter.

- **Terminal Adapter (TA).** A component external to a TE1 which allows for access into the ISDN network.

- **Network Termination Device 1 (NT1).** NT1 is the device that connects the CPE with the service provider. This device could be a CSU/DSU converting the signals between the LAN and the WAN.

- **Network Termination Device 2 (NT2).** NT2 is the ISDN switching device and may or may not be located at the CPE.

ISDN REFERENCE POINTS. Each connection in an ISDN configuration is given a reference point to describe its logical connection within the network design. There are four reference points covered here:

- **Reference point "R."** Represents the connection between the TE2 and a terminal adapter (TA).

- **Reference point "S."** Represents the connection between the TE1 or the TA and the NT2. S and T reference points are electrically the same, therefore they can be represented as S/T.

- **Reference point "T."** Represents the connection between an NT1 and the NT2. S and T reference points are electrically the same, therefore they can be represented as S/T.

- **Reference point "U."** Represents the connection between the NT1 and the ISDN network. If the router has a built-in NT1 component it can connect directly to the ISDN network.

In Figure 6-5, view the hardware and reference points used in an ISDN connection.

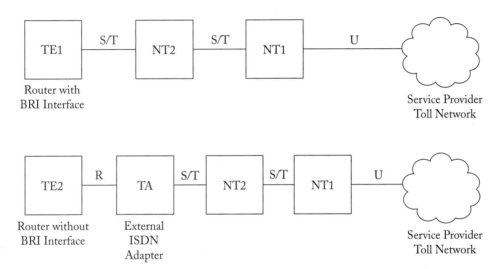

Figure 6-5. *ISDN Reference Points*

ISDN CHANNELS. ISDN uses multiple channels of signaling to transmit voice, video, and data. ISDN is a synchronous communication standard and reserves one channel of the communication medium for signaling. ISDN supports two communication standards: *Basic Rate Interface (or BRI) and Primary Rate Interface, or PRI.*

Basic Rate Interface (BRI). BRI consists of three signaling channels. Two of the channels are called *Bearer* or *B channels* and are used to transmit data. The third channel is a *Delta,* or D channel, and is used for control and signaling, including call setup and termination. The two B channels can carry up to 64 Kbps of data, so it stands to reason that while using BRI ISDN the data rate is 128 Kbps. The D channel can carry 16 Kbps of control and signaling information and is not included in the aggregate total of bandwidth available. The D channel works with the Link Access Procedure on the D channel (LAPD) protocol, which is a data-link protocol that complies with the signaling standards of ISDN.

Primary Rate Interface (PRI). PRI can handle more data than the BRI. PRI has different standards throughout the world. For example, in North America and Japan it can handle up to 23 B channels at 64 Kbps and 1 D channel using 64 Kbps. In Australia and Europe, PRI uses 30 B channels with 64 Kbps and 1 D channel at 64 Kbps.

X.25

Although X.25 has a strong history, all good things must come to an end. As stated, X.25 was built in the early 1960s and because of this, the protocol is considerably outdated. It has paved the way, however, for newer, robust technologies, such as *frame relay* and *ATM*. X.25 packet switching still exists in the public Internet, and is also supported by many vendors. However, in the United States its use has diminished considerably. In Europe X.25 is still a fairly popular technology, but as costs of other equipment are driven down, its days are limited.

One of the shortcomings of X.25 is the fact that it was developed at a time when hardware, such as switching facilities and communication lines, were very unreliable. Since the protocol had to be transmitted over unreliable communication lines, a great deal of overhead was built into the X.25 packet structure, ultimately slowing the protocol down. Analog lines are giving way to digital lines and fiber optics throughout much of the world. These reliable lines do not need to use protocols that are weighted down with overhead in the form of error detection and correction. Even in Europe (where X.25 is still popular), analog lines are slowly being replaced, which will eventually provide the infrastructure for newer frame and cell relay technologies.

X.25 Operations

X.25 was standardized by the CCITT (now the ITU-T) in the mid 1970s. When X.25 was standardized, there were several X dot standards defined. For example:

- **X.21 and X.21bis**—X.21 and X.21bis define the physical layer DTE to DCE connectivity.

- **X.121**—X.121 defines the network layer protocol addressing.

- **X.3, X.28, and X.29**—These X dot standards define how an asynchronous DTE, such as an analog modem, can interface with the X.25 public data network through the use of a packet assembler disassembler (PAD). A PAD can convert asynchronous signals from a modem into synchronous X.25 packets before forwarding them to the X.25 switching device.

The protocol had to be standardized because many vendors were developing their own implementation of X.25, and normally when this happens, each vendor's equipment only works with their own equipment resulting in proprietary networks. The X.25 protocol stack is shown on the following page.

X.25 Packet Layer Protocol (PLP)	Layer 3 Network
LAP-B	Layer 2 Data Link
X.21	Layer 1 Physical

Figure 6-6. *X.25 Protocol Stack*

X.25 was the first standardized packet switched protocol that operated over a public data network. It provides DTE to DTE communications through the X.25 network using *permanent virtual circuits (PVC)* or *switched virtual circuits (SVC)*, which are considered virtual calls (VC) in X.25 terminology. Virtual circuits are logical connections that give the impression of a dedicated line through the PDN. The difference between a PVC and a VC or SVC is that the PVC is established and available all of the time. The SVC, on the other hand, is established at the beginning of a communication and is torn down at the end of it (see below).

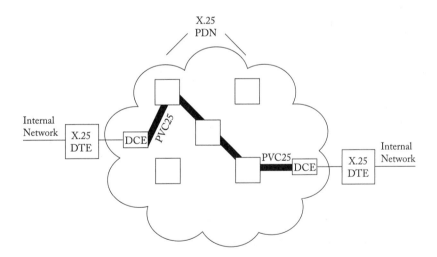

Figure 6-7. *DTE to DTE Over a PVC Communications*

PVCs and SVCs will be further explained while discussing frame relay, as it is a much more relevant technology. A single X.25 physical interface can handle 4095 virtual circuits. Each virtual circuit is given a numerical identifier, described as a *logical channel number (LCN)*. The logical channel number is locally significant, and the X.25

protocol uses search algorithms to map the local logical channel number with a remote logical channel number to successfully transmit data (see below).

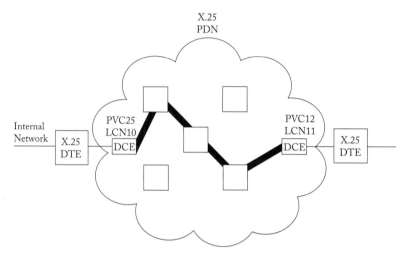

Figure 6-8. *X. 25 PVCs with LCNs Established*

During normal X.25 operations, every packet that is sent by every switch in the X.25 network is acknowledged. This causes a tremendous amount of congestion on the lines. These acknowledgements are the result of having unreliable lines (see below).

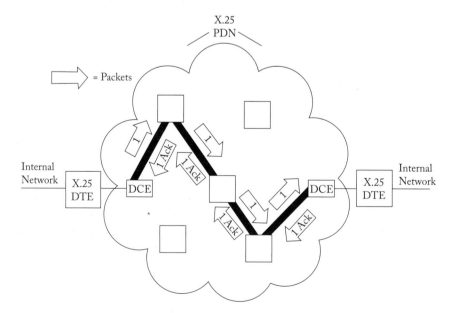

Figure 6-9. *X. 25 Acknowledgements*

X.25 Drawbacks

There are advantages to using X.25. However, they are far outdated and its popularity in the data communication world will continue to dwindle until it has finally been completely replaced. That time is not near for many countries, and X.25 will continue to be the stable protocol that it has been for the past thirty-plus years. The disadvantages of the protocol are based on the fact that it is being replaced by far better protocols. For example, frame relay is the successor to X.25. In the frame relay protocol, much of the overhead has been removed, primarily because communication lines are becoming much more reliable.

X.25 has seen its time and must be given credit where credit is due. X.25 has spawned these new technologies but is prone to several drawbacks. Primarily, it is now considered a legacy network with many vendors abandoning the development of new X.25 technologies. It has low-speed transmission, normally reaching speeds no higher than those of a T1 line. X.25 has a high delay and, once again, a very high overhead, especially compared to the newer frame and cell relay technologies.

Frame Relay

Frame relay is an ITU and ANSI standard that is used to forward frames through a public data network (PDN). The PDN is comprised of many frame relay devices that forward frames from one location to another. To send data into the PDN, a frame relay service provider is needed. Once the data is sent into the frame relay cloud, the service provider's frame relay switches the data forward to the destination through the use of virtual circuits.

Frame Relay Features. The *frame relay* protocol is a layer 2 encapsulation protocol that sends data through the serial port of a Cisco router to a frame relay service provider. frame relay providers allow customers to buy the amount of bandwidth needed. The terms that relate to the frame relay technology are listed here:

- **Virtual circuits.** A virtual circuit is a logical connection between two endpoints in a frame relay network. The service provider's frame relay switches provide the means to create a virtual circuit between two sites. There are two types of virtual circuits, *permanent virtual circuits (PVC)* and *switched virtual circuits (SVC)*.

  - **Permanent Virtual Circuit (PVC).** A PVC uses the same path all of the time to transfer data through the PDN from one location to another. It is configured in advance, is always available to the subscriber, and normally used for a connection that is consistently sending data across the frame relay connection.

- Switched Virtual Circuit (SVC). SVC is a virtual circuit that is dynamically created at the outset of a transmission and is torn down at the conclusion of the transmission, much like the process of setting up a telephone connection. These are used for sporadic transmission of data and are less popular than PVCs.

- **Committed Information Rate (CIR).** The *CIR* is the guaranteed amount of bandwidth allocated to the customer in bits per second. The CIR is a quality-of-service mechanism that ensures subscribers are receiving a guaranteed minimum amount of bandwidth requested. It is also used as a pricing mechanism and can be sold in blocks of as small as 4 Kbps. However, many companies will not sell frame relay in such small increments, and they require a minimum purchase such as 64 Kbps and sometimes as high as 184 Kbps. The CIR for a PVC is unidirectional.

- **Bursting.** Statistically speaking, not all subscribers will be sending data across the service provider's frame relay line at the same time. Therefore providers allow for the bursting of data over the CIR when the line is not congested. For example, assume a frame relay provider is using a T1 access circuit to a user's location but the subscriber has paid for a CIR of 64 Kbps. In a non-peak time the subscriber can send data over the CIR at approximately 1.5 Mbps (the line capacity of a T1 circuit). When bursting data over the CIR it is a non-guaranteed transmission. For example, if bursting data over your CIR and another subscriber accesses the line, the bursting data may be lost. This is based on the DE bit, which is described next.

Asynchronous Transfer Mode (ATM)

Asynchronous Transfer Mode (or *ATM* as most people refer to it) is the premier technology for implementing WANs. ATM uses a cell relay technology, which adds to the technological success of both packet and frame relay technologies. ATM has the capability to transfer data up to 622 Mbps and is becoming an excellent complement to the SONET/SDH standards implemented by the ITU-T. ATM can also be brought to the desktop by implementing ATM hardware throughout the network.

ATM Defined. ATM was designed and is continuously discussed by the ATM Forum. The ATM forum is a group that was established in 1991 by the ITU-T to continue the development of an intelligent switching technology that began in 1980. It is possible to read about new and emerging ATM technologies by visiting the ATM Forum's web site, which is currently WWW.ATMFORUM.ORG.

ATM can handle connection-oriented or connectionless traffic through the use of application adaptation layers. It is an intelligent technology since it can support multiple Quality of Service (QoS) classes for differing application requirements.

The definition of ATM can be, and is often based on, its role in an internetwork. For example, it can be referred to as:

- **A protocol**—It provides the basis for communication over a predefined communication medium.

- **A technology**—ATM conforms to hardware and software standards, therefore vendors can develop equipment based on these standards allowing for interoperability with other vendors' equipment.

- **An infrastructure**—Entire networks can be designed and implemented based on ATM standards.

The ATM Cell Structure. ATM uses a *cell relay* technology. This feature of ATM is what makes the service a success, because cells are fixed length. In comparison, frame relay uses variable length packets. The payload in a frame relay packet varies based on what is being sent. Packets can be as large as 8182 bytes and beyond. Since packets are variable length, the devices in the network must calculate the size before forwarding or reading the packet. This additional calculation adds to the delay time associated with packet-switched networks.

Cell relay avoids these additional delays by ensuring that every cell placed onto the network media is a predefined size. ATM cells are 53 bytes in length. Of those 53 bytes, 5 bytes are overhead and 48 bytes are data or payload. Ironically enough, the length of the payload (48 bytes) was the result of a great debate in the ATM Forum. The discussion of which would be better, a 32-byte cell or a 64-byte cell resulted in a compromise of 48 bytes. The 5-byte header was the compromise of a debate on a 3-byte or 8-byte header.

SYNCHRONOUS OPTICAL NETWORK (SONET)

SONET or *Synchronous Optical NETwork* is a networking standard that was developed by the Exchange Carriers Standards Association (ECSA) for the ANSI. It governs *Optical Carrier (OC)* standards in North America. The *synchronous digital hierarchy (SDH)* is a parallel standard to SONET, and it governs the OC standards for the entire world. SDH was put in place after SONET. However, SONET is a subset of the SDH standard, which is put in place by the ITU-T. When implemented, these standards were expected to remain active in the telecommunication industry for twenty to thirty years.

The SONET standard was created because telecommunication providers in different countries had little or no standards available to provide connectivity with providers in different countries. Providers used proprietary equipment, architectures, and line codes. The need for a standard method of connecting fiber optic systems was obvious.

SONET Signals

SONET multiplexes signals of different capacities into the synchronous optical hierarchy. The signaling method is called *synchronous transport signal (STS)* for SONET and *synchronous transfer module (STM)* for SDH. The signals are categorized into levels. Each STS and STM level offers a different bandwidth capacity, each higher than the one below it. For example STS-1, which is more frequently referred to as OC-1, can handle 51.840 Mbps. It is equivalent to 28 DS1 lines or 1 DS3 line. The SONET hierarchy offers bandwidth capacities much higher than OC-1. Here is a list of OC-*N* standards, also known as the SONET hierarchy, the *N* is the variable that will be replaced by a number:

OC-*N/STS*	STM	Mbps
OC-1	STM-0	51.840
OC-3	STM-1	155.520
OC-12	STM-4	622.080
OC-48	STM-16	2488.320
OC-192	STM-64	9953.280
OC-768	STM-256	39813.12

Each signal level of the SONET hierarchy is comprised of multiple signals from the level below it. This is accomplished through multiplexing the signals. For example, OC-12 is comprised of twelve OC-1 channels of 51.840.

INTERNET ACCESS TECHNOLOGIES

When discussing WAN technologies, it is important to understand how business and home users access the Internet. Although companies can have T service and/or frame relay access to the Internet, those are not the only available options. Companies may opt for a more cost-effective service to access the Internet. In addition to the good old reliable POTS (plain old telephone service, also referred to as the public switched telephone network/PSTN), two low-cost solutions available to them are the digital subscriber lines (DSL) and broadband cable (cable modem) access. In addition to these, other technologies such as satellite and even wireless services are being offered by some Internet Service Providers. These technologies are covered in the following paragraphs.

POTS/PSTN. POTS and/or PSTN refer to the existing international telephone system based on the copper wire infrastructure still available today. POTS lines are differentiated from other types of lines available (such as ISDN) by available line speeds. Access to the Internet through POTS is done via a dialup connection from a modem. Modem technologies are based on the *mo*dulation of digital signals into analog signals going up, and the *demod*ulation of analog signals to digital signals on the way down; hence, the term *modem*. Modems usually connect to POTS at a line speed of 56Kbps.

xDSL. DSL comes in several varieties. Since its inception DSL has continued to grow in popularity, simply because it runs over the existing POTS/PSTN copper lines. The

DSL technology utilizes modulation techniques that allow it to run over pre-existing wires. This is a huge advantage to small businesses and home users of DSL because the installation requirements usually do not include any rewiring. DSL can run over the same line as a two-pair Cat 1 wiring scheme in a home. The beauty of DSL from an end user perspective is that it will not interfere with the telephone system. Therefore, it is possible to be on the telephone and connected to the Internet at the same time. DSL comes in several varieties, which are discussed below:

- Asynchronous DSL (ADSL). ADSL is a popular standard used for access to the Internet from homes. In ADSL, the download or downstream bandwidth will be greater than the upload or upstream bandwidth simply because most Internet users download more data than they upload. Maximum upload speed is 800Kbps and the maximum download speed is 8Mbps.

- Synchronous DSL (SDSL). SDSL is often used as a business connection. The SDSL standard provides a dedicated telephone line to the Internet connection. Therefore, it is not possible to utilize the line for both telephone calls and Internet access. The speeds for SDSL, however, support businesses in a more effective manner. The maximum speed for SDSL is 2.3Mbps upstream and downstream.

- High-Data-Rate DSL (HDSL). HDSL sends data at a rate of 1.54Mbps upstream and downstream. It does require a separate line from your existing home telephone line.

- Very High DSL (VDSL). VDSL is a DSL technology that supports very high rates of data. The VDSL standard can support a connection of 52Mbps upstream (from your home) and 16Mbps downstream (to your home). The technology is not yet as available as other DSL services. Currently, VDSL only works over short distances.

Broadband Cable. Broadband cable service is offered to users and businesses alike from cable TV providers. The infrastructure of a cable company may consist of coaxial cable or fiber optic cable. The cable that runs into a businesses or a home is, however, coaxial. This coaxial cable will run to a cable modem, which is responsible for modulating and demodulating the data that runs through the cable. In many instances the same cable that carries cable television into a user's home will carry the Internet service through the cable modem. One drawback of broadband cable Internet service is that many homes in the same geographic area will be utilizing the same bandwidth of the cable service provider. This may reduce the available bandwidth to users in that area. The maximum bandwidths available through a cable modem are 27Mbps downstream and 2.5Mbps upstream. This is certainly an optimistic number for users, as the cable service provider normally provides the customers with speeds much lower.

Satellite. Satellite Internet service is becoming a popular choice for users who are in rural locations that do not have support for DSL or broadband cable. Satellite Internet service is a good alternative to a dialup modem. The speeds of a satellite Internet connection are 500Kbps downstream and about 50Kbps upstream. Satellite Internet works similar to the operation of satellite television service. The user must have a satellite dish that will align with a service provider's satellite. A coaxial cable will run from the dish to the PC similarly to the way satellite television works.

Wireless. Wireless Internet access is becoming a desire of many consumers. The technology for wireless Internet access continues to be developed. Cell phones and PDAs can take advantage of the wireless Internet services available, and some companies are even offering PCMCIA cards that can connect laptops to existing wireless networks. As time goes by, however, the service will eventually become more available and more mainstream.

CHAPTER SUMMARY

Chapter 6 focused on two important technologies related to internetworking multiple LANs together: routing and wide area networking. To successfully connect two or more networks together, it is required that several of the technologies covered in this chapter be used. The organization is often limited to the services provided by the local telephone service providers when dealing with WAN technologies. However, there is great flexibility in the choice of routing protocols that will be implemented. Before going on to the next chapter, be sure to complete the Knowledge Test.

KNOWLEDGE TEST

1. How many channels are available in an ISDN BRI connection, available for data transmission, and what are their speeds?
   A. 2 channels at 44 Kbps each
   B. 1 channel at 156 Kbps
   C. 2 channels at 64 Kbps each
   D. 1 channel at 16 Kbps

2. Which dial-up protocol supports authentication and can transmit IPX/SPX, TCP/IP as well as NETBEUI?
   A. AFS
   B. SLIP
   C. PSN
   D. PPP

3. Your company is connecting two of its sites together. The company needs at least 1.5 Mbps between the two sites. What type of line should they use?
   A. E1
   B. DS1
   C. DS0
   D. T3

4. Your company has requested an OC-3 line from a service provider to carry a massive amount of voice and video. Approximately how much bandwidth will your organization have?
   A. 54 Mbps
   B. 1.5 Mbps
   C. 155 Mbps
   D. 622 Mbps

5. How many 16 Kbps channels does a BRI ISDN connection support?
   A. 1
   B. 2
   C. 12
   D. 23

6. Which protocols have the ability to use distance-vector routing algorithms? (Choose two.)
   A. DLC
   B. NETBEUI
   C. TCP/IP
   D. IPX/SPX

7. What statements are used to describe ISDN? (Choose all that apply.)
   A. ISDN provides 2 56k lines and 1 16k line with the BRI.
   B. ISDN supports voice and data.
   C. ISDN uses frame relay as its encapsulation method.
   D. ISDN offers basic rate services and primary rate services.
   E. BRI offers more speed over PRI.
   F. Provides end-to-end digital connectivity.
   G. ISDN supports voice only.
   H. ISDN supports data only.

8. What network is considered unreachable when using RIP routing.
   A. The 14th network.
   B. The 15th network.
   C. The 16th network.
   D. The 17th network.

9. For a router to successfully route a packet to a network that is directly or indirectly connected to it, what must the router know?
   A. The source router address.
   B. The destination address of the packet.
   C. The packet's network source address.
   D. The next hop address.

10. What are the correct statements about dynamic routing? (Choose all that apply.)
    A. Dynamic routing has less processor overhead than static routing.
    B. Dynamic routing has less administrative overhead than static routing.
    C. Dynamic routing is best suited for large internetworks.
    D. Dynamic routing is best suited for small internetworks.
    E. Dynamic routing was Cisco's response to the shortcomings of RIP.

11. RIP is susceptible to routing loops. What mechanism does RIP have in place to avoid the count-to-infinity problem? (Choose two.)
    A. Horizon adjust.
    B. Route poisoning.
    C. Split horizon.
    D. Route adjust.
    E. Link-state routing algorithm.

12. Which statements are characteristics of the link-state routing algorithm? (Choose all that apply.)
    A. Routing tables are broadcasted to all routers in the internetwork.
    B. Only changes to the route tables are sent to other routers in the internetwork.
    C. RIP uses link-state routing algorithm.
    D. Link-state routing has a maximum hop count of 15.
    E. Link-state routing has high processor overhead in comparison to static routing.

13. Which protocol uses a packet-switching technology?
    A. Frame relay
    B. ISDN
    C. SONET
    D. T1

14. What are some characteristics of ATM? (Choose all that apply.)
    A. Circuit-switched technology.
    B. Uses a cell relay technology.
    C. Cells are 48 bytes in size.
    D. Cells are 53 bytes in size.

15. Your company has set up a public web site. You anticipate a massive amount of traffic. While you are planning the capacity needed you determine an access connection of at least 40 Mbps is needed. What type of line will you choose?
    A. TI
    B. DS0
    C. T3
    D. DSI

16. What terms are related to frame relay? (Choose two.)
    A. Cell
    B. CIR
    C. PVC
    D. PRI

17. What standard governs the fiber optic hierarchy in North America?
    A. SDH
    B. Frame relay
    C. ATM
    D. SONET

18. To connect a router to a local service provider you normally need to have a CSU/DSU carry the signal. The CSU/DSU often represents the exchange of responsibility for the data from the subscriber to the provider. If the connection is down yet the provider insists their portion of the network tests fine, where can the problem lie?
    A. Between the CSU/DSU and the CO.
    B. Between the CSU/DSU and the subscriber's modem.
    C. Between the CSU/DSU and the subscriber's router.
    D. In the CSU/DSU.

19. Which mechanism does a distance-vector routing algorithm use to avoid routing loops by falsely advertising routes as 16 or unreachable?
    A. Triggered updates.
    B. Holddown timers.
    C. Split horizon.
    D. Route poisoning.

20. Which mechanism does a distance-vector routing algorithm use to avoid routing loops by not advertising the route to the interface where it learned it?
    A. Holddown timers.
    B. Poison reverse.
    C. Triggered updates.
    D. Split horizon.

CHAPTER 7

Operating Systems

OBJECTIVES

After reading this chapter you will be able to:

- Identify the features of network operating systems.

- Understand basic features of authentication services.

- Explain and implement security services for the major network operating systems in the industry.

- Understand printing services.

INTRODUCTION

Chapter 7 focuses on network operating systems such as Windows NT Server, Windows 2000 Sserver, Novell NetWare, UNIX, and Apple. It will also cover the client operating systems that are used to connect to the servers. Many organizations will run several operating systems. This chapter attempts to prepare you for just that by explaining file services, directory services, printing services, and security.

7.1 NETWORK OPERATING SYSTEMS (NOS)

The server is a key element in a networking environment. Physically, servers come in many different sizes. They can also run several different versions of network operating systems. A single network can have hundreds of servers running in it. Small companies normally have between three and ten servers. The number of servers in a company depends on the role of the organization. However, there has to be at least one server if the network will be administered centrally. In this section, Windows NT Server, Windows 2000 Server, Novell NetWare, UNIX, and Apple are covered.

WINDOWS NT 4.0 SERVER

Microsoft has two popular server products worth mentioning: Windows NT and Windows 2000. Microsoft has recently released Server 2003, which is not yet covered in the Network+ objectives. Server 2003, however, is similar to Windows 2000. Windows NT 4.0 was released in the early to mid 1990s and was Microsoft's premier server product until the release of Windows 2000 Server. Much of the Windows 2000 platform was developed from Windows NT technology. The preferred protocol used by Microsoft products is TCP/IP but Windows NT's native protocol is NETBeui. Microsoft's file and print services are based on the Server Message Block (SMB) protocol.

Windows NT Server comes in two versions: NT Server for the small- to medium-sized company, and NT Server Enterprise Edition for large organizations. Since NT Server does not fully support plug-n-play, it is essential to check the Hardware Compatibility List (HCL) when preparing to install NT or adding hardware to the network. The HCL is located on Microsoft's website and lists all tested hardware. You may have a difficult time receiving support for Windows NT since it is becoming an outdated technology. Windows NT does, however, offer a stable, secure environment, which can run on up to four microprocessors without any additional configuration. During the installation of NT Server, you have the option of installing the server as a *Primary Domain Controller (PDC)*, *Backup Domain Controller (BDC)* or a *Standalone Server*.

The PDC maintains the NT directory services, or NTDS, which is the directory service for the network. Remember, directory services provide for a single, centralized logon by users in the network. The BDC holds a copy of the NTDS and is used for fault tolerance. A standalone server acts as an application, file, print or e-mail server. It does not have a copy of the NTDS on it but is a member of the network.

Directory Services

Windows NT directory services are based on a *domain* model. A domain, which is the logical grouping of users and computers, is created during the installation of the

PDC. There can only be one PDC per domain. For fault tolerance there should be at least one BDC installed (see Figure 7-1).

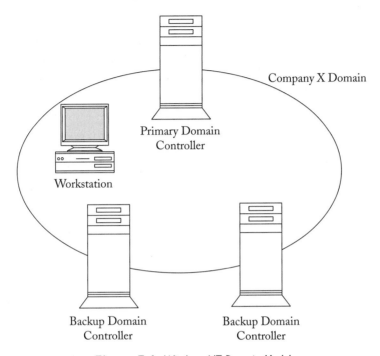

Figure 7-1. *Windows NT Domain Model*

 Test Tip: Domain = Logical grouping of users and computers. One PDC per domain, multiple BDCs per domain.

Each user and each computer that will be a member of the domain must have either a user account or a computer account created for them in the domain. The database that maintains the directory service cannot grow larger than 40 megabytes. Since each user, computer, and group account is between one half and one megabyte in size, the database can handle approximately 26,000 users. To overcome this limitation, domains can be linked together through logical connections called *trusts*. There are four different domain models used by Windows NT. They are listed here:

- **Single domain.** In a single domain, all users and computers are created in the same domain (see Figure 7-2).

- **Single master domain.** In a single master domain model there are at least two domains. All users are in the master domain, and all computer accounts are in the resource domain (see Figure 7-2).

- **Multiple master domain.** In a multiple master domain model there are at least three domains. All users are in the master domains, and all computer accounts are in resource domains (see Figure 7-2).

- **Complete trust.** In a complete trust there are normally several domains all trusting one another. This is not recommended. It can be very difficult to administer and is usually the product of two companies merging together (see Figure 7-2).

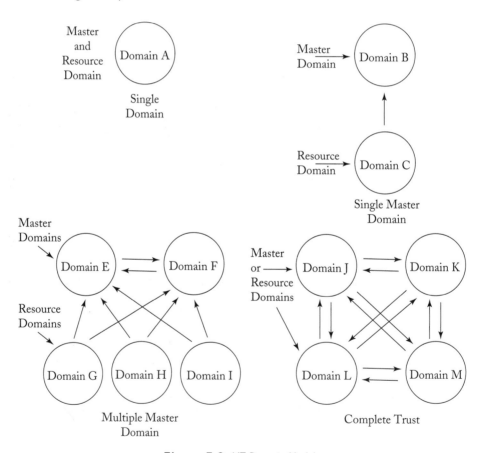

Figure 7-2. *NT Domain Models*

User and Group Management

In Windows NT, user accounts are created using the User Manager for Domains utility in a domain environment. On a Windows NT workstation, the utility is called User Manager. To open the utility, click the Start button, Program Files, Administrative Tools, and then select User Manager or User Manager for Domains (see Figure 7-3).

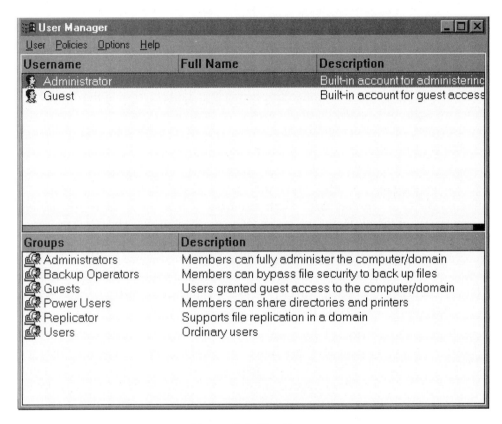

Figure 7-3. *User Manager*

During user creation, passwords (which can be up to fourteen characters long) can be assigned, group membership can be given, and a home folder can be configured for the user. A home folder is a private area of disk storage located on a network server for the user. Group accounts are also created from the User Manager for Domains. Groups are used to categorize users to simplify administration.

File Services

Windows NT supports two file systems: FAT 16 and NTFS. When formatting drives with FAT 16 in Windows NT, the size limitation is 4 gigabytes. NTFS partitions can be as large as 16 hexabytes. NTFS allows you to control the access of files and folders by placing permissions on them that allow or disallow specific users from accessing them. Auditing the access of files, and compressing files and folders is also supported on an NTFS partition.

File System Security. File system security in Windows NT consists of two primary security mechanisms: shared permissions, which only protect data if the user is connecting to it remotely, and NTFS permissions, which are set on the local file or folder and protect against users connecting remotely and users accessing the data locally. Before we begin this discussion on file system security, it is important to understand how the operating system monitors file system security. It is done through the use of an access control list.

Access Control List (ACL). All users and groups are given an identification number that is unique among all other users and groups in the network. This number is called a *security identifier* or *SID*. Each resource, such as a file, folder, or printer, maintains a list of the SIDs that can or cannot access the resource. This list is the access control list (ACL). Each time a user or group is granted or denied permissions to a particular resource, an *access control entry*, or *ACE*, containing the user's SID is added to the ACL. When a user attempts to access the resource, the resource compares the user's SID with the ACL. If a match is made, the user is given access or denied access based on the permissions assigned to the user.

Share Permissions. Sharing folders allows users to give other users in the network access to resources on their local machine. Only folders can be shared. If there are specific files that need to be accessed by remote users, the files must be placed in a shared folder. Once a folder is shared, all files and folders within the shared folder become available to users over the network. There are four share permissions available in Windows NT. They are:

- Full Control. Allows users to perform any function on the folders and files located in the share, including deletion and creation.

- Change. Allows users to read, execute executable files, modify, and delete files and folders located in the share.

- Read. Allows users to read folders and files as well as execute executable files. However, the user cannot change or delete anything from the share.

- No Access. Denies users access to the folder. No access overrides any other share-level permission.

Sharing folders only allows users the ability to protect the folders and files within the folders from users connecting to the folder remotely. Therefore, if a user who is given the No Access permission sits down at the computer where the folder is actually stored and logs on, he has full control of the folder and its contents.

There are some rules to follow when creating shares. First, to share a folder, right click the folder and select Sharing. From here, assign the resource a shared name and select the users that will have access to the folder by clicking permissions (see Figure 7-4).

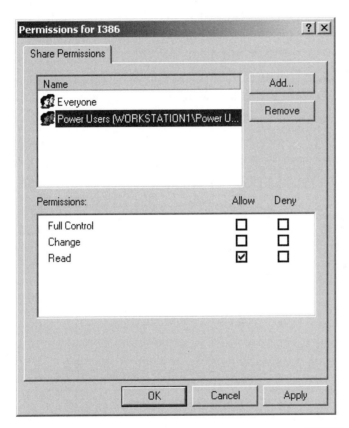

Figure 7-4. *Share Tab and Permissions Dialog Box on a Windows 2000 Workstation*

Notice the Everyone group has the full control permission. This is the default permission. Be sure to remove the Everyone group from the permissions tab rather than assigning the No Access permission. Do not ever assign the Everyone group No Access because none of the users in the Everyone group will have access to the resource if this is done. Further, the Everyone group includes <u>everyone</u> in the network, even the administrator. If a group or user is not in the ACL of a folder, the operating system assumes they have no access.

NTFS Permissions. NTFS permissions are set locally. They protect folders and files from remote users, as well as local users. A local user is a user physically sitting at the computer, accessing data on it. In Windows NT, the user must have a user account created on a particular machine to log on to the local machine. However, if logging onto the network, the user only has to have an account in the domain. Therefore, if User A saved data on the C: drive of a workstation and then User B logged on to the network from that workstation, User B would have access to the file User A saved on drive C:.

NTFS permissions are slightly more complicated than share level permissions. NTFS permissions can be assigned to both folders and files. The following shows the permissions that can be assigned to both folders and files:

NTFS FOLDER PERMISSIONS

- Read. View files and folders within the folder as well as its attributes, who is the owner is, and permissions set on it.

- Change. Create files and folders within the folder and change the folder's attributes.

- List. View the names of the folders and files within the folder and execute files.

- Add and Read. Allows users to read, write, execute files in the folder.

- Add. Write and execute new files in a folder; cannot view the files.

- Full Control. Combination of all previously-mentioned permissions, coupled with the ability to change the permissions on the folder and take ownership of the folder.

- No Access. Denies access to the folder for specified users.

NTFS FILE PERMISSIONS

- Read. Read the file, view its attributes, the owner, and permissions set on it.

- Change. Delete and modify the file.

- Full Control. Perform all actions to include changing permissions and taking ownership.

- No Access. Denies the user access to the file.

There are some rules to be aware of when working with NTFS permissions. Here is a list of them:

- Permissions that are set directly on the files within a folder override the settings on the folder itself.

- The Everyone group is given the Full Control NTFS permission to the root of a volume as soon as it is formatted as or converted to NTFS.

- The No Access permission overrides any other permissions. Because of this, never assign the No Access permission to the Everyone group.

- When copying and moving folders or files with NTFS permissions assigned to them, the folder or file will always inherit the permissions of the destination directory unless it is being *moved* within the same volume, in which case it will retain its current permission assignment.

The last rule to be discussed is the rule of NTFS permission inheritance. By default, when an NTFS permission assignment is made to a folder, the folders and files within that folder inherit those assigned permissions. There is, however, an option to prevent this from happening.

Effective Permissions. A user's SID can be listed in a resource's ACL through individual or group permission assignment. When this happens, the user normally accumulates different NTFS permissions, as well as different share level permissions. Sometimes, a user can end up with a combination of both NTFS and share level permissions. The combination of permissions is called *effective permissions*.

Once again, there are rules to follow when calculating effective permissions. For example, if user Joe was given read permission to a directory, and Joe is a member of a group that has the Write permission to the folder, Joe's effective permissions to the folder and files within it would be Read and Write, or just Write since Read is implied with the Write permission.

When a user has more than one NTFS permission assignment to a resource, the least restrictive permission is the user's effective permission. The exception to this rule is when the user is given the No Access permission to the resource (in any of his permission assignments). No Access will always take precedence over any other permission. On the same note, if a user has multiple share level permissions to a shared folder, the user's effective permission to the folder will be the least restrictive share permission. Again, the exception is if No Access is given to the user (in any of his share level permission assignments).

One important note to remember is that NTFS folders can be shared out. This means that both shared permissions and NTFS permissions can be set on a resource for specific users or groups of users. When both share level permissions and NTFS permissions are assigned to a user, the **MOST** restrictive permission in any assignment (share level or NTFS) will be the user's effective permission to the resource. Here is a simple method used to remember this rule:

EFFECTIVE PERMISSIONS RULE

Share Permission + Share Permission = Least Restrictive

NTFS Permission + NTFS Permission = Least Restrictive

Share Permission + NTFS Permission = Most Restrictive

The exception to this rule is that **NO ACCESS** always outweighs all other permissions.

User Rights and Password Policies

User Rights allow you to protect the operating system, and password policies allow you to dictate when users must change their passwords, and how long the passwords must be. The assignment of user rights and password policies are both configured from the User Manager for Domains utility.

To set NT password policies, go to User Manager for Domains, click Policies, then Account. From there you can assign a password policy for the entire domain. There are several settings available. For a secure password policy, ensure users change their passwords on a regular basis and require unique passwords.

Client Support

NT Server can support many clients. The client that works best with NT Server is NT Workstation, which is built on the same technology as NT Server. NT workstations have their own local database. User accounts should only be created on NT workstations if operating in a peer-to-peer or workgroup environment. Avoid local user accounts in a domain model.

To log on to the machine, press the ctrl-alt-del keys simultaneously and the logon dialogue box will appear. Click the drop down arrow and you can choose to log on to the domain or the local workstation. Windows XP, Windows 2000 Professional, 95, 98, 98 SE, and ME are capable of logging onto Windows NT domains.

There are NT services available that allow for other operating systems to connect and utilize NT services as well. If you have UNIX or Macintosh users in your network, you must ensure that you load the proper services on the NT Server to support them. Go to Control Panel, Network applet, Services tab, and click Add. You will see the client services there.

NT Server can interoperate with Novell NetWare servers as well. However, for the NT Server to connect you must install Gateway Services for NetWare (GSNW) and the NWLink protocol if the NetWare server is using IPX/SPX. GSNW can be loaded from the Network applet, Services Tab. The file and printer sharing protocol used by Windows is Server Message Block (SMB); that used by Novell's IPX/SPX is Remote Connection Protocol (RCP). The GSNW service is responsible for converting SMB calls to RCP.

Remote Connectivity

NT Server also supports Remote Connectivity through the Remote Access Service. To install RAS, go to the Services tab of the network applet and click add. Microsoft RAS can support a combination of 256 incoming and outgoing calls. It can be configured to transport TCP/IP, IPX/SPX, and even NETBeui by using the Point-to-Point Protocol. RAS also supports secure transfers of data by creating a virtual private network with the point-to-point tunneling protocol (PPTP). Finally, RAS also gives the option of utilizing PPP's multilink protocol. Multilink protocol allows one machine to utilize two modems to double the available bandwidth. If a client cannot dial into an RAS server over the public telephone system, be sure the provider is not having line trouble before assuming the RAS server is not working.

WINDOWS 2000 SERVER

Windows 2000 server comes in three versions, Server for the small company, Advanced Server for the medium to large company, and Data Center Server for specialized companies involved in e-commerce. Windows 2000 was developed based on NT and many of the features are similar, however there are plenty of differences, beginning with the fact that 2000 has not lost any of its security or stability but is now plug-n-play compliant. Windows 2000 uses TCP/IP as its native protocol and has abandoned the primary domain controller and backup domain controller modes. Servers are installed as servers, and if you choose to load directory services on a server, that server becomes a domain controller. There is no hierarchy between domain controllers since each one of them can make changes to the directory. In NT, all changes were made on a single server, the PDC.

Directory Services

Windows 2000's directory service is called Active Directory. It is an X.500, LDAP-compliant database that can handle over one million objects. The directory service is based on a forest, tree, domain model with a single namespace. There can only be one forest with multiple trees in a 2000 directory. Within each tree there can be multiple domains. Figure 7-5 shows an example of a Windows 2000 Active Directory forest.

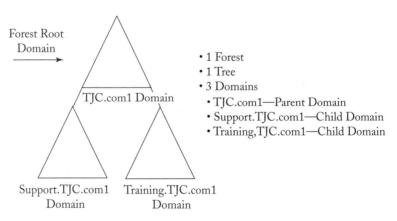

Figure 7-5. *Forest, Tree, Domain Structure*

The single namespace means that if there is a single domain named TJC.COM1 and another domain is added to the network, the name of the new domain would be SUPPORT.TJC.COM1.

User and Group Management

To create users, groups, and computers in the active directory, go to administrative tools, Active Directory Users and Computers.

File Systems

Windows 2000 supports FAT 32, FAT 16, and NTFS version 5.0. There is also an encrypted file system that allows users to encrypt files. The user-level permissions that pertain to NT are similar to Windows 2000 but not exact. For example, share permissions in 2000 are Read, Change, and Full Control. Notice there is no longer a permission called No Access. However, the ability to Deny or Allow permissions is available. Therefore, assigning No Access is done by using the Deny Full Control permission. Denied permissions take precedence over any other permissions.

In Windows 2000, shares can be created at the folder or by using the Create Shared Folder wizard. To utilize this utility, navigate to the Computer Management utility in Control Panel, Administrative Tools applet. Once the utility is open, expand the System Tools and the Shard Folders icon by clicking on the "+" sign of each (see Figure 7-6).

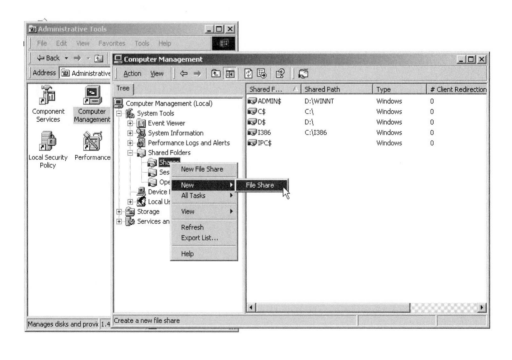

Figure 7-6. *Computer Management*

NTFS. NTFS 5.0 is available with Windows 2000. Some of the changes include disk quotas and the encrypted file system (EFS). Disk quotas allow the administrator to dictate the amount of space a user has on a drive. EFS allows users to encrypt their own files for an additional level of security.

The NTFS permissions are slightly different. They can be denied or allowed, and there is not a No Access permission. NTFS 5.0 permissions are listed here (changes are noted):

NTFS FOLDER PERMISSIONS

- Read. View files and folders within the folder as well as its attributes, who the owner is, and permissions set on it.

- Write. Create files and folders within the folder and change the folder's attributes.

- List Folder Contents. View the names of the folders and files within the folder.

- Read and Execute. Performs the actions of List Folder Contents and Read. It also allows for the traversing of folders. Assume a user executes a file from within a folder. If that executable calls an additional file from within another folder that the user is denied access to, traversing will allow the executable to run.

- Modify. This permission is a combination of Read and Execute and Write. It also allows for the deletion of the folder itself.

- Full Control. Combination of all previously-mentioned permissions coupled with the ability to change the permissions on the folder and take ownership of the folder.

NTFS FILE PERMISSIONS

- Read. Read the file. View its attributes, the owner, and permissions set on it.

- Write. Write to the file and change its attributes.

- Read and Execute. Run applications.

- Modify. Delete and modify the file.

- Full Control. Perform all actions including changing permissions and taking ownership.

Security

Windows 2000 security is very comprehensive. When working with 2000 there are two types of security policies defined: domain policies, and local policies that pertain to the individual machine. The policies are set cumulatively, first the local policy is applied, then the domain security policy is applied. To set these policies, go to Administrative Tools and select the policy you want to configure. From the policy you select you can set password age limits, password minimum length, and password uniqueness (see Figure 7-7).

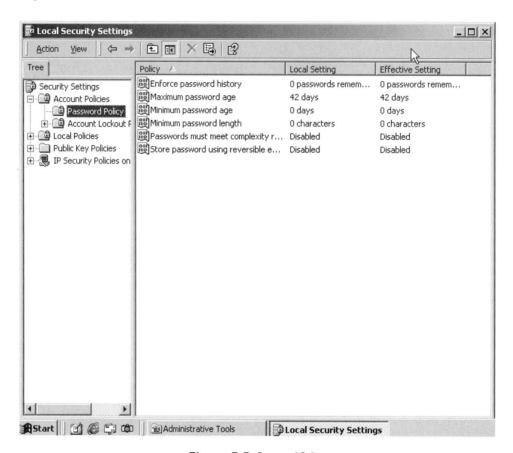

Figure 7-7. *Password Policy*

Client Support

The clients that best support Windows 2000 server are Windows 2000 Professional and Windows XP Professional. Other Microsoft products are supported, but Windows 2000 Professional is recommended to gain the full benefits of working with Active Directory.

WINDOWS SERVER 2003

Windows Server 2003 is the next edition of Microsoft's Windows NT/2000 operating system. This version of the server operating system is more of a revision than a rewrite. Although there are some very good enhancements to the operating system, they are certainly not massive changes as seen with the NT to 2000 changes. Windows Server 2003 is available in four versions: Standard, Enterprise, Data Center, and Web.

Enhancements

The major enhancements to the operating system include the following:

- The Enterprise and Data Center Edition have 64-bit versions available that will run on 64-bit microprocessors.

- The ability to change domain names in the Active Directory and server names of domain controllers.

- Robust support of the Distributed File System (DFS) provides support to a hierarchy of shared folders located on several machines that provide fault tolerance and load balancing.

- Remote Desktop administration.

- Shadow Copy Service for files, folders, and entire volumes that can automatically move data from a fixed disk to a removable or remote storage area when fixed disk space reaches critical levels. This benefits users because they can recover data that has been moved.

- Virtual Disk Service provides an interface to manage multiple vendors' storage components.

- Group Policy Results allows administrators to locate the effective policies on an object in Active Directory.

- Increased hardware support, as shown below:

EDITION	MAX MEMORY	MAX PROCESSORS
Web	2 GB	2
Standard	4 GB	4
Enterprise (32 bit)	32 GB	8
Enterprise (64 bit)	64 GB	8
Data Center (32 bit)	64 GB	32
Data Center (64 bit)	512 GB	64

NOVELL NETWARE

Novell's NetWare is one of the most widely-used network operating systems. There are several versions available on the market today. The most recent version of NetWare released is NetWare 6.5. NetWare's native proprietary protocol was IPX/SPX until version 5 was released, at which time it changed to TCP/IP.

Directory Services

NetWare's first attempt at directory services included the use of the bindery service, which was a database that resided on a single server. Currently, NetWare uses a distributed database called NDS that works best for large organizations. The NDS is an X.500, LDAP-compatible database that can be divided into separate partitions. The partitions can then be strategically located throughout a geographically-dispersed company. Changes made to partitions are replicated throughout the organization. This ensures that the database is never out of synchronization.

NetWare began using the NDS with NetWare version 4.11. The database is object oriented, which means each object in the database has a set of properties and values. The directory service is logically organized as an inverted tree with the root at the top. The tree is named during installation of the first server and containers that logically group users and groups together are created. Network designers often organize and name containers based on geographic location or business unit function.

 Test Tip: NetWare 3.12 used the bindery directory service. NetWare 4.11 and better use the NDS.

NetWare's file systems is the Novell Storage Services, or NSS. This is a high-performance file system that offers many benefits. Novell migrated to this file system from the traditional NetWare File System in NetWare 5.0. Beginning with NetWare 5.0, the print service of choice is Novell's Distributed Print Service (NDPS) for printing. NetWare 4.11 and below used a queue-based service which was slightly different from NDPS.

NetWare Rights

NetWare has two sets of rights to become familiar with: NDS rights, and file system rights. NDS rights give users the ability to manipulate NDS objects. For average users, the default assignments should be fine. Here is a list of NDS rights:

NDS RIGHTS

- Supervisor
- Browse
- Create
- Delete
- Rename

File system rights give users the ability to manipulate the NetWare file system. Here is a list of NetWare file system rights:

FILE SYSTEM RIGHTS

- Supervisor

- Read

- Write

- Create

- Erase

- Modify

- File Scan

- Access Control

User and Group Management

Several utilities are used to administer NetWare. Traditionally, most of the administration is done from a client. However, Novell has slowly been moving in the direction of allowing the server to be managed from the server. Four of the most popular utilities are:

- **Console One.** Allows you to create users, groups, and other NDS objects.

- **NWAdmin.** Allows you to administer users, groups, printers and NDS objects from a client or the server.

- **NDS Manager.** Allows you to manage and partition the NDS.

- **RCONSOLE.** Allows you to administer the server remotely.

Recent versions of NetWare have also implemented web-based utilities that allow for the configuration of services through a web browser. The utilities are based on the NetWare Remote Manager web service, and they include iManage, iMonitor, iPrint.

 Test Tip: ConsoleOne and NWAdmin can both be used to manage an NDS tree.

Client Support

To gain the full functionality of the NDS, it is recommended that you use Novell's Client 32. It is an application that can be loaded onto many different operating systems. For example, there is a client application that can be loaded on OS/2, UNIX, Macintosh, Windows NT, 2000, 95, 98, ME, and DOS. Microsoft operating systems have a Novell client built into them.

In Windows NT and Windows 2000 install Client Services For NetWare. In Windows 9x, add the Microsoft Client for NetWare Networks from the network applet in control panel. In either operating system it will be necessary to install the NWLINK protocol if the Novell server is running the IPX/SPX protocol.

When logging into a NetWare network, there are several parameters that must be configured. For example, the tree name, the context of the user (which is where the user is located in the tree), the server name, the user's name, and the user's password are all required. The client usually remembers the tree, the context, and the server. Therefore, when the user logs in, the only parameters that must be entered are the username and password.

UNIX

UNIX, by far, is the grandfather of networking. This operating system was developed and released in the late 1960s and early 1970s as an open standard. Since it has been an open standard for so long, many companies have developed their own versions of it. UNIX is primarily a command line-based shell operating system. However, a graphical user interface called X-Windows is used to assist in administration. UNIX uses TCP/IP as its native protocol. As a matter of fact, it was the UNIX operating system that began using TCP/IP first. Popular versions of UNIX include Red Hat Linux, Sun Solaris, Digital UNIX, HP-UX, and IBM AIX.

UNIX's file and print services are based on the TCP/IP suite of protocols. The file service used is the Network File System, or NFS. For printing, UNIX relies on Line Printer Daemon (LPD), which is a TCP/IP service that runs on the server. The client uses a Line Printer Request (LPR) service to connect to the LPD. UNIX directory service is made up of a series of files and programs called Network Information Service, or NIS. It was once known as the Yellow Pages but has since been renamed. Currently, there is also a version of NIS called NIS+.

Administration

The administrative account for UNIX is known as ROOT. This user has permissions to manipulate all areas of the operating system. To administer a UNIX system, become familiar with that version's utilities. Here is a list of some UNIX administrative commands.

Command	Results
Linuxconf	Opens utility that allows for configuration of entire system
Useradd	Add users
Adduser	Add users
Usermod	Modify users
Userdel	Delete users
Chown	Change owner of file
Chmod	Change permissions on file or folder

File System and Permissions

The Unix file system is a tree structure that begins with a forward slash to identify the root directory. Permissions available are read, write, and execute. They are shown as a series of nine letters and dashes. The first three characters pertain to the file's owner, the second three to the file's group, and the last three to everyone else or other. An example is shown here:

```
-rwxr--r--
```

The dash in the first position means that this set of permissions pertains to a file. If the first position held a "d," it would mean directory. The first RWX means that the owner has read, write, and execute permissions. The second set of letters consists only of the read permission, which pertains to the file's group. The last three letters give read permission to all others. A dash in place of a letter is representative of denying access.

Client Support

There are many clients that can log in to a UNIX server. Popular clients include DOS, Windows, Macintosh, and the multitude of UNIX clients available. When configuring clients to connect to the UNIX server, the settings to connect are typical of any TCP/IP network. The workstation must have an IP address on the network in which the user is logging onto, the domain name for the NIS database must also be placed in the client, and the node must have a unique name. In addition, the user that is attempting to log on must have a user account created in the centralized UNIX database. If all of these parameters are not met, connectivity is likely to fail.

File Services. Once a client has logged on to the network, she can access files located on the UNIX server by utilizing the Network File System, or NFS, which is a protocol within the TCP/IP suite. All major client operating systems have support for TCP/IP and NFS.

Printing Service. Any clients successfully logged into the network can access printers installed on the server by utilizing TCP/IP printing services, specifically LPR and LPD. For example, if using a Windows 2000 client, simply install TCP/IP printing services and then create a TCP/IP printing port with the IP address of the UNIX-based network printer. To do this, use the Add Printer Wizard located in the Settings option off of the Start button.

LINUX

An extremely popular spin-off of Unix is the Linux operating system. Linux was developed as an open source operating system. An open source operating system is one that makes the source code available to the general public for free. Linux can run on any hardware platform, and because of this it has become a popular alternative to other operating systems such as Mac and Windows based systems.

There are several versions of open source Linux. One popular version is Red Hat. A Red Hat Linux installation can contain all programs needed for a user to create documents, spreadsheets, slideshows, and even to edit graphics. Linux can be networked with other Linux clients or with other vendors' clients, such as Windows or Macs.

If file and print sharing are to be done with a Linux-based computer, the Samba service can be installed. Samba hosts an open source version of the SMB protocol that other popular operating systems use for file and print sharing. Once Samba is installed in Linux, user accounts can be created through the *useradd* command or through the User Manager utility. Since Linux is a version of the Unix operating system, many of the features are the same.

APPLE

Apple Computers was created in the 1980s and quickly became one of the major developers and competitors in the PC market. Apple has a client OS as well as a server OS. They have also developed the AppleTalk protocol which is a proprietary protocol suite. In an Apple network, however, AppleTalk is not the only protocol that can be run. Apple networks also support access protocols such as Ethernet, Token Ring, and FDDI. Apple does support TCP/IP services as well and can integrate with other major operating systems such as Windows and UNIX.

Macintosh OS X Server

Macintosh OS X Server is the name of the Mac server. Currently in version 10.2, it offers much of the same services that are mentioned above including directory services, file, and print services. It uses the Kerberos protocol for authentication (Kerberos is covered in Chapter 8). It is heavily integrated with TCP/IP and uses several TCP/IP applications for file and print capability. For file sharing, FTP, NFS, AFS, and Microsoft's SMB are all supported. Print services include LPD/LPR, as well as SMB services for Microsoft clients.

Client Support

Macintosh OS X server can handle a multitude of clients trying to access the different services available. Some of them include, but are certainly not limited to: file services, web services, e-mail services, and printing services. To log on to an Apple file server, there are different requirements for each client.

Accessing Files. The clients supported include Macintosh clients, Windows clients, and UNIX clients. If logging on via Macintosh, the Mac client should have either the AppleTalk protocol or TCP/IP installed. Windows clients can access the Macintosh file server through the use of the server message block (SMB) protocol. SMB is the native file and print-sharing protocol used in the Windows environment. Although SMB is bundled up into the application layer of the TCP/IP model, it performs the role of presentation-layer protocol. UNIX clients that access a Mac file server must be running the Samba service and will also use SMB to connect.

Accessing Printers. When a Mac server is configured as a print server, all three popular vendor operating systems can be configured to print to it. For example,

Windows, UNIX, and Mac clients can all print to the Mac server using LPR, which is a TCP/IP standard. LPR stands for line printer request, and it works in conjunction with the line printer daemon (LPD) server service.

Additional Services. If the MAC server is running additional services such as e-mail, web, or FTP services, clients from all vendors can connect provided they are using the proper application. For example, to access the web or FTP service, any popular web browser will work. To access the e-mail service, any POP or IMAP e-mail program will suffice since they are supported by the Macintosh server.

AppleShare IP. AppleShare IP is a product offered by Apple that can greatly enhance the IP resources of an Apple network. AppleShare IP is basically an application suite that provides file and printer sharing support over an IP-based network. It does not stop there, however, but offers a web server that can handle many different locally hosted web pages and an e-mail server. The e-mail server can support both IMAP and POP clients. This product can integrate with just about all clients in the network that operate on TCP/IP.

7.2 DESKTOP OPERATING SYSTEM CONFIGURATION

Since most client/server implementations use TCP/IP as the primary protocol, it is important to know how to set the TCP/IP parameters of clients. In this lesson you will learn how to configure the TCP/IP parameters of three desktop operating systems: Windows 98, Windows NT, and Windows 2000.

WINDOWS 98

To view the TCP/IP parameters of Windows 98, click Start, Run, then type WINIPCFG in the Run command line. Click the enter key and the parameters will be returned. If DHCP is used in the network and the IP address is to be renewed, click the release and then the Renew button from this dialogue box (see Figure 7-8).

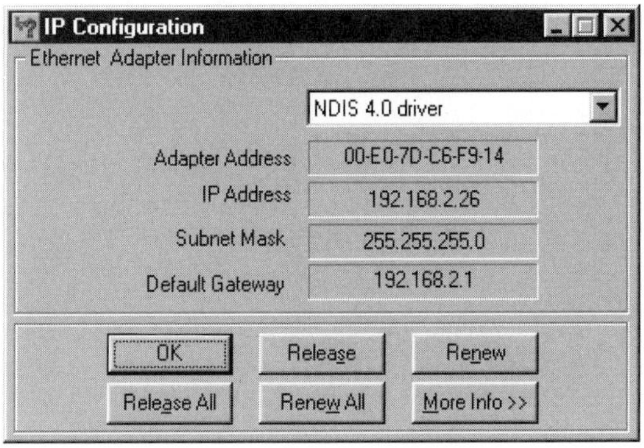

Figure 7-8. *WINIPCFG Results*

To change the TCP/IP parameters, right click Network Neighborhood, go to Properties, from the Configuration tab select TCP/IP, and click the Properties button. The TCP/IP Properties dialogue box appears (see Figure 7-9).

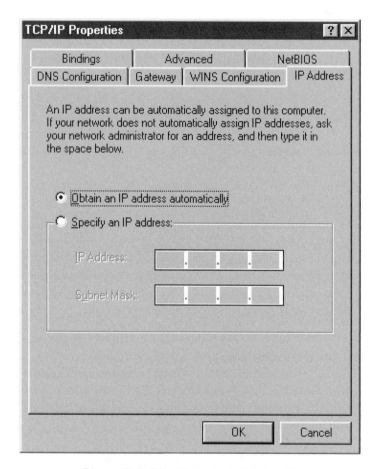

Figure 7-9. *TCP/IP Properties for Windows 98*

From here, IP information can be obtained automatically through DHCP, or an IP address can be configured statically. A default gateway can be assigned, as well as DNS, WINS, and other information.

If static IP addressing is to be used (and it should be on some nodes in the network, usually critical servers), enter the IP address and the subnet mask being used. To configure DNS there are three mandatory settings needed: the computer's host name, the company's domain name, and the IP address of the DNS server in the company (see Figure 7-10).

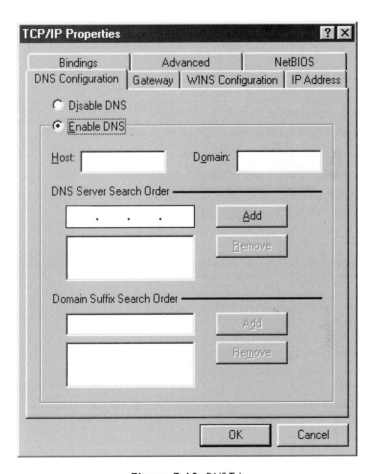

Figure 7-10. *DNS Tab*

To configure WINS, select enable WINS, and then enter the IP address of the WINS server (see Figure 7-11).

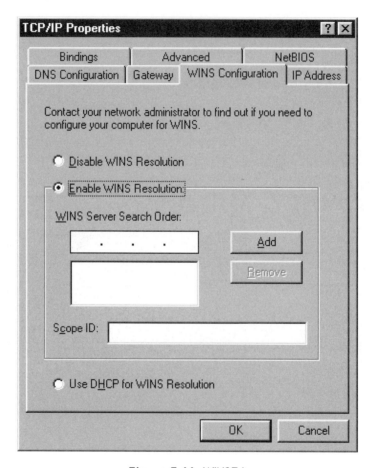

Figure 7-11. *WINS Tab*

WINDOWS NT WORKSTATION AND WINDOWS 2000 PROFESSIONAL

To learn the IP configuration information on a Windows NT or Windows 2000 computer, go to the Command prompt and type IPCONFIG (see Figure 7-12).

Figure 7-12. *IPCONFIG*

The screen output gives basic TCP/IP parameters. To learn more, type IPCONFIG /ALL (see Figure 7-13).

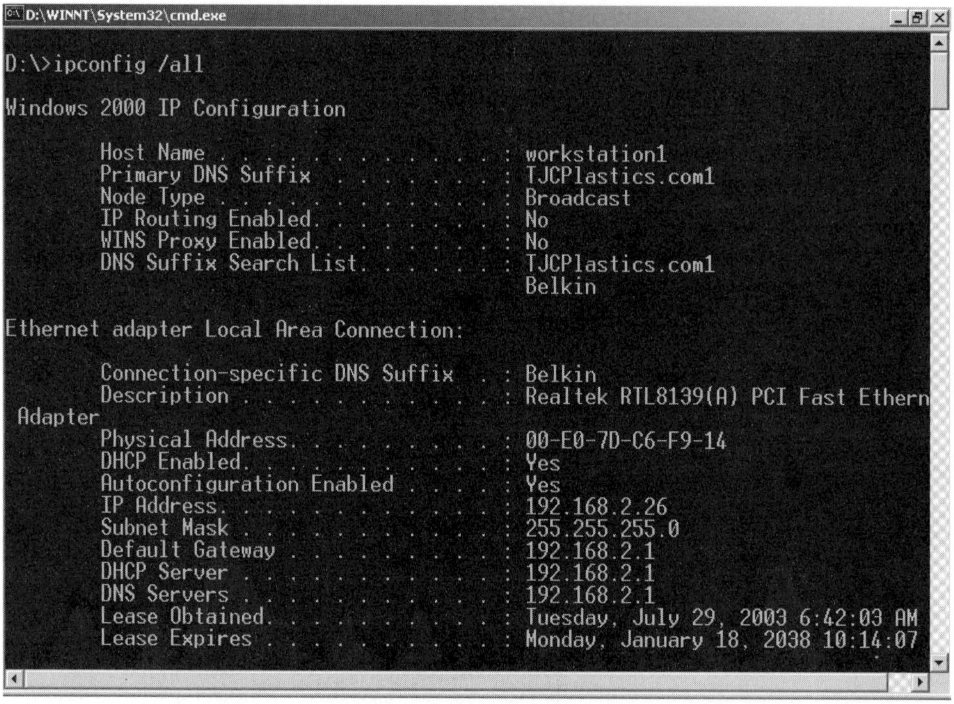

```
D:\WINNT\System32\cmd.exe                                              _ 8 X

D:\>ipconfig /all

Windows 2000 IP Configuration

        Host Name . . . . . . . . . . . . . : workstation1
        Primary DNS Suffix  . . . . . . . . : TJCPlastics.com1
        Node Type . . . . . . . . . . . . . : Broadcast
        IP Routing Enabled. . . . . . . . . : No
        WINS Proxy Enabled. . . . . . . . . : No
        DNS Suffix Search List. . . . . . . : TJCPlastics.com1
                                              Belkin

Ethernet adapter Local Area Connection:

        Connection-specific DNS Suffix  . : Belkin
        Description . . . . . . . . . . . : Realtek RTL8139(A) PCI Fast Ethern
Adapter
        Physical Address. . . . . . . . . : 00-E0-7D-C6-F9-14
        DHCP Enabled. . . . . . . . . . . : Yes
        Autoconfiguration Enabled . . . . : Yes
        IP Address. . . . . . . . . . . . : 192.168.2.26
        Subnet Mask . . . . . . . . . . . : 255.255.255.0
        Default Gateway . . . . . . . . . : 192.168.2.1
        DHCP Server . . . . . . . . . . . : 192.168.2.1
        DNS Servers . . . . . . . . . . . : 192.168.2.1
        Lease Obtained. . . . . . . . . . : Tuesday, July 29, 2003 6:42:03 AM
        Lease Expires . . . . . . . . . . : Monday, January 18, 2038 10:14:07
```

Figure 7-13. *IPCONFIG/ALL*

This screen output will give more information. IPCONFIG is a useful utility. If the network is using DHCP, the IPCONFIG /RELEASE command will release the current IP address, and the IPCONFIG /RENEW command will begin the DHCP lease request process.

To configure TCP/IP parameters on NT, go to the network applet in Control Panel and double click it or right click Network Neighborhood and choose Properties. Click the Protocols tab, select TCP/IP, and click Properties (see Figure 7-14).

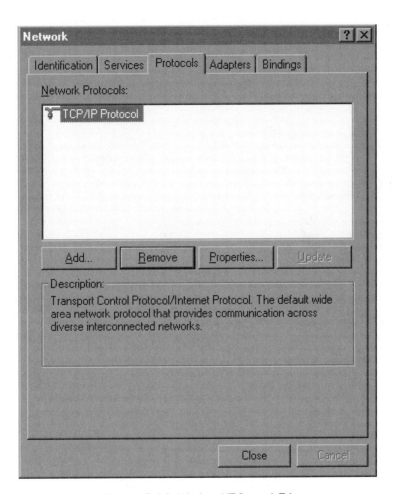

Figure 7-14. *Windows NT Protocols Tab*

In Windows 2000, go to Control Panel, double click My Network Places, and right click the connection you are configuring. From here, select TCP/IP and go to Properties (see Figure 7-15).

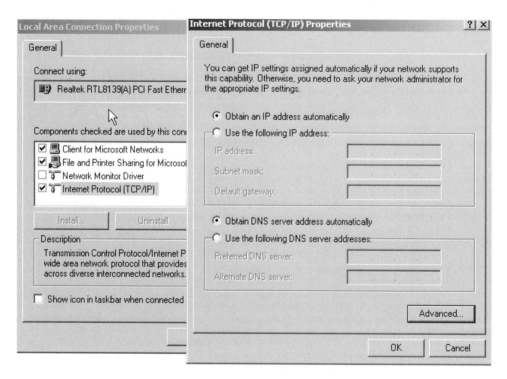

Figure 7-15. *Windows 2000 TCP/IP Properties*

7.3 NETWORK PRINTING

Network printing consists of connecting a printer to the network and allowing users in different locations of the network to print to it. There are several steps to configuring a network printer. There are also several devices that are needed, including the print server, the print queue, and the print device or physical printer. Microsoft also uses a logical printer. The logical printer is the icon located on the print server that allows for the configuration of the print device.

The first step is to setup a *print server*. The print server does not necessarily have to run on an NOS, however the print drivers must be installed on the print server. The print driver is a software program installed from either a floppy disk or CD. Some operating systems, such as NT workstation and 2000 Professional, can be configured as the print server. The print server allows or denies the access of users to the printer. This is based on the permissions that are set up by the administrator. Some printer permissions include: Print, Manage Documents, Manage Printer, and No Access.

The print server often has the *print queue* residing on it. The print queue is simply hard drive space where network jobs being sent to the printer can be stored or spooled while waiting for the print device to become available. Current technologies have been developed that allow print servers and print queues to be embedded into the printer itself.

In the following figure, different network printing terminology and configurations are shown. In Figure 7-16 there is a print device connected to a workstation or server through the parallel port (local printer). The print server and the print queue are both located on the node that the printer is connected to. The printer is then shared out so other users in the network can access it.

The network printer diagram shows the print device connected directly to the network. This type of printer has a NIC installed in it, and the print queue may be embedded in the printer itself or on an administrative computer in the network. The print server is the workstation identified. This allows the administrator to grant and deny permissions to users.

Figure 7-16 also shows the print server and the print queue both on a print server. It is also possible to utilize a vendor's print server or an existing server in the network. The vendor's print server is usually a small device connected directly to the network.

The printer, in this instance, would be administered from a program offered by the manufacturer, usually a web-based program that resides inside the print server.

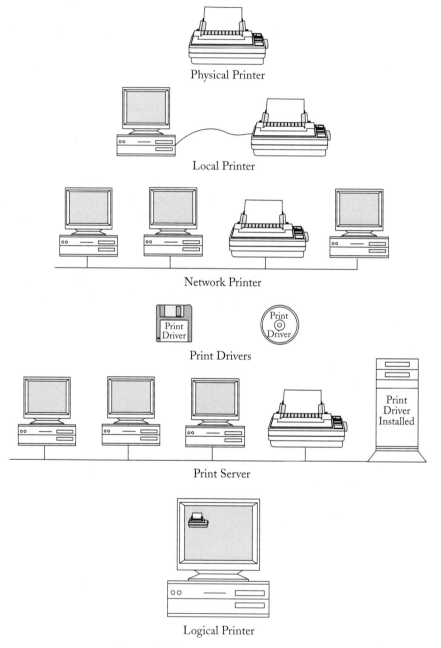

Figure 7-16. *Diagram of Printing Technology*

NETWORK PRINTER INSTALLATION (LOCAL MACHINE)

To install a printer on a Windows-based workstation, use the Add Printer wizard. If the machine is going to be the print server, then click on local printer. Be sure to share the printer out so all clients can connect to it. Also, permissions can be set so users and groups will have access to the printer. Once it is set up properly, it is possible to view the queue by double clicking the printer. If any print jobs are in the queue that are not supposed to be, it is possible to delete them individually, purge all of them, or pause the printer for maintenance.

NETWORK PRINTER INSTALLATION (REMOTE MACHINE)

From a client PC, use the Add Printer wizard. Select the option that allows for a networked printer, and browse for the shared printer.

CHAPTER SUMMARY

Network operating systems and their features were discussed in this chapter. Directory services, administrative utilities, file systems, and many other technologies were explained. You learned how to install printers on the network and how clients connect to them. There were many concepts discussed. In the next chapter you will build on what you have learned here. However, before going on to the next chapter be sure to complete the Knowledge Test in this chapter.

KNOWLEDGE TEST

1. What are the directory services called in Windows 2000?
   A. NDTS
   B. Active Directory
   C. NDS
   D. Bindery
   E. NT Domain Model

2. In Windows 2000 network, a user is unable to access a specific folder. Other users in his department can access the data. He calls the Help Desk to tell them of the problem. What could the problem be?
   A. The user has the Full Control permission to the data.
   B. The user has the Deny Full Control permission assigned to the folder.
   C. The user's network motherboard has failed.
   D. The data has become corrupt.

3. Which dial-up protocol does Windows NT/2000 Server support?
   A. TCP/IP
   B. SLIP
   C. PPP
   D. L2TP
   E. NETBeui

4. What three keys do you press simultaneously to log on on to a Windows NT computer? (Choose three.)
   A. Del
   B. Shift
   C. Tab
   D. Alt
   E. Ctrl

5. What three parameters must you enter in the Windows Logon dialog box to log on to the XYZ domain? (Choose three.)
   A. The workgroup you belong to.
   B. The domain you belong to.
   C. Your user name.
   D. Your e-mail account.
   E. Your password.

6. Which command is used to check the IP configuration on a Windows 9x computer?
   A. inconfig
   B. ipconfig
   C. winipcfg
   D. winipconf

7. What protocol must be installed in a mixed Novell 4.11 and Microsoft environment to access the Internet?
   A. NWLINK
   B. NETBeui
   C. TCP/IP
   D. IPX/SPX

8. A user in a mixed environment needs access to both a NetWare 3.11 server and the Internet. He is using Microsoft's client for NetWare. What two protocols must be installed on the Windows NT workstation?
   A. IPX/SPX
   B. DLC
   C. TCP/IP
   D. NWLINK
   E. NETBeui

9. If a Windows NT workstation using NETBeui is moved from segment A to segment B of a network, what resources will be available?
   A. Resources on segment A will be available.
   B. Resources on segment B will be available.
   C. Resources on segment A and segment B will be available.
   D. No resources will be available.

10. How many PDCs can be in a Microsoft Windows NT 4.0 domain?
    A. 1
    B. 2
    C. 3
    D. Only limited based on hardware

11. To enable WINS on a Windows 9x machine, what should you do from the WINS tab? (Choose all that apply.)
    A. Enter the host name.
    B. Type IPCONFIG /renew from the command prompt first.
    C. Click the enable WINS resolution button.
    D. Enter the IP address of the WINS server and click add.

12. When a user complains that she cannot print to a network printer that she should be able to print to, what should your first step as the administrator be?
    A. Go check to see if the print server is off line.
    B. Reboot the printer.
    C. Reboot the workstation the user is sitting at.
    D. Check that the user's access permissions are set correctly.

13. What command would return the following output?

    A. IPCONFIG
    B. WINIPCONFIG
    C. IPCONFIG /ALL
    D. WINIPCFG /ALL

14. What client software can be used to connect a Windows 9x machine to a Novell NetWare network? (Choose two.)
    A. Microsoft's Client Services for NetWare (CSNW)
    B. Microsoft Client for NetWare Networks
    C. Novell's Client for Mac
    D. Novell's Client 32 for Windows

15. What is needed to configure DNS resolution on a computer? (Choose all that apply.)
    A. LMHOST file
    B. Host name
    C. Scope name
    D. IP address of the DNS server
    E. Domain name

16. Your network consists of several different operating systems. Currently there is one UNIX server, three NT servers, and a NetWare 6.0 tree with five servers in it. What protocol suite would be used for all of them to work together?
    A. TCP/IP
    B. IPX/SPX
    C. NWLink
    D. NetBEUI

17. You have a Windows NT 4.0 network. Your manager has asked you if it is possible to configure dial-up access to the server for the mobile sales staff. He goes on to explain that the data they will be sending and receiving over the connection is confidential. What protocol will allow this to work?
    A. PPP
    B. TCP/IP
    C. RAS
    D. SLIP
    E. PPTP

18. To authenticate to a NetWare network, what parameters are required? (Choose all that apply.)
    A. The domain name
    B. The correct context of the user account
    C. The username
    D. The user's password
    E. The tree name

19. A user cannot access an application that she is supposed to be able to access.
Her coworkers can access the application without a problem. What is most
likely the problem?
A. The server crashed.
B. The user does not have the correct access permissions.
C. The user forgot her password.
D. The user is clicking on the wrong application.

20. Where is the RAS service installed from in Windows NT?
A. Control Panel, Network applet, Protocols tab
B. Control Panel, Dial-Up networking
C. Control Panel, Network applet, Services tab
D. Network Neighborhood, Services, Dial-Up Services

CHAPTER 8

Supporting a Network

OBJECTIVES

After reading this chapter you will be able to:

- Understand several aspects to supporting a network.
- Describe the functions behind address assignment.
- Understand why name resolution techniques are employed.
- Understand methods available for remote connectivity.
- Define what RAID is.
- Explain what a proxy server is.
- Describe popular methods of securing a network.

INTRODUCTION

Chapter 8, Supporting a Network, deals with some very important concepts related to networking and the Network+ exam. Supporting a network consists of being able to utilize multiple services so the network continues to operate, regardless of the situation. There are many services available to assist in the administration of a network, and they will be covered within this chapter. For example, there are six main areas of support: address assignment, name resolution, remote connectivity, network address translation, data loss prevention, and security. Each of these will be discussed in relation to the TCP/IP protocol stack since it is the most popular.

8.1 ADDRESS ASSIGNMENT

In a TCP/IP-related network, one of the most critical tasks accomplished by an administrator is assigning IP addresses to the hosts in the network. There are two methods for address assignment. The first is manual allocation, which consists of physically entering the IP address, subnet mask, and other parameters into the operating system of each host. The second method is by dynamically allocating IP addresses through protocols such as DHCP and BOOTP. Regardless of the method to assign addresses, the *Network Address Translation* service is often used in a private network to gain access to the public Internet. This service is also discussed within.

DYNAMIC HOST CONFIGURATION PROTOCOL (DHCP)

DHCP is a client/server program that allows for the dynamic allocation of TCP/IP addresses. Some of the advantages of using DHCP include:

- Simplifies administration.
- Reduces typographical errors, which can lead to greater problems.
- Eliminates communication problems.
- Manages and maintains database of which node has which IP address.

The operations include the DHCP lease process, lease parameters, lease configuration and renewal, monitoring IP address assignment, and how DHCP deals with broadcast messages. These issues are discussed within.

The DHCP Lease Process

The process involves two entities: client and server. The client must be configured to request an automatic address, and the server must be configured to hand IP addresses out. The DHCP clients broadcast requests for IP addresses from DHCP servers. All DHCP servers in the network will respond to the client with an address lease offer. The client will request to keep the first DHCP lease that it receives by sending a request packet back to the DHCP server. The DHCP server will then send the client an acknowledgment confirming the DHCP lease acceptance. The four steps involved in the DHCP process are Discover, Offer, Request, and Acknowledgement (see Figure 8-1).

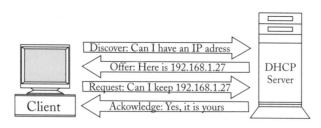

Figure 8-1. *DHCP Process*

Lease Parameters

Clients in an internetwork normally need to have several IP parameters configured for successful communication. For example, if DNS is used in the network, the clients need to know the IP address of the DNS server. If they do not they will not send queries to the correct servers. Also, all clients must have a default gateway if the internetwork consists of more than one network or if the network is connected to the Internet. DHCP servers have the capability of informing client computers about these addresses.

Lease Configuration and Renewal

The DHCP lease can be configured to last for a specific amount of time. For example, the lease can be set up to expire after three days or even thirty days. This is based on how the network administrator chooses to implement DHCP. It is a good idea to configure long leases if all of the nodes in the network are permanently set up thereby reducing unnecessary traffic. However, if the network has a great deal of mobile users, short leases may be more suitable.

Regardless of the length of the lease, when a DHCP client is given a lease it attempts to renew the address at specific intervals. DHCP clients request to renew their lease assignment when 50 percent of the lease interval is up. For example, if the lease assignment is four days, after two days the client will request to renew the lease. If the DHCP server is unavailable to renew the lease, the client will then wait until 87.5 percent of the lease interval is up. At 87.5 percent, the client simply requests a new address rather than attempting to renew its existing address.

Monitoring IP Address Assignment

It is possible to monitor the lease assignment from the client by using the IPCONFIG command line utility. The IPCONFIG command line utility can show many parameters about the lease assignment. For example, if IPCONFIG is typed on the command line, the output will include the IP address, subnet mask, and default gateway. If IPCONFIG is used with the /ALL switch, there is much more information given.

IPCONFIG can also be used to release or renew existing DHCP leases. The commands are:

> **IPCONFIG/RELEASE**—Releases the current DHCP lease.

> **IPCONFIG/RENEW**—Requests a new DHCP lease. Before renewing a lease, any existing leases must be released.

DHCP Broadcasts and Relay Agents

As stated, DHCP clients broadcast for DHCP address leases upon bootup or when manually released and renewed with the IPCONFIG command. This causes some concern in large routed internetworks because routers, by default, filter broadcasts.

If client computers on one subnet are to obtain addresses from a DHCP server on a separate network, additional configuration must be considered. For example, it is possible to implement routers that are BOOTP compatible. BOOTP compatible routers are compatible with and are described in RFC 1542. However, this is not always an economical choice. A second method of achieving this objective is to implement DCHP relay agents. A *DHCP relay agent* is a server located on a remote network that handles all client DHCP-discover broadcasts. The relay agent then forwards the client request to the DHCP server located on the other subnet (see Figure 8-2).

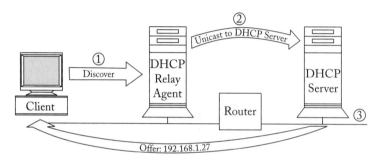

STEP 1: Client sends broadcast for IP address
STEP 2: Relay agent intercepts discover packet, and forwards request as
           a unicast directly to DHCP server
STEP 3: DHCP sends offer directly to workstation

Figure 8-2. *DHCP Relay Agent in Action*

Essentially, relay agents turn broadcasts into unicasts and direct the unicast to the DHCP server.

BOOTStrap PROTOCOL (BOOTP)

BOOTP is closely related to DHCP, and both have their ties to the Reverse Address Resolution Protocol. BOOTP and RARP deliver configuration settings to diskless workstations during initialization. However, they differ from one another because RARP only delivers IP addresses and cannot traverse a router. BOOTP can assign additional configuration settings, and its broadcasts can be forwarded by BOOTP-compatible routers.

NETWORK ADDRESS TRANSLATION (NAT)

NAT is a service that has become increasingly popular since its inception. NAT has helped the industry in overcoming one of its most severe shortcomings: the depletion of IP version 4 addresses. There are two general categories of IP addresses: public and private. Public addresses are those that are registered with ICANN/IANA and allow users to browse the Internet. Private addresses are not registered with ICANN/IANA and only allow hosts to browse their company's private network. NAT provides a link between the two. NAT is a service that can convert thousands of private IP addresses into one public address so all hosts in a private network can browse the public Internet (see Figure 8-3).

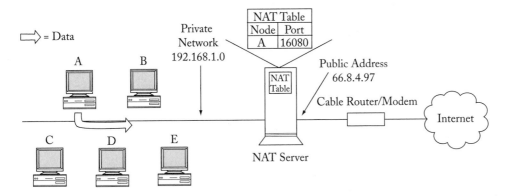

1. Node 'A' attempts to browse Internet.
2. The NAT Server intercepts packet.
3. NAT server then maps Node 'As' IP address to specific port and forwards the packet to the Internet.

Figure 8-3. *NAT Service*

NAT is a service often offered by *proxy servers*. A proxy server normally has two network adapter boards installed in it: one for the public network and one for the private network. This way, all hosts that browse the Internet are now represented by the network's proxy server. In this design, the proxy server also acts as the default gateway for clients of the IP network. A default gateway is a central node for all clients on the local network to send data to if the destination address is not located on the local network. Proxy servers can also cache web pages to speed up the web page search process for hosts as well as prevent public nodes on the Internet from gaining access to the private network.

Internet Connection Sharing, or *ICS*, is a form of NAT used in small business or home networks. This service allows multiple computers to use the modem of one computer to dial out to the Internet and surf the web.

8.2 NAME RESOLUTION

It is already known that IP networks use numbers as their unique identifiers between all nodes, but for many years people have been able to identify hosts by using names rather than numbers. This is done by using some form of name-to-IP address resolution method. During the early days of the Internet, a simple file called HOSTS provided name-to-IP address resolution. The Internet became so popular it was impossible to manage the HOSTS file. Therefore, a database called the Domain Name System was created to keep track of all of the hosts and IP addresses on the Internet. DNS is still in use today and is one of the most widely-used services. The other name resolution service that will be discussed in this chapter is Microsoft's Windows Internet Naming System (WINS).

DOMAIN NAME SYSTEM

DNS is an *X.500*-based distributed database, which means that it can be split up and reside on many servers for fault tolerance and load balancing. DNS was developed in 1984 in response to the difficult task of managing a text file called the HOSTS file. HOSTS files are still in use today, but in a limited capacity. UNIX, Windows 2000, and Windows NT store the HOSTS file in the *etc* directory. Windows 9x stores its HOST file in the Windows directory. Figure 8-4 shows an example of the HOSTS file from a Windows 9x machine. Notice the valid entry in the file is the 127.0.0.1 address which is mapped to the name *localhost*.

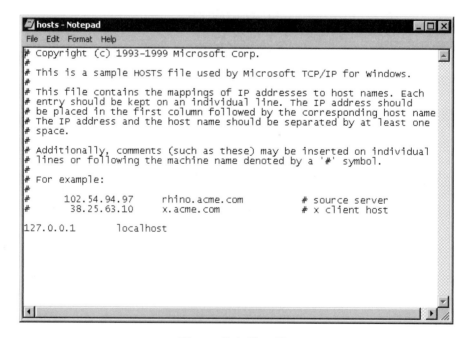

Figure 8-4. *Hosts File*

DNS Structure

DNS is a hierarchy designed as an inverted tree with the root at the top. The hierarchy is represented as three domain levels: the root level, top level, and second level. The *root-level domain*, or the top of the DNS, is represented by a dot. There are several root servers strategically located throughout the world. Each root server has an entry for the other root servers in its DNS database. *Top-level domains* are represented by categories found at the end of domain names that characterize their nature, such as COM, ORG, NET, EDU, or country codes, for example, US for the United States or CH for Sweden (see Figure 8-5).

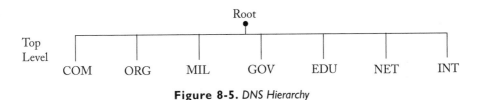

Figure 8-5. *DNS Hierarchy*

Here is a list of the original top-level domains and what they represent. This list represents domains that primarily relate to the United States.

COM	**Commercial Organization**
ORG	**Organization**
MIL	**Military**
GOV	**Government Organization**
EDU	**Educational Institution**
NET	**Network-Related Organizations**
INT	**International Organization**

Finally, *second-level domains* are assigned to companies that would like to register their company name in a top level of the DNS. To register a name in the DNS you must contact ICANN/IANA and request the name. For them to register the name it must be unique, and there will be a yearly fee associated with the registration. For example, when Delmar Learning registered its company name in the COM domain, its domain name became delmarlearning.com. If business needs require it, Delmar can subdivide its own domain name into smaller domains such as electronics.delmarlearning.com and support.delmarlearning.com. The hosts in the Delmar domain now have a *fully-qualified domain name*, or *FQDN*, that consist of their host name and their domain name. An example of an FQDN is workstation1.Delmarlearning.com or fileserver1.support.Delmar.com (see Figure 8-6).

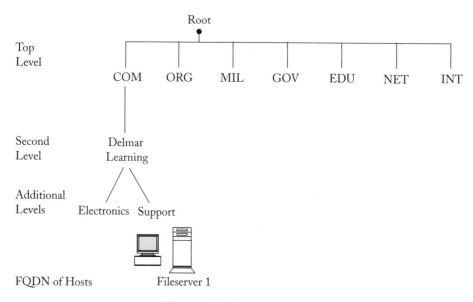

Figure 8-6. *Hosts in Domains*

The DNS Process

The DNS process is based on queries. A *resolver* is a client that queries a DNS server to find out the IP address of an FQDN it is trying to reach. If the local DNS server does not know the IP address to the FQDN being sought, it will query a server above it in the hierarchy. This process will continue until the client receives its requested information or an error occurs.

Here is an example of how a DNS server is queried by a resolver. A user located in the support.TJC.COM domain attempts to access a website that is located in the store.com domain. The user types the Universal Resource Locator (URL) in the web browser and hits the go button. The user's computer will first query the closest DNS server to see if the local DNS server knows the IP address of the requested website (see Figure 8-7).

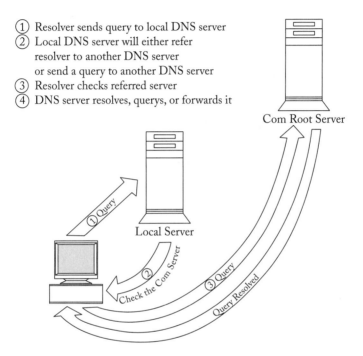

Figure 8-7. *User Query*

If the local DNS server is aware of the IP address, it will give the requesting user the IP address. If it does not know the IP address of the destination it will forward the query on to another DNS server. If the next DNS server does not know the IP address either, the query will be forwarded to one of the top-level domains, which should know about one of the domains in the path. It will forward the query to the next domain and, finally, the IP address will be returned to the user requesting the website. The user's machine will then contact the website by IP address rather than URL (see Figure 8-8).

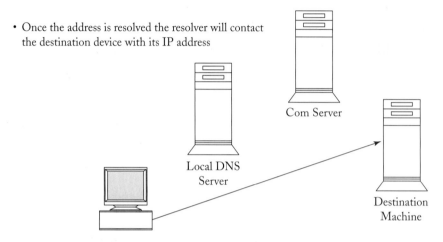

- Once the address is resolved the resolver will contact the destination device with its IP address

Com Server

Local DNS Server

Destination Machine

Figure 8-8. *Example of DNS Process*

DNS Server Roles

There are several servers involved in the DNS process.

- **Root Server.** Root servers maintain the master list of the top-level domains on the Internet. Currently, there are thirteen root servers distributed throughout the world. Different organizations, including the United States government, maintain these servers.

- **Primary or Master Server.** This is the server in a second-level domain that maintains the DNS database, known as a zone file. To successfully utilize DNS, records are created that map the FQDN to the IP address of the hosts on the network. A server can be the primary DNS server for multiple domains, as well as the secondary server for other domains.

- **Secondary or Slave Server.** Secondary servers maintain a copy of the zone file and service client requests.

- **Caching Server.** This server does not store the zone file. It learns about DNS entries by querying primary or secondary servers. It will keep the DNS information it learned from the query in cache until the Time To Live expires.

- **Forwarding Server.** Forwarders can be a primary, secondary, or caching server that forward requests to servers if they cannot be resolved locally.

DNS Records

The DNS hostname resolution process works based on DNS records. DNS records are added to the DNS database to show what the IP address-to-hostname resolution is supposed to be for servers and workstations in the internetwork. There are many records available for creation in DNS. Here is a sample of the most popular used.

- **NS Record.** A Name Server Record identifies a DNS name server.

- **SOA Record.** The Start of Authority Record is the Primary DNS server in a domain.

- **A Record.** An Address Record identifies computer hostnames to IP address mappings.

- **CNAME Record.** Canonical Name Record creates an alias for a host.

- **MX Record.** The Mail Exchanger Record identifies an e-mail server for a domain.

- **PTR.** A Pointer Record allows for IP-to-FQDN reverse DNS lookups, rather than FQDN-to-IP lookups.

Dynamic DNS

One of the limitations of DNS in the past was that it had to be manually configured. All records were created and deleted by administrators. This was not a problem if node IP addresses were configured manually, but if the network used DHCP, addresses of hosts constantly changed. Therefore, the DNS database would be out of synchronization unless the administrator consistently updated DNS records. This problem has been addressed by the creation of Dynamic DNS. DDNS automatically creates and removes DNS records based on lease assignments of the DHCP server. DDNS greatly reduces the administrative effort used to manage DNS and DHCP in the same network.

WINDOWS INTERNET NAME SERVICE (WINS)

WINS is a name resolution program used by Microsoft operating systems. WINS is a dynamic database that maintains records for NETBIOS name to IP address resolution. Nodes register their NETBIOS names and their IP addresses with a WINS server upon bootup. WINS grew out of a text-based file called LMHOSTS. The LMHOSTS file is stored in the same directory as the HOSTS file and was used for the static mapping of NETBIOS names to IP addresses. Here is an example of a LMHOSTS file (see Figure 8-9).

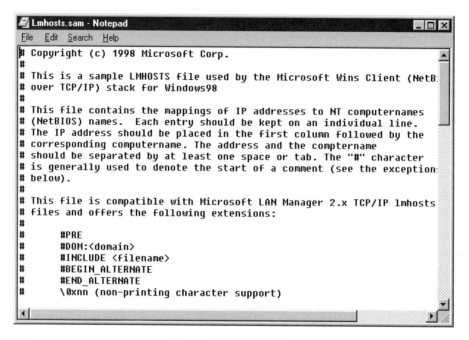

Figure 8-9. *LMHOSTS File*

TCP/IP ports 137 and 138 are the well-known ports used to forward WINS data. It is possible to implement WINS and DNS in the same environment so if a DNS entry for a host does not exist, the WINS server can be queried.

Choosing the Right Service

When discussing network services it is important to understand that choosing the correct services to use at first will save great amounts of time in the future. For example, assume you are the administrator of a small network. Due to the size of the network you decide to use the LMHOSTS file for NETBios name resolution and the HOSTS file for host name resolution. This option may work fine for the time being, but consider if the network expands by forty computers. It will be very difficult to keep adding entries to the files during an expansion. It may be beneficial to you to install WINS and DNS to help with the administration of the network.

Test Tip: When taking the Network+ exam you will be required to make these decisions to answer some of the questions.

ZERO CONFIGURATION NETWORKING (ZEROCONF)

Zeroconf, also known as Rendezvous, is a technology that allows devices to establish a network or connect to an existing network without utilizing traditional networking services such as DNS and/or DHCP. It is intended for use in small networks where security is low. It works on the following principles: Automatic Private IP Addressing, Multicast DNS, and Service Discovery.

Automatic Private IP Addressing (APIPA). Basically, APIPA was designed as a fail-over mechanism for a client when it attempted to get a DHCP address from a server that was unable to provide the address. In Zeroconf, APIPA has a different function. Its function here is to give an automatic address to the client in the 169.254.0.0/16 address range that will allow it to connect to and interoperate with another host, server, or an existing network. Remember, each IP address on a network must be unique. Therefore, the service must check with other devices on the network to ensure its APIPA-issued address is unique.

Multicast DNS. In traditional DNS technologies, the client machine is given an IP address of a DNS server. This address can be added manually or through a DHCP server. When the client queries a DNS server it will look to the address that was added earlier. This is essentially a unicast (one node talking directly to another). In multicast DNS the client queries for the DNS service on a multicast address. The DNS server(s) listens for requests destined for that multicast address and responds to the client when queried.

Automatic Service Discovery. Automatic Service Discovery works similarly to the multicast DNS. When a client requests a print server, the Automatic Service Discovery service will query for that service. The service type should be stored in the DNS server as a .SRV record. The client is then able to connect to the device.

8.3 REMOTE CONNECTIVITY

Remote connectivity consists of allowing users the ability to access the network from a location other than the organization's main site. For example, many companies allow their sales staff the ability to "dial in" to the network over a remote access service. This service allows the users to connect to the network and gain access to the resources that are available to them when they are sitting in the building where the network resides. Another example may be allowing an injured worker to work from home over the remote access service until he or she is feeling well enough to physically come back to work.

TYPES OF REMOTE CONNECTIVITY

There are primarily two types of remote connectivity. They include remote control and remote user.

- **Remote Control.** The user logs into the network from a distance and gains control of the node that he has logged in as. Terminal service is a service that offers this type of remote connectivity. Some popular terminal service programs include Microsoft's terminal server which is shipped with Windows 2000 Server and Advanced Server, as well as Citrix' Metaframe, and Norton's PC Anywhere. The protocol that supports terminal server connections on a Microsoft Server is the Remote Desktop Protocol or RDP.

- **Remote User.** The user connects to the network from a distance but does not remotely control any nodes. He simply has access to the resources available on the network. This will be elaborated on further.

The server service that must be running for a remote workstation to connect to the network is the Remote Access Service. Many vendors offer this with their operating system, but here we will discuss Microsoft's version.

ROUTING AND REMOTE ACCESS SERVER (RRAS)

Remote access has two portions to it: a client portion which is known as dial-up networking, and a Windows 2000/2003 server component known as Routing and Remote Access Service, which is located on the Administrative Tools menu. When configuring a remote access solution, there are many parameters that must be configured. For example, during the configuration of the server you have the option to set the type of protocol the user will use to connect to the server.

DIAL-UP PROTOCOLS

Popular protocols consist of PPP, PPTP, and PPoE. PPP and PPTP have already been discussed. PPoE, on the other hand, has not. PPoE is the point-to-point protocol over Ethernet and is slightly different from PPP and PPTP. PPTP and PPP are installed on each client that needs to dial and connect to the network. PPoE uses characteristics of Ethernet, therefore multiple LAN users should technically be able to connect to a remote server through a single device. This protocol is used when trying to access a remote access server through a cable modem or a DSL connection. PPoE supports PAP, CHAP, PPP, and PPTP.

CONFIGURING REMOTE ACCESS

It is imperative that the proper protocols be available when configuring remote access. For example, if your internal network uses IPX, the remote access client must be set up to use IPX. This is, however, set at the server because the client will be dialing in using a TCP/IP-based protocol. Once the client connects to the RRAS server, it will encapsulate the client data in IPX/SPX so the client can access data on the internal network. If the protocol is not configured correctly, the user will not be able gain access to the data on the internal network.

VIRTUAL PRIVATE NETWORKS (VPN)

VPNs are a popular technology for connecting to corporate sites. Using specific devices, a VPN provides a connection to a defined location over the public Internet. Several vendors sell VPN-capable components. VPNs can also be set up with popular vendor operating systems. There are primarily two types of VPNs: client-to-site VPNs and site-to-site VPNs.

Client-to-Site VPN. A client-to-site VPN is a VPN that allows designated users to have access to the corporate network from remote locations. These types of VPNs are extremely popular with companies that allow users to telecommute to work or have a traveling sales staff. The requirements for a client-to-site VPN include a permanent Internet connection at the corporate site and an Internet connection for the user. The user's Internet connection does not necessarily have to be a permanent connection. It can be a dial-up connection or an Internet connection in a public area.

Site-to-Site VPN. A site-to-site VPN is a VPN that allows multiple corporate sites to be connected together over low-cost Internet connections. The requirements for a site-to-site VPN include a permanent Internet connection and VPN-compatible services at each location. VPNs can also be used with encryption-based technologies to secure the virtual tunnel over which data travels. Two popular protocols used with VPNs are L2TP and PPTP. Figures 8-10 and 8-11 show both types of VPNs.

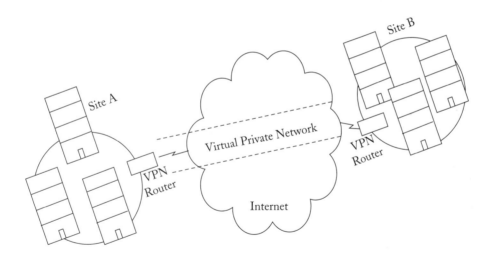

Figure 8-10. *VPN Site to Site*

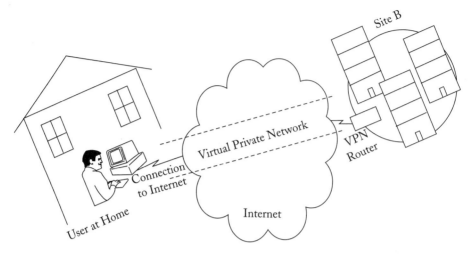

Figure 8-11. *VPN Remote User*

8.4 DATA LOSS PREVENTION

As a network administrator, you must be prepared to protect your data against unpreventable natural disasters and equipment failure. Obviously it is impossible to prevent disasters from occurring, however it is possible to preserve your network's data in the event a disaster occurs. Two popular data loss prevention methods used today include: Backups and Redundant Arrays of Inexpensive Disks (RAID). These technologies, along with how to protect against power loss, will be explained in this section.

BACKING UP THE DATA

Backups simply consist of making a copy of the network's critical data. This allows for the preservation of data in the event of a server crash or other unforeseen event. There are many different types of media to back your data up to. The most common is tape because it is a mature technology that can handle large amounts of data. Once the organization has a backup system in place, it is time to determine what *backup strategy* will be used. The backup strategy first consists of choosing to back up all nodes locally (which is not recommended), or backing up all machines over the network.

Local Backup

A local backup strategy is only recommended in specific situations because the administrator will be responsible for backing up data at each workstation in the network. If the administrator is not backing up the data, then the users will be responsible for it. Users are often preoccupied with their own job responsibilities, and backing up their data will not be a high priority.

Over the Network Backup

To simplify network administration, advise all users to save their data to a network file server. This way, only a few servers will have to be backed up. The backup strategy will also include a *backup method* that may consist of using a combination of the following four backup methods. Backup methods are based on the archive attribute bit of each file. If the archive attribute is on or set to one, it means that the file has changed since the last backup and it requires backup again. Some backup methods reset the archive bit to zero after the file is backed up, others do not.

Backup Methods

There are basically four backup methods available with most popular backup software. They include: *normal or full; incremental; differential;* and *copy.*

- **Normal or Full.** This method copies all selected files and resets the archive bit to zero. It is the most lengthy backup method and uses the most tape.

- **Incremental.** This method copies all files that have the archive bit on. Once an incremental backup runs, it resets the archive bit to zero for files backed up. This method uses less tape and less time than a full.

- **Differential.** This method does not reset the archive bit after copying a file. This method uses more tape and time than an incremental, but less than a full.

- **Copy.** The copy backup method allows you to copy all data and not reset the archive bit.

Backup Implementations

There are several different ways to implement the backup methods described. The different implementations allow for companies to tailor the backup strategy to the requirements of their data. The popular implementations of backup methods include:

Full Every Night. In this example, all of the files used every day are backed up every night. This implementation requires the most support and utilizes more tapes than the next two methods (see Figure 8-12).

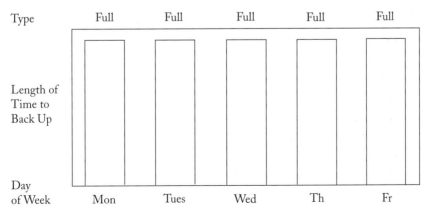

• Full Backup = All files backed up every day

Figure 8-12. *Full Every Night*

Full and Incremental. While using this strategy, a full backup will be completed on the first night of the backup cycle. On the second night and the nights thereafter, an incremental backup will be performed. When the incremental is run, only the files that have been used since the last successful backup are backed up. This method provides the shortest time to back up the files because only the files that have changed on the day of the incremental will be backed up. Remember, the incremental backup resets the archive bit. The full and incremental restoration will be the longest restoration because all of the tapes in the cycle will have to be restored. For example, assume Company X is using this method, a full backup is performed on Monday and then an incremental is performed on Tuesday, Wednesday, and Thursday (see Figure 8-13).

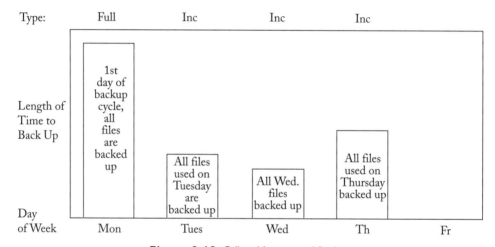

Figure 8-13. *Full and Incremental Backup*

On Friday morning there is a problem with the system, and a restoration must be performed. The tapes that must be restored include the full from Monday and all three of the weekday incremental backups (see Figure 8-14).

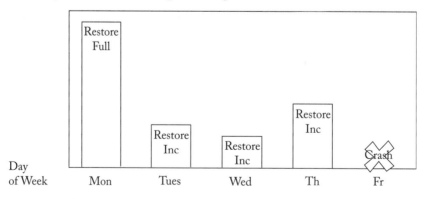

• Restore Mon, Tues, Wed, and Th tapes to get data that was lost

Figure 8-14. *Full and Incremental Restoration*

Full and Differential. A full backup with a differential backup works similarly to the full and incremental, but the key difference is that the differential does not reset the archive bit. Therefore, each day a differential backup is run it will copy the files that have the archive bit set to one. In other words, when a differential backup runs, it will back up all files used since the full backup ran. That means that the backup time each night will increase, but the restoration time will decrease (see Figure 8-15).

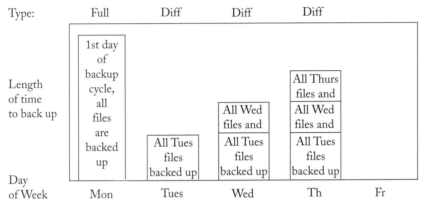

Figure 8-15. *Full and Differential*

Assume the company completes the full backup on Monday and a differential for the days thereafter. Each day the differential is performed it will copy the files that were used the day of the backup, as well as the files used the day before because the archive bit was never reset. So, if the first differential was completed on Tuesday, when the Wednesday differential is performed it will back up Tuesday's and Wednesday's files. If there is a system crash on Friday, only Monday's full backup and Thursday's differential backup need to be restored since Thursday's differential has the changes from Tuesday as well as Wednesday. Differential backups reduce the amount of time it takes to restore a system, yet they increase the amount of time the backup takes and the amount of tape used (see Figure 8-16).

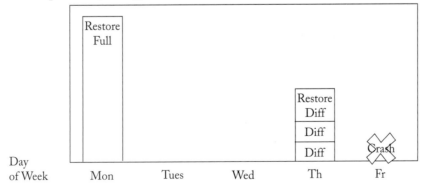

• Only two tapes (Mon and Th) have to be restored to retrieve data that was lost

Figure 8-16. *Restoring a Full and Differential Backup*

Backup Maintenance

Backup maintenance is one of the most important aspects of a company's data loss prevention plan but it is also one of the most overlooked practices. The three most neglected practices of a data loss prevention plan are:

- Keeping a copy of the data off site.
- Verifying the backups by completing a test restore.
- Cleaning the tape drives periodically.

The final concern for backing up data is to backup the data during off-peak hours since the process of backing up data often takes up much of the resources available on a network. For example, the backup server's CPU and RAM will be utilized to run the backup program. Also, if backups are being completed over the network, bandwidth usage will be increased drastically. Try to schedule the backups when no other services are running.

REDUNDANT ARRAY OF INEXPENSIVE (INDEPENDENT) DISKS (RAID)

RAID is a mechanism used to provide fault tolerance. Fault tolerance consists of having the ability to sustain the failure of one hard disk and still operate. It can be implemented in a network as a hardware solution or a software solution. In a hardware solution, special hard disk RAID controllers are used. In a software implementation, standard hard disk controllers can be used, and RAID software controls them. Some operating systems such as Microsoft Windows NT and Windows 2000 have RAID software support built into them. However, hardware RAID is much more reliable and should be used rather than software RAID in most situations.

A hardware RAID implementation often includes a separate tower that stores the additional hard disks. The RAID tower is then connected to one of the network servers through an external interface. Hard disks in RAID implementations must be the same size, unless the RAID setup is taking place at the partition level. If the RAID setup is taking place at the partition level, then the partitions must be the same size. In hardware RAID configurations, the drives will most likely be the same size.

RAID implementations are available in several different configurations. RAID configurations are categorized by different levels: Level 0, 1, 5, and 10 are the most popular.

RAID 0: Disk Striping

Although RAID level 0 does not provide fault tolerance, it is still considered a type of RAID. It consists of connecting two to thirty-two hard disks together to act as one hard disk. RAID 0 is used to improve I/O speeds (see Figure 8-17).

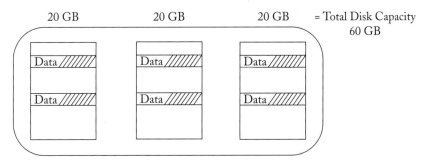

• No fault tolerance
• 2-32 disks acting as one
• Speeds up I/O requests

Figure 8-17. *Striping (RAID Level 0)*

If the RAID 0 implementation has four hard disks of 40 GB each, the usable disk space is 160 GB. If a drive fails in this implementation, all data will be lost. In general, RAID does not replace a reliable backup system and is not implemented to prevent data loss. It is implemented to allow a system to continue operations if hardware fails.

RAID 1: Disk Mirroring

RAID level 1 consists of having two hard disks with an exact mirror image of each other. When data is written to one of the disks, the same data is written to the second disk. If a mirrored set consists of two 20 GB hard drives, the usable space is only 50 percent of the total (or 20 GB) because the second drive is only used to store a copy of the data. It is recommended that you implement disk duplexing when using a mirrored set. Duplexing consists of installing a second hard disk controller to avoid a single point of failure (see Figure 8-18).

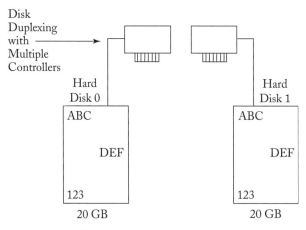

Figure 8-18. *Mirror with Duplexing (RAID Level 1)*

RAID 5: Disk Striping with Parity

RAID level 5 consists of a striped set of three to thirty-two drives. Each drive must be the same size. Data is striped across the drives in 64 KB blocks. As it is written, a parity block corresponding to the data that has just been striped is placed on a separate disk. The parity is created and compressed through the use of a complex mathematical algorithm. To determine the amount of usable space in a RAID 5 design, multiply the space on each disk by the number of disks and subtract the amount of space associated with one hard disk. For example, if there are four drives of 40 GB each, the total giga-byte available is 160. However, since the amount of space associated with one drive is used for parity, the total usable space is 120 GB, or 75 percent. The more drives in the implementation, the more space available.

The data and its parity information are never stored on the same disk. Therefore if one disk fails, the original data can be restored from the remaining disks and the parity data (see Figure 8-19).

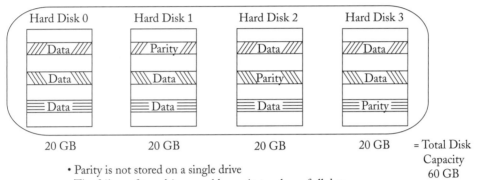

- Parity is not stored on a single drive
- The failure of two drives would constitute a loss of all data
- 3-32 drives acting as one

Figure 8-19. *Striping with Parity (RAID Level 5)*

RAID 10: Mirrored Stripe Set

RAID level 10 is one of the most expensive RAID implementations because it uses the most hard disks. The usable storage space will be 50 percent of the total amount of drives used in this setup. RAID level 10 consists of a RAID 0 stripe set, however the entire stripe set is mirrored. This will prevent the stripe set from losing data if a single drive crashes (see Figure 8-20).

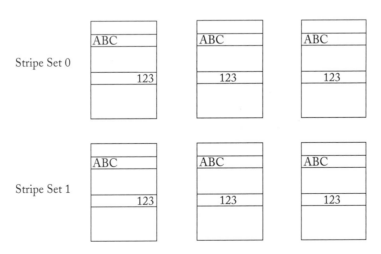

- All data written to stripe set 0 is written to stripe set 1

Figure 8-20. *RAID Level 10*

Most RAID towers allow for the removal and replacement of a failed drive without powering down. This is known as hot swappable. Once the bad drive is replaced, the data that was on the drive can then be regenerated. Regeneration of data can be a slow process based on the amount of data that is on the RAID system.

Other Redundant Solutions

Redundancy in a network goes beyond having redundant hard drives in a disk array. Many new strategies are being used to prevent the loss of connectivity as well as the loss of services.

Loss of Connectivity. To prevent the loss of connectivity, organizations are implementing dual or redundant links between critical servers and critical sites. It is not uncommon now to purchase servers with at least two network interface cards in them. Utilizing both network interface cards can have a positive impact on the network in two ways. First, if one network interface card becomes damaged or corrupt, the other card will continue to operate. Second, if a server offers multiple services, network interface cards with different IP addresses can be used to load balance the amount of requests sent to the server.

Loss of Service. Having all of your data backed up to a RAID device or a storage area network will do you no good if the services that need the data are unavailable. A popular trend in the day and age of fault-tolerant networks is to utilize clustering services to ensure the availability of a server's services. For example, if you have a single e-mail server in your network and it goes down, there will be no e-mail for any users. To solve this problem, add a second server to the network. Both servers would then run cluster services as well as the e-mail service. When the cluster is established, one server will continue to process client requests if the other server goes down, as if nothing happened. In most clustered networks, the two servers will share a data store, such as a storage area network, that should be able to provide the data that the server will request.

STORAGE AREA NETWORKS AND NETWORK ATTACHED STORAGE

An alternative to RAID is currently taking the network industry by storm. Storage Area Network (SAN) and Network Attached Storage (NAS) devices are among the hottest internetworking trends. These two devices are similar in concept and will both be referenced as a SAN.

A SAN is a component that connects to the IP network through a network interface card. It is assigned an IP address and acts as an independent node in the network. SANs are managed by a server in the IP network. The speed associated with a SAN is often faster than that of RAID devices because a RAID tower is limited to the transfer speed of the external interface of the server in which it is accessed through. The speed of a SAN is based on the speed of the network, which in popular implementations is between 100 Mbps and 1000 Mbps

Users can save data directly to the SAN. The amount of data that a SAN can handle is far greater than any other storage devices mentioned thus far. Capacities can well exceed hundreds of terabytes. An estimate of the future capabilities of SANs is incalculable. It is a leading technology, and vendors are in constant competition to increase the capabilities of the technology.

PROTECTING AGAINST POWER

The two most common power problems include power surges and power sags. When preparing a data loss prevention plan, these issues must be accounted for.

- **Power surge.** A *power surge* or power spike is the unexpected increase in voltage supplied to a component. Power surges often occur after a power outage or a power sag, which is the unexpected drop in line voltage. Power surges can destroy components in a PC or server without leaving a trace.

- **Power sag.** A *power sag* or brownout occurs when line voltage drops. It seems that a drop in the line voltage may not harm a PC or a server. However when a power sag occurs, the components within the node must work harder to maintain the acceptable performance level, ultimately reducing the life of the hardware.

Uninterruptible Power Supply (UPS)

A *UPS* is a battery-type device that can regulate the flow of electricity to components. Consider utilizing an uninterruptible power supply to continue operations during a power outage and prevent the unexpected increase in line voltage caused by power surges. A UPS is absolutely necessary for critical servers and routers in the network. Operating without a UPS or some other type of backup power device (such as a generator) can lead to problems that may result in large financial expenditures.

PROTECTING AGAINST TEMPERATURE

A room with many computers in it, such as a server room, can become very hot. Servers and critical nodes such as routers and switches should not be stored in a room with a poor ventilation system. A specific room temperature is not recommended, however it should be cool to you. Operating critical nodes in a hot room will attribute to their overheating and, ultimately, the failure of the node.

MAINTAINING SPARES

One practice that most administrators should become familiar with is the storage of spare components. All of the redundancy and fault tolerant technologies available could become useless if a simple component in a network fails. To prevent this, take a proactive approach in trying to determine which network components may fail. It is nearly impossible to guess which may fail, but there are certainly a few that you can be prepared to replace. For example, power supplies tend to burn out over time, hard drives fail, and network adapters can be damaged through power spikes.

Spares can be maintained as either hot spares or cold spares. A hot spare is a second device that is basically ready to take over when the primary device fails. For example, purchasing servers with dual power supplies is very popular now. If one of the power supplies fails, the other continues to work. Hence the term "hot spare." On the other hand, a cold spare is a component in reserve that is sitting on a shelf waiting to be used if something goes bad. For example, it is good practice to keep a drive of the same standard and size of the drives located in a RAID array. This way, if a drive in the RAID array fails, all that has to be done to keep the network running is to replace the failed drive with the cold spare that you had on hand.

DISASTER RECOVERY (DR)

Disaster Recovery, or DR as it has come to be known in the networking industry, is the ability to recover data after some sort of disaster. The entire basis of DR is to respond to the dreaded question "What if something happens?" On a fundamental level, DR provides insurance that, if a natural disaster or some other type of disaster destroys equipment and data, the company as a whole will still be able to operate. DR sites are often set up at locations remote from where the primary business is taking place. Some companies will now host a DR site for other companies. The sites that are set up can be designated as Hot sites, Cold sites, or Warm sites.

Hot Site. A hot site is a site that is 100 percent ready to go with computers, data, telecommunications services, and business functions in the event something happens to the primary site.

Cold Site. A cold site is a remote site that is physically prepared to start recovery operations but does not necessarily have the support equipment, services, or personnel ready to go.

Warm Site. A warm site is normally equipped with some of the necessary equipment, services, and data, and would need some additional support to be up and running.

8.5 SECURITY

The first level of security in any network is physical security. This means keep your critical servers in a locked area with access limited to trusted employees and administrators. However, you still have to protect the data on the network. There are primarily two threats to protect against: hackers and viruses.

VIRUS PREVENTION

Virus prevention, from an administrator's point of view, consists of maintaining up-to-date virus software on all nodes in the network. Also, user training can help prevent viruses. Many viruses occur because users are unaware of how they can be transmitted. For example, teach users to screen floppy disks from untrusted sources, and do not open e-mails from unknown sources. By utilizing proper antivirus software you will be able to track and prevent the spread of viruses in your network. Cleaning a network that has been infected can take countless man hours, which often results in the loss of both money and data.

HACKER PREVENTION

Hacker prevention needs to be applied at two levels. First, it is important to protect against the hacker intrusion. In other words: KEEP THE HACKER OUT. Second, if the hacker is able to find a way into the network, it is important to minimize the amount of damage that can be done to the network and user data by protecting it through the use of permissions, encryption, and authentication.

Keeping the Hacker Out

The primary method of keeping hackers out of your network if it is connected to the Internet is to implement a *firewall*. Firewalls are normally placed between a private LAN and the public Internet. They should act like the choke point to the private network. If set up in this manner, all data will have to go through a single point. Firewalls can filter packets based on source address, destination address, port numbers, and other criteria. There are four firewall topologies that can be implemented in a network.

- **Packet-filtering router.** This is the least protective of the four mentioned and consists of a router monitoring IP packets as they enter the router from the public side and then allowing or denying them access to the network based on defined rules or criteria (see Figure 8-21).

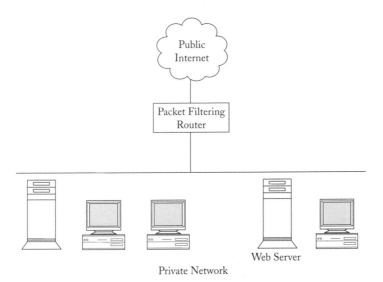

Figure 8-21. *Packet-Filtering Router*

- **Single-homed bastion.** This process consists of the packet-filtering router forwarding all incoming packets to the firewall software on a bastion host. Once through the router, the bastion host determines whether or not the data can be forwarded to a host on the network (see Figure 8-22).

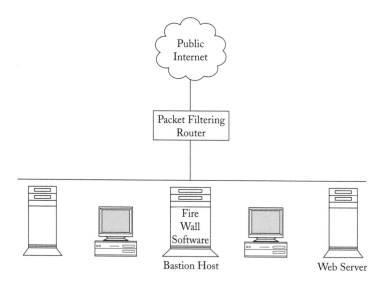

• All traffic is screened by the Bastion Host

Figure 8-22. *Single Homed Bastion*

- **Dual-homed bastion.** A dual-homed bastion works like a single-homed bastion, however it has two network adapter cards in it. One attaches to the packet-filtering router and the other connects to the internal network. This physical division of networks adds increased security or defense in depths (see Figure 8-23).

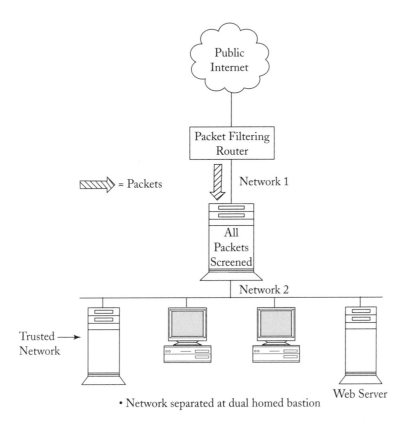

• Network separated at dual homed bastion

Figure 8-23. *Dual Homed Bastion*

- **Demilitarized Zone (DMZ).** A DMZ consists of having two packet-filtering routers, one from the Internet to the Internet-accessible servers in a screened subnet, and a packet-filtering router connecting the internal network to the screened subnet. This is the most secure firewall solution (see Figure 8-24).

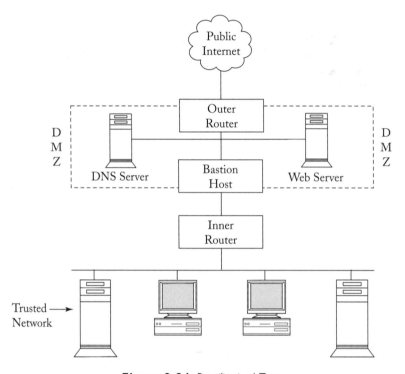

Figure 8-24. *Demilitarized Zone*

PERMISSIONS, ENCRYPTION, AND AUTHENTICATION

If a hacker is able to find a line of attack through the firewall implementation, there are other mechanisms available to protect the data including permissions to access network resources, encryption of data, and the authentication of a user's identity.

Permissions

The use of *permissions* in general networking security simply means that users must be given the approval to access a resource. Setting permissions on files and folders not only protects data from hackers breaking into the network, but they also protect data from users within the network. After all, approximately 80 percent of all malicious hacking of resources takes place from users within the internetwork.

Encryption

Encryption at the network level often consists of using security algorithms to scramble and descramble data. Some algorithms used include symmetric-key encryption and asymmetric-key encryption.

- **Symmetric key.** *Symmetric key* encryption is a single key-encryption method. A message can be encrypted and decrypted through the use of one key. The drawback of this method is that if an unwanted user learns the single key, all messages encrypted are now compromised (see Figure 8-25).

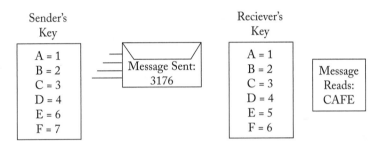

Figure 8-25. *Symmetric Key Encryption*

- **Asymmetric key.** *Asymmetric* or *public key* encryption is more secure than symmetric key encryption. Public key encryption uses a mathematically-matched key pair. In this instance, each user would have a public and a private key. The private key remains private to the individual user, whereas the public key can be shared. Now as data is encrypted with the private or public key, it must be decrypted with the opposite key (see Figure 8-26).

- Message is encrypted with user A's private key
- User B must have user A's public key to decrypt the message

Figure 8-26. *Asymmetric Key Encryption*

If a hacker attempts to steal data off the network through the use of a packet sniffer, encryption keys will not allow the data packets to be read unless the user has the correct key.

- **Secure sockets layer.** SSL is a means of encrypting a session between two hosts through the use of digital certificates, which are essentially asymmetric keys. Digital certificates can provide authentication, as well as assign responsibility to organizations that transmit data over the Internet.

Encryption Protocols. There are also protocols that create secure encrypted tunnels for data to go through. They include, but are not limited to, IP Security (IPsec), L2TP, and PPTP.

- **IPsec.** IPsec is a group of protocols that supports the secure exchange of IP-based packets. It uses two encryption methods, transport and tunnel. Transport encrypts the data, and tunnel creates a secure tunnel to send the data through.

- **L2TP.** L2TP stands for the Layer 2 Tunneling Protocol. It is an extension of the point-to-point protocol and is used to create a secure tunnel for data to go through when dialing in to a network.

- **PPTP.** PPTP creates a secure tunnel for data to go through when dialing in to a network. Microsoft's version of PPTP allows multiple transport protocols to be sent through the tunnel, even NETBeui which is a non-routable protocol.

- **ICA.** ICA is a protocol that provides compression and security for clients using terminal services, such as Citrix's MetaFrame product.

- **Wireless Equivalent Privacy (WEP).** WEP is a security mechanism used in wireless LANs (WLAN) that prevents unwanted users from connecting to, and browsing in, a wireless network. The basic premise of WEP is that it prevents users from accessing the radio waves that often extend beyond the physical walls of an organization. When WEP is enabled, network users are configured with the same WEP information that the WEP-enabled WAPs utilize.

- **Wi-Fi Protected Access (WPA).** WPA is the WLAN security that replaces WEP. WEP had fallen short in some areas, and hackers were capable of capturing packets and learning the WEP key. WPA, which is based on the same WEP engine (and can scale back to WEP if a component does not support WPA), has put such mechanisms in place as a Message Integrity Check (MIC) to prevent forgery. WPA has also incorporated sequence numbers into the data packets and encryption keys to prevent unwanted users from accessing the network.

- **802.11i.** 802.11i is a standard that was ratified in June 2004 and provides improved encryption for the current WLAN standards such as 802.11a and 802.11b. Like WPA, 802.11i supports key encryption. It also supports key caching (for fast reconnection), and pre-authentication to speed up the roaming process. Another standard supported is Advanced Encryption Standard (AES), which requires a hardware chip to be installed; this is a downfall of the standard.

Authentication

Authentication is the process users verifying to a directory service server in the network that they are who they say they are. There are several types of authentication that prevent hackers from pretending they are someone in the network who has rights when they really are not. For example, the password authentication protocol (PAP), the challenge handshake authentication protocol (CHAP), and MSCHAP are all authentication protocols used when dialing in to a network. The kerberos protocol is used when authenticating to a directory services server.

- **PAP.** PAP uses plaintext passwords, is the least sophisticated authentication protocol, and only uses a two-way handshake.

- **CHAP.** CHAP is a challenge-response authentication protocol that uses a three-way handshake and is based on the Message Digest 5 (MD5) to encrypt the response.

- **MSCHAP.** Microsoft's version of CHAP.

- **Kerberos.** Kerberos is an authentication protocol that uses a key management scheme to vouch for entities that want to communicate with one another. When two parties attempt to communicate, they must both authenticate to the kerberos server, which will issue a session key to the parties and allow for a communication dialogue to occur. Kerberos is the default for Windows 2000.

- **RADIUS (Remote Authentication Dial-In User Service).** The RADIUS service is available to organizations that have the need to authenticate many users over a dial-in connection. RADIUS provides a database of user sites as a backend server to the frontend dial-in server. The RADIUS service may be available to many servers that handle the incoming calls. When one of the incoming callers enters his/her username and password, the dial-in server will check with the RADIUS service to see if the user's username and password are valid.

- **Extensible Authentication Protocol (EAP).** EAP is an extension to PPP. EAP can be used with certificate-based technologies. EAP requires both the client and the server to authenticate a connection and to communicate that verification to one another. If a certificate is not sent or is invalid, the connection will not take place.

Password Policy

Most network operating systems require users to log in to the network. Based on the security of the network, there should be some rules to follow or a *password policy* in effect. Password policies often require users' passwords to be a specific length, to be changed every thirty, sixty, or ninety days, and to be different each time they change them.

> ## CHAPTER SUMMARY
>
> Chapter 8 covered many topics related to maintaining and supporting a network. Network services such as DHCP, NAT, DNS, and WINS were described. You also learned about the HOSTS and LMHOSTS files that were once used to provide for name-to-IP address resolution. Also explained in this chapter were methods to prevent the loss of data and how to keep your network data secure. In the next chapter, you will learn about troubleshooting techniques. But first, complete the Knowledge Test that follows.

KNOWLEDGE TEST

1. What is the purpose of having a proxy server in your network? (Choose all that apply.)
   A. It protects the network from users on the public Internet.
   B. It resolves names to IP addresses.
   C. It can allow your network to use a single public IP address.
   D. It protects hardware from failure.

2. What should you do to check to ensure your backups have completed successfully?
   A. Test the RAID system.
   B. Test the backup by completing a restoration.
   C. Clean the tape drive.
   D. Crash the server and attempt to restore it.

3. What two methods are used for host name-to-IP address resolution? (Choose two.)
   A. SAP
   B. LMHOSTS
   C. DNS
   D. HOSTS
   E. WINS

4. What data are you to backup in your disaster recovery plan?
   A. Operating systems
   B. Applications
   C. Workstation data
   D. Critical data

5. A user attempts to log on to the network from a Windows NT workstation. Since he is having trouble logging on to the network, he decides to bypass the logon. He uses the WINIPCFG command to check his IP address, and it returns an IP address of 0.0.0.0. What is the most likely cause of this problem?
   A. DNS server is down.
   B. WINS configuration tab is wrong.
   C. DHCP server is down.
   D. The user cannot log on to local workstation.

6. Your company is migrating from using the HOSTS file to a DNS database. Once the DNS is installed in the network, what is the next step?
   A. Correct the entries in the HOSTS file.
   B. Stop the clients from using the LMHOSTS file.
   C. Create a new HOSTS file.
   D. Stop the clients from using the HOSTS file.

7. What is the difference between fault tolerance and disaster recovery? (Choose two.)
   A. Disaster recovery is being able to recover data from a crashed server.
   B. Fault tolerance is being able to recover data from a crashed server.
   C. Disaster recovery is being able to continue to operate if a component fails.
   D. Fault tolerance is being able to continue to operate if a component fails.

8. What service is needed to map NETBIOS names to IP addresses?
   A. WINS
   B. DNS
   C. DHCP
   D. NAT

9. You are using a full and incremental backup strategy. On Sunday night, the full backup runs every week. The incremental backup runs nightly. What data would be backed up on Thursday night?
   A. The changed files from Monday, Tuesday, Wednesday, and Thursday.
   B. The changed data from Thursday.
   C. All of the data.
   D. None of the data.

10. How can you make a global DNS change to all users in your network?
    A. Make the change at each workstation.
    B. Make the change by using an automated script.
    C. Share out the HOSTS file.
    D. Make the change in the DHCP configuration, and have all users renew their IP addresses.

11. What tunneling protocol can be used to carry multiple transport protocols?
    A. PPTP
    B. L2TP
    C. IPsec
    D. HTTPS

12. Your network manager has told you it is time to implement a fault tolerant and disaster prevention system. You propose to him that you buy a new backup system and use the full and incremental backup strategy. You also recommend putting in a RAID 0 system. What does your proposal accomplish?
    A. Both objectives.
    B. Neither objective.
    C. One objective.
    D. There is no need to waste the money.

13. What is SSL based on?
    A. Session encryption
    B. Tunneling protocol
    C. Packet encryption
    D. Key management

14. You have an internetwork with three subnets separated by two routers. On one of the segments you install a DHCP server to assign addresses to all nodes. Only nodes on the same segment are receiving addresses. What is the problem?
    A. DHCP requests are prevented by the switch.
    B. DHCP cannot work in an internetwork.
    C. Your users did not shut APIPA off.
    D. Routers filter broadcasts.

15. When configuring DNS to receive e-mails from the Internet, what type of record must be created?
    A. SOA
    B. MX
    C. EML
    D. PTR

16. You are the administrator of a small network. You believe your workstations are showing signs there is a problem with the amount of electricity they are drawing from the wall outlets. What can you do to eliminate this problem?
    A. Install a surge protector.
    B. Move the PCs to a different room.
    C. Call the power company and complain.
    D. Install a UPS.

17. A firewall works well when protecting private network data from the public Internet. What method is used to protect private data from users within the network? (Choose all that apply.)
    A. Packet filtering
    B. Encryption
    C. Authentication
    D. NAT
    E. DMZ
    F. Passwords

18. What are the features of RAID level 1? (Choose all that apply.)
    A. You are limited to only 50 percent of disk space used in the implementation.
    B. You can have two to thirty-two disks.
    C. Data is striped with parity.
    D. You can only have two disks.
    E. An exact duplicate of the data is placed on multiple disks.

19. Your network currently uses DNS for IP address-to-name resolution for internal operations. Because DNS records have historically been created statically, you cannot use DHCP. What can you do to try to automate the process?
    A. Use IPX/SPX.
    B. Set up DDNS.
    C. Implement DWINS.
    D. Start using DDHCP.

20. What are the three most overlooked practices when performing backup maintenance? (Choose three.)
    A. Keep multiple copies of the backups on site.
    B. Keep a copy of the backup off site.
    C. Clean the tape drive.
    D. Ensure the parity on the stripe set is working.
    E. Periodically bring down the entire network to ensure your plan works.
    F. Test your backups.

21. You are the administrator for the network shown in the exhibit that follows. Your user cannot access the network after booting up successfully. You open the user's command prompt and type IPCONFIG.

The following information is learned:

IP address 0.0.0.0
Subnet Mask 0.0.0.0
Default Gateway 0.0.0.0

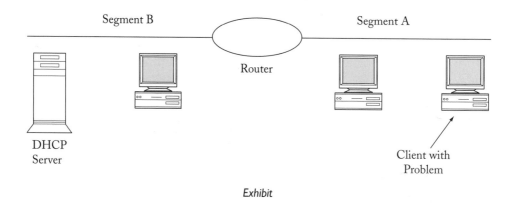

Exhibit

What could the problem be?
A. The client has the wrong DHCP server parameter set.
B. The client is not on the same segment as the DHCP server.
C. DNS is wrong.
D. WINS is wrong.

CHAPTER 9

Troubleshooting a Network

OBJECTIVES

At the end of this chapter you will be able to:

- Recognize the steps involved with troubleshooting a network.
- Utilize several hardware-based troubleshooting tools.
- Describe and utilize software-based troubleshooting tools.

INTRODUCTION

Chapter 9 is a very important chapter in relation to studying for the Network+ exam. The exam is troubleshooting oriented, and you should have a good understanding of what step to take at what stage of the troubleshooting process you are at. Learning how to troubleshoot includes two processes. First, you must learn how to ask the right questions to find the answers that you need, and second you must gain experience. This chapter focuses on some of the questions you can ask and what tools are available to help diagnose the problem. Gaining the experience will only come from working with the actual equipment. The Network+ objectives state specific troubleshooting scenarios in which you should become familiar.

The Network+ objective 4.9 lists the steps that should occur in any troubleshooting scenario from the problem identification to the last step. Shown below is the objective 4.9 from the Network+ objectives:

4.9 Given a network problem scenario, select an appropriate course of action based on a general troubleshooting strategy. This strategy includes the following steps:

1. Identify the symptoms and potential causes.
2. Identify the affected area.
3. Establish what has changed.
4. Select the most probable cause.

5. Implement an action plan and solution including potential effects.

6. Test the result.

7. Identify the results and effects of the solution.

8. Document the solution and process.

This process should be utilized each time a problem is encountered. The Network+ exam will have several troubleshooting questions. The questions will not be as clear-cut as you would like. It is your responsibility to read through each question and apply the above process. There will be questions that present a situation and then ask what step is next. In this chapter, a typical troubleshooting scenario is described and subsequently analyzed.

9.1 ASKING THE RIGHT QUESTIONS

Troubleshooting a computer network is similar to finding a problem with any other object, such as an automobile. Not all problems are easily identified. The problem, however, can usually be defined by asking the simple questions of who, what, when, and where. The answers to these questions should provide you with enough clues to begin the troubleshooting process.

It is important to become skilled in probing for answers when troubleshooting a connectivity problem. Ensure that the obvious is not overlooked when trying to narrow down the problem, and do not forget to ask the following questions.

WHO IS HAVING THE PROBLEM?

Answers to this question may reveal whether or not this particular user often has problems. For example, if the user often loses his password, it is a good possibility the user has lost it again. Users who often load software on their workstation without the approval of the IT department will be identified by this question as well. This answer may also determine whether or not multiple users are experiencing the same problem. If a commonality between multiple users is found, pinpointing the problem may be easier.

An answer to this question may even lead to additional troubleshooting requirements. For example, if the user is using remote connectivity software and is dialing in to the network over PPP, PPTP, or PPoE to connect remotely, several other problems could have been generated. One such problem may be the fact that authentication has been configured incorrectly. Often times when a remote client requests authentication to a dial-up or VPN server, the authentication types can be different. You must ensure that both the remote client and the server have the same configuration parameters. A good troubleshooting technique is to configure both the client and the server with the lowest type of authentication and test it. If it works, increase the authentication. Remember, when dialing in some options include authenticating over CHAP, MSCHAP, and clear text.

WHAT ARE THE SYMPTOMS?

Determine whether any logs or error messages are available. Users should be trained to record all error messages they receive. Sometimes it is not easy to recreate an error message. Users should know how to use the print screen key on the keyboard because when an error occurs they can simply print out the error and give it to the support staff rather than writing it down. This will help dramatically when beginning the troubleshooting process.

Be sure to look at the server and workstation logs to see if any unusual activity occurred at the time the user could not connect. Answers to this question will give an idea of where to begin the troubleshooting process. For example, has any hardware or software been installed to cause the issue? Are other computers on the same cable link troubled? Is the problem sporadic or consistently occurring?

WHEN DID THE PROBLEM OCCUR?

The answer to this question should aid in determining if this is a recurring problem. If the user cannot connect to the network between 6:00 P.M. and 7:00 A.M., perhaps the user's account has been restricted between those hours. Find out if the user could log on to the network at an earlier time or date. Also, determine when the last time the computer was working correctly. Perhaps a system update or service pack that was loaded on the machine is causing irregular behavior.

WHERE IS THE NODE WITH THE PROBLEM LOCATED?

The answer to this question will help determine whether or not the problem is an isolated issue or if several users are affected. Use this question to determine whether or not this is the only node having the problem on this cable segment. If there are additional connections or third-party service providers involved, be sure to examine the problem objectively. The service provider may be experiencing down time.

9.2 A TYPICAL TROUBLESHOOTING SCENARIO

In a typical troubleshooting scenario there is a sequence of events that can be followed to make the problem discovery and resolution simple. Always remember to begin with the easiest solution first and work down to the more difficult solutions. Assume in a normal network scenario a user calls the administrator because she cannot connect to one of the file server's shared folders.

STEP 1

Be sure the user's account has the correct permissions to see the resource before proceeding. If the user does not have permissions to access the folder, then the problem is solved. Be polite when explaining to the user that she does not have access to the folder, and there seems to be no problem.

STEP 2

Assuming the user does have permissions to access the folder, attempt to log on as the user. Although the user should not reveal her password to anyone, there are other steps that can be taken to accomplish this. For example, change the user's password and then attempt to log on. (When you are done troubleshooting, be sure to let the user reconfigure the password.) If the logon is successful, attempt to access the folder. If the folder is accessible, the problem exists between the user's PC and the server that she cannot access. If a user is having a problem logging onto the network and this step is completed successfully, the user may be typing her name incorrectly. Be sure the users understand that passwords are case sensitive and if the CAPS LOCK key is on, their passwords may not work.

STEP 3

Assuming that it is impossible to access the server's folder once logged on as the user, have another user in the network try to connect to the resource. It is possible that the server is down. If the server is down, go to the server closet and check it to make sure. Keep in mind, though, if the server were down, more than one user would be having issues. Use the PING utility to check connectivity between workstations and servers in the network. This will eliminate simple problems such as cabling and protocol installations.

STEP 4

Determine if other machines are affected by the problem or not by asking a nearby user on the same segment to log on to the server. If the second user cannot log on, find the commonality between the two and expose it. For example, if both nodes are connected to the same central device such as a switch or a hub and neither node can connect, the central device may be the problem.

STEP 5

Once the problem is isolated to the workstation, go to the workstation and check the connectivity. Once you arrive at the workstation, check the lights on the back of the NIC. In normal operation the lights should be blinking. If the lights are not blinking, there are several steps to take. If any of the methods produce blinking NIC lights, stop what you are doing and attempt to log on to the network with either your account or the user's account:

1. Check the patch cable at both ends to ensure it is properly connected to both devices.

2. Change the port the cable is connected to at the central device. Replace the hub if all ports are down.

3. Replace the cable.

4. Check to ensure that the NIC is properly configured with an IRQ and DMA.

5. Open the computer and reseat the NIC.

6. Remove the NIC and its driver and reinstall them both.

7. Install a known good network interface card.

The above steps should be followed in the order they were introduced. There is no need to open the workstation case as the first step unless the problem certainly resides in the case.

STEP 6

The last step in the troubleshooting process is the most difficult to accomplish: document your findings. This is one of the most overlooked practices because many people do not have the discipline to actually do it. Many administrators become caught up in troubleshooting the next problem before following up with the documentation on the problem they just fixed. It would not be a bad idea to develop a database that has all of the problems that have occurred and the fixes that solved them. This would be time consuming to create. However, it will help tremendously in the long run.

Obviously, not all troubleshooting scenarios will be as easy to troubleshoot as the scenario described. As a matter of fact, most of them are not. Troubleshooting is a skill just like any other, and the best way to become efficient in it is to experience it. However, troubleshooting means something went wrong or will not work. These are often stressful situations. Try to remain calm, and always look at the problem objectively. If the problem is overlooked in an early phase of the process, the time it takes to solve the problem will be multiplied tenfold. It is nearly impossible to prepare future administrators for every troubleshooting scenario. However, there are some utilities that may help in the troubleshooting process that are covered next.

9.3 NETWORK UTILITIES

There are utilities available to help narrow down possible causes of network failures. In this section, a few of them will be described. Troubleshooting utilities serve many different purposes and can help in several different ways. There are three categories of troubleshooting utilities described within: hardware utilities, software utilities, and TCP/IP utilities.

HARDWARE UTILITIES

Hardware utilities are often used to check the continuity of the network infrastructure, such as the cabling and the connectivity components. The hardware troubleshooting devices listed here include the hardware loopback, the tone generator, the crossover cable, the punch-down tool, the crimper, and the cable tester.

Loopback

There are primarily two types of loopbacks: a hardware loopback and a software loopback. A *software loopback* is often a component of the NIC's properties. Navigate to its properties and find the hardware loopback radio button or check box. This option usually allows the NIC to send and receive a signal to ensure it is operating properly. A hardware loopback is a physical component that is plugged into the port on the NIC, and it tests the electrical signal that physically comes out of the NIC.

Tone Generator and Tone Locator

A *tone generator and locator* are often used together when installing network cables. The generator is placed at one end of the wire, the locator on the other. The generator sends a signal, and the locator finds it. These tools help when labeling cables in a network that travel through walls and between floors.

Crossover Cable

The *crossover cable* is one of the most versatile and inexpensive tools available. It consists of an unshielded twisted pair cable that has the transmit wires and the receive wires crisscrossed within the casing. Therefore, the cable connects one node that is sending with another node that is receiving. Crossover cables are often used in networking. When two like devices are connecting together, a crossover cable is often needed. Without a crossover cable, two PCs using UTP must connect to a central device (such as a hub) to send data to one another. If you suspect a hub is bad, use a crossover cable between two of the machines that are connected through the hub. If the two machines see each other, the problem probably lies within the hub or the wires connecting to it.

Punch-Down Tool

A punch-down tool is used to connect twisted pair cable to a punch-down block (see Figure 9-1).

Figure 9-1. *Punch-down Tool*

In Ethernet, implementations, all cable runs coming from wall jacks are supposed to terminate in a punch-down block. The punch-down tool is simply the tool that pushes the individual wires within the casing into a slot on the punch-down block. If these wires come loose, connectivity problems may arise.

Wire Crimper

Wire crimpers are used to attach the different connectors to the end of the wire. For example, a crimper is used to connect the RJ45 connector to the end of a category 5 UTP cable. If a connector is too loose on the cable, you may need to cut the cable before the connector and crimp a new connector onto the cable.

Cable Tester

A cable tester is used to test the continuity of the connector that has been crimped onto a wire. For example, it is possible to use the cable tester to test whether or not RJ45 connectors were crimped onto category 5 cable properly or not. A cable tester normally has two ports, and both ends of the cable to be tested are plugged into the tester. It tests the cable by sending signals down each of the lines. A series of lights will blink in a specific order if the cable is good. Figure 9-2 shows a crimper and cable tester.

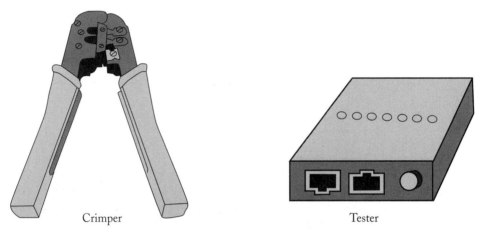

Crimper   Tester

Figure 9-2. *RJ45 Crimper and Tester*

 Test Tip: When given a wiring task, you must be able to identify what tool is needed. For example, if you are required to terminate UTP wires in a punch-down block, the tool required is a punch-down tool. Another example consists of utilizing a pair of crimpers and a cable tester to connect a client workstation to a UTP network.

SOFTWARE UTILITIES

Software utilities are used to troubleshoot the network with a program. There are two software utilities described here: the protocol analyzer and server logs.

Protocol Analyzer

Protocol analyzer, also known as *packet sniffers* and *network monitors,* allow administrators to capture data as it travels on the network. Analyzers can be set up to capture traffic from all machines or from suspected problem nodes that are sending too much data. Network monitors are very useful in finding and solving network bottlenecks, network trends, and network overutilization. Packet sniffers can also identify network viruses that multiply themselves throughout the network.

Each packet captured can be examined to determine where the packet is coming from and where it is going. A great deal of time can be spent analyzing packets. Packet monitors can either monitor a single network interface card, or they can monitor every network interface card on the network.

Server Logs

One of the most useful software utilities to use is log files. Log files are available on workstations as well as servers. However, since the focus here is to troubleshoot the problems associated with the network, server logs are discussed. Log files can come in many different forms. For example, Windows 2000 records several logs in the Windows 2000 Event Viewer.

TCP/IP UTILITIES

There are several utilities available that work with the TCP/IP protocol suite. Most of them are command-line based. Explained within are the arp, nbtstat, netstat, route, ping, tracert ipconfig, winipcfg, and nslookup commands. How to use the telnet program and FTP are also covered. Telnet, as a matter of fact, is a great utility to use when testing the entire protocol stack from the network interface layer through the individual application being used.

Here is a tip for using command line utilities. The utilities often generate more data than can fit in the command prompt window. To prevent this, use the pipe more (|more) switch. To generate the pipe more switch, use the Shift backslash (\) key sequence. The data will now scroll screen-by-screen.

The ARP Command

ARP is the address resolution protocol. It deals with IP-address-to-MAC address conversions. ARP stores addresses it has learned temporarily in the ARP cache of the local machine. ARP tables can be statically built by using the correct ARP commands. Building ARP tables statically is not a common practice because they are usually built dynamically. It is possible to view the ARP cache and check for invalid or duplicate entries with the ARP utility. To learn what the syntax is for using the ARP command, simply type arp. Here is a list of the more frequently used arp commands.

- **arp -a or -g**—Displays the current contents of the arp cache.
- **arp -d**—Deletes an arp entry.
- **arp -s**—Adds a static entry to the cache.

To see an arp table, see Figure 9-3.

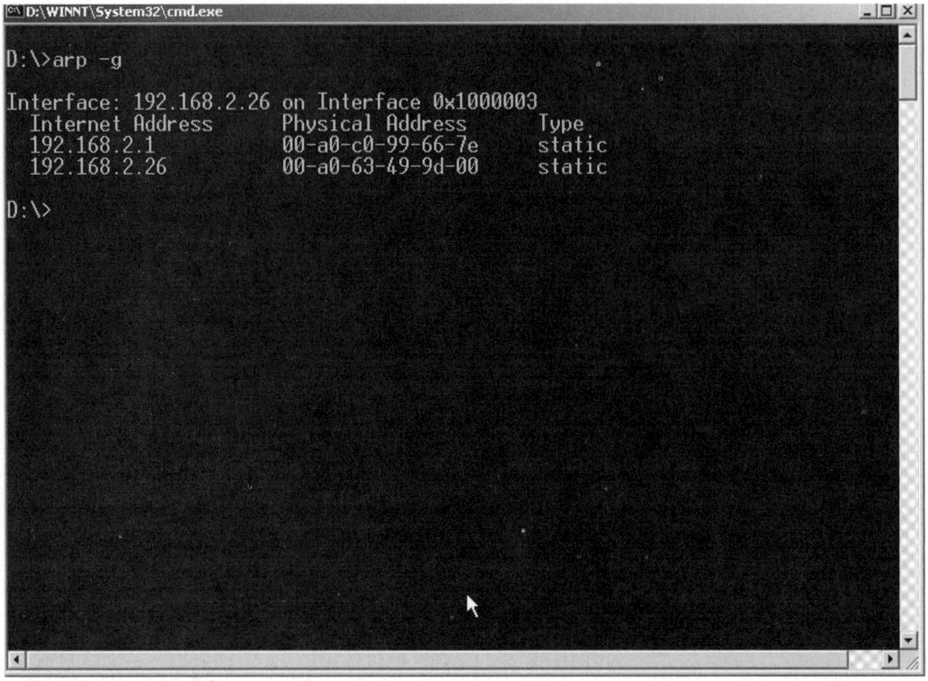

```
D:\WINNT\System32\cmd.exe

D:\>arp -g

Interface: 192.168.2.26 on Interface 0x1000003
  Internet Address       Physical Address      Type
  192.168.2.1            00-a0-c0-99-66-7e     static
  192.168.2.26           00-a0-63-49-9d-00     static

D:\>
```

Figure 9-3. *ARP Table*

The NBTSTAT Command

The nbtstat command is another command that allows you to troubleshoot name resolution. It stands for NetBIOS over TCP/IP statistics. NetBIOS names are often used to name workstations, servers, and other nodes in the network. There has to be a name resolution method to convert NetBIOS names into IP addresses, especially in large Windows NT networks. The method used in small networks simply consists of nodes broadcasting for other nodes. However, in large internetworks where routers are involved, additional configuration is required. The method that was once popular was to use a file called an LMHOSTS file. This file is stored in the System32\drivers\etc directory on Windows NT and 2000 computers. The LMHOSTS file maps NetBIOS names to IP addresses to allow nodes the capability of browsing for other nodes on different cable segments.

When a node learns the NetBIOS name of another node, it stores the information in the NetBIOS cache. It is possible to view the NetBIOS cache, add entries to it, and purge it with the nbtstat command. To see the command line syntax for the nbtstat command, simply type nbtstat from the command line prompt. The nbtstat available switches are case sensitive. Here is a list of some of the commands available and what they do:

- **Nbtstat -c**—Lists the contents of the name cache, mapping each IP address to a name.

- **Nbtstat -n**—Lists local NetBIOS names.

- **Nbtstat -R**—Purges the name cache and reloads it from the LMHOSTS file if any entries have been entered there.

An example of Nbtstat is shown in Figure 9-4.

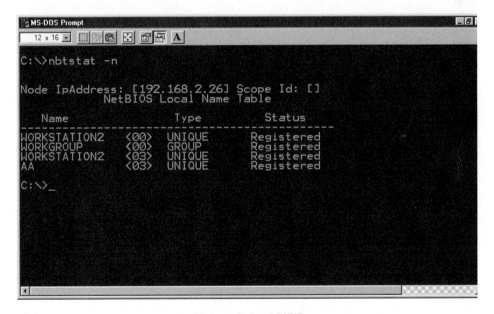

Figure 9-4. *NBTSTAT*

The NETSTAT Command

Netstat displays current protocol statistics and receives information about TCP/IP connections. To see the commands available while using netstat, use the help switch, which is /?. When using netstat, it is possible to list connections by protocol, port, or active connection. Here is a list of the switches available with netstat:

- **Netstat -a**—Displays connections and listening ports and their current state.

- **Netstat -n**—Displays active connections, listed by IP address.

- **Netstat -s**—Displays per-protocol statistics for IP, ICMP, TCP, and UDP.

- **Netstat -r**—Displays the contents of the routing table which can also be learned by typing **Route print.**

Figure 9-5 shows an example of the Netstat command.

Figure 9-5. NETSTAT

The ROUTE Command

The route command can also be used to add and remove routing table entries to a Windows-based machine. To see the command line syntax available, type Route as shown here.

        C:\>Route

The PING Command

PING stands for Packet Internet Groper, and it sends ICMP echo packets to verify connections to local or remote hosts. The PING command is used to test for connectivity. If pinging the local host, use the 127.0.0.1 address. It will test the local TCP/IP protocol stack as well as the local network adapter board. PING is one of the most useful utilities when testing a failed link. It can provide enough information as to where the problem may be and is a good starting point when troubleshooting problems that may be related to connectivity. For example, if a user cannot access a network resource, the first course of action is to ping the machine in which the user is logged onto, often referred to as the local host. The command is:

C:\>Ping 127.0.0.1

If the message received is a successful REPLY, then try to ping the default gateway (if there is one), which is usually the near side of a router or a proxy server in the network. If this is successful, ping the far side of the router, which should be the router's interface connecting to another network in the internetwork. Finally, ping the node with the resource on it that the user cannot access. If the ping is successful and the user is still unable to access the resource, try an alternate solution because the problem does not exist in the first two layers of the TCP/IP suite. To see the different arguments that work with the ping command, simply type ping. Here is a list of some of the options available:

- **Ping -t**—Ping until interrupted.

- **Ping -a**—Ping address and resolves host name.

- **Ping -n count**—Send number of echo packets.

- **Ping -l length**—Send echo packets of a specified size; by default they are 32 bytes.

A sample PING command is shown in Figure 9-6.

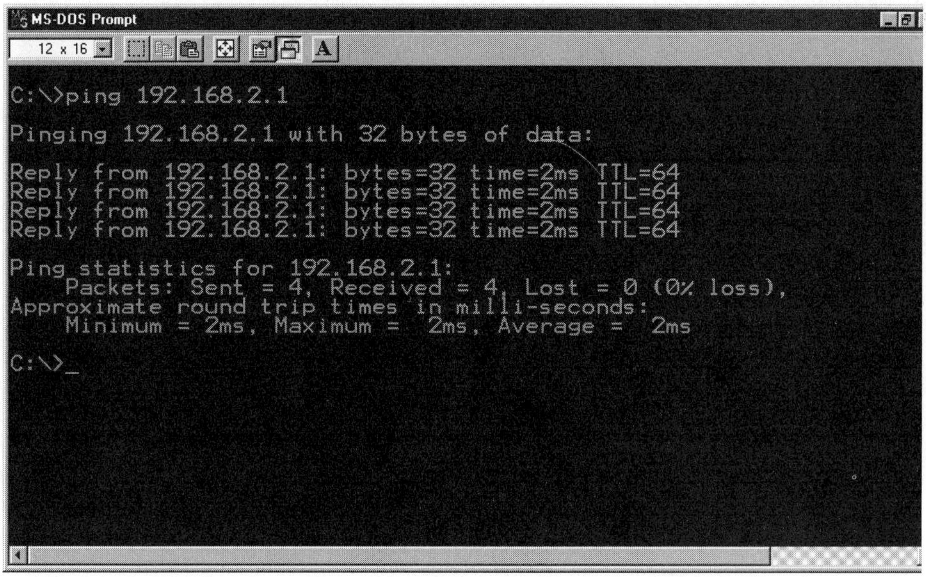

```
C:\>ping 192.168.2.1

Pinging 192.168.2.1 with 32 bytes of data:

Reply from 192.168.2.1: bytes=32 time=2ms TTL=64
Reply from 192.168.2.1: bytes=32 time=2ms TTL=64
Reply from 192.168.2.1: bytes=32 time=2ms TTL=64
Reply from 192.168.2.1: bytes=32 time=2ms TTL=64

Ping statistics for 192.168.2.1:
    Packets: Sent = 4, Received = 4, Lost = 0 (0% loss),
Approximate round trip times in milli-seconds:
    Minimum = 2ms, Maximum = 2ms, Average = 2ms

C:\>_
```

Figure 9-6. *PING*

The TRACERT/TRACE ROUTE Command

Tracert is used to determine the route a packet takes to reach its destination. Tracert is very useful when trying to find which router in a series of routers is not forwarding packets appropriately. It can also identify bottlenecks between LANs. Tracert is another utility that makes use of the ICMP protocol. When trying to determine if a router is down within a series of routers, type:

C:\>tracert *[IP ADDRESS OF DESTINATION or FQDN]*

The output will explain all of the routers the packet goes over with a time to live of 30 hops, which again is a trip over a router. Each time a packet crosses a router, the TTL will be decremented by one. If the packet is decremented to a value of zero, it will no longer be forwarded, and you will receive a Destination unreachable or Destination unknown ICMP message. If tracing a route to a known path and the packet is failing to make it past a certain router, there is a good chance the router is not performing packet forwarding operations correctly, it is down, or the router is experiencing unusually heavy congestion.

To see the actual command line syntax that works with the tracert command, from the command line type tracert and press enter. It is possible to use FQDNs in place of IP addresses when using tracert. However, the client being used to type the command must have access to a DNS server somewhere in the private or public network (see Figure 9-7).

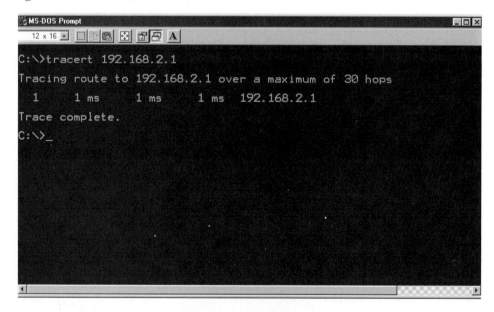

Figure 9-7. *TRACERT*

The IPCONFIG and WINIPCFG Commands

To learn the IP configuration information on a Windows 2000 or Windows NT computer, go to the command prompt and type IPCONFIG. Basic TCP/IP parameters such as IP address, subnet mask, and default gateway will be identified. To learn what additional configurations have been made, type IPCONFIG /ALL. This command will return the IP address of the DHCP Server, DNS Server, WINS server, and MAC address of the node. IPCONFIG is a useful utility. If your network is using DHCP, the IPCONFIG /RELEASE command will release the current IP address, and the IPCONFIG /RENEW command will begin the DHCP lease request process. The Win 9x family uses the WINIPCFG command. The WINIPCFG command can be executed from the Run Dialog box.

The NSLOOKUP Command

NSLOOKUP is a utility that retrieves the IP address of an FQDN queried or the FQDN of an IP address entered. Another command that works similar to NSLOOKUP is the DIG command.

File Transfer Protocol

Although FTP can be used through web browsers, it can be used as a command line utility as well. This utility is used to transfer files between clients and servers in a TCP/IP network, including UNIX, Microsoft, and recent versions of NetWare networks. It is a reliable method of transferring data because it uses TCP as its transport protocol. To access an FTP site through the command line utility, type:

> ftp.ftpsite.com

Replace *ftpsite* with the destination ftp site. Once at the ftp site, type ? to learn the ftp commands used to transfer files. Some of the popular commands are:

- Ls—Lists the directories and files available.
- Get—Downloads a file.
- Put—Posts a file.
- User—Allows for authentication, if required.
- Bye—Log out of the FTP session.

The Telnet Program

Telnet is a terminal emulation program that will allow you to execute commands on a remote server. Telnet is an excellent utility to test the entire TCP/IP protocol stack of a remote node. It allows you to open a remote session and execute commands as if you were sitting at the machine locally. You can telnet through a specific port of a remote host to test the network application running on that node, such as HTTP port

80, POP3 port 110, or SMTP port 25. For example, you can telnet into the mail server over the SMTP port 25 to verify the service is running properly. The procedures for using Telnet differ between operating systems. In Windows NT, for example, click the Start button, select Run, and type telnet in the run dialog box.

KEEPING SYSTEMS UPDATED

Operating system and application vendors often update their software. It is very important to maintain the most updated software available. This is done simply by monitoring the websites of the vendors' software running in the network. For example, use the Windows Update option located on the Start menu on a regular basis. This will help keep the system updated and with the newest software and security patches. For third-party software vendors, frequently visit their websites and perform a search of downloadable versions of their software updates.

These practices may seem like a waste of time, but they are not. It is very important to update the systems in a network. It should be taken seriously, and time each day should be set aside for it. Be sure to have a backup of the network's data before running untested updates. If an untested software update conflicts with system files, network data could be lost. One method to prevent this is to run all software and system updates on a test machine before implementing them in the production network.

CHAPTER SUMMARY

In this chapter you were exposed to some of the popular utilities network administrators and engineers use to troubleshoot networks. Other topics included the questions that should be asked when trying to determine what the cause of a problem is, as well as steps to take to solve the problem. Remember, in the Network+ exam you will be tested thoroughly for troubleshooting skills. Be sure to read the questions objectively, and sort through all of the possible answers eliminating those that you are sure are not the answer and selecting the best answer available. In the following Knowledge Test, several troubleshooting-related questions are given to you. Take your time as you go through and answer them. Before registering for the Network+ exam, you should be scoring at least a 95 on all nine of the Knowledge Tests in this book. Thanks for reading, and GOOD LUCK!

KNOWLEDGE TEST

1. You are the administrator of a network. None of your workstations can access the Internet. However, they can log on to the servers within the network. Upon examination of the network components, you notice that all lights are blinking except for the uplink light of the hub and the router's port it is connected to. What is your next course of action to determine what the problem is?
   A. Switch the hub with a known good one.
   B. Switch the patch cable that connects the hub to the router.
   C. Switch the hub out with a layer 2 switch.
   D. Switch the router with a known good one.

2. There is a workstation in your network that is not working properly. You have gone through the normal troubleshooting steps. None of them seemed to reveal a problem so you have replaced the network interface card. Now the workstation cannot see the network or log on to the server. What utility is available for you to check to see if the NIC that you installed is a good NIC?
   A. Tone generator
   B. Crossover cable
   C. Cable tester
   D. NIC diagnostics

3. Which command's output is shown in the exhibit?

```
Active Connections

  Proto  Local Address           Foreign Address        State
  TCP    workstation2:135        WORKSTATION2:0         LISTENING
  TCP    workstation2:1025       WORKSTATION2:0         LISTENING
  TCP    workstation2:1048       WORKSTATION2:0         LISTENING
  TCP    workstation2:137        WORKSTATION2:0         LISTENING
  TCP    workstation2:138        WORKSTATION2:0         LISTENING
  TCP    workstation2:nbsession  WORKSTATION2:0            LISTENING
  UDP    workstation2:1048       *:*
  UDP    workstation2:nbname     *:*
  UDP    workstation2:nbdatagram *:*
```

Exhibit

   A. Nbtstat -r
   B. Netstat -s
   C. Netstat -a
   D. Nbtstat -n

knowledge TEST

4. If the software loopback is not producing the results needed when testing a NIC, what other component can be used to test the electrical signals sent out of the NIC?
A. Hardware loopback
B. Crossover cable
C. Tone amplifier
D. Signal generator

5. If your network utilization increases to an unacceptable level, what could the problem be associated with? (Choose all that apply.)
A. Faulty cable
B. Faulty hub
C. Virus
D. Faulty NIC
E. Users

6. Which command line utility should be used to troubleshoot NETBIOS?
A. Ipconfig
B. Tracert
C. Netstat
D. Nbtstat

7. What command line utility would you use to check the DHCP settings to determine if your Windows NT workstation is using the correct default gateway address?
A. Winipcfg
B. Tracert
C. Netstat
D. Nbtstat
E. Ipconfig

8. Your internetwork consists of multiple network segments located in the same building. One of the clients has seemed to have lost connectivity. What is your first course of action?
A. Replace the NIC.
B. Identify the network segment the user is on.
C. Remove the failed workstation.
D. Fix the broken device.

9. A user seems to be having problems gaining access to the company's internal web site. Choose the best answer that would allow you to determine if it is the user's workstation.
A. Have the user log on to another machine and access the site.
B. Tell the user to give his password to another employee and let the other employee log on as the user and access the website.
C. Attempt to PING the web server from the user's computer.
D. Use the ipconfig utility.

10. Your customer reports that none of the thirty-five workstations (connected by two hubs and two switches) inside the network can access the Internet. Based on this statement, where do you think the problem may reside?
    A. The workstations.
    B. The cabling.
    C. The router.
    D. The switch.

11. What command line utility produces the following output?

```
  1      1 ms     1 ms     1 ms   192.168.2.1
  2     11 ms    10 ms    24 ms   10.118.80.1
  3     22 ms    19 ms    11 ms   srp4-0.albynyhmn-rtr01.nyroc.rr.com [24.29.33
7]
  4     31 ms    11 ms    27 ms   srp5-0.albynywav-rtr01.nyroc.rr.com [24.29.33
5]
  5     14 ms    13 ms    13 ms   srp0-0.albynywav-rtr02.nyroc.rr.com [24.29.33
6]
  6     11 ms    12 ms    13 ms   alb-24-29-32-105.nyroc.rr.com [24.29.32.105]
  7     13 ms    14 ms    14 ms   pop1-alb-P6-0.atdn.net [66.185.133.225]
  8     13 ms    14 ms    16 ms   bb2-alb-P0-0.atdn.net [66.185.148.98]
  9     26 ms    28 ms    22 ms   bb2-new-P6-0.atdn.net [66.185.152.195]
 10     22 ms    29 ms    24 ms   bb1-nye-P4-0.atdn.net [66.185.152.196]
 11     18 ms    21 ms    23 ms   pop1-nye-P0-0.atdn.net [66.185.151.49]
 12     32 ms    24 ms    24 ms   204.255.173.33
 13     20 ms    20 ms    20 ms   0.so-6-0-0.XL1.NYC4.ALTER.NET [152.63.21.78]
 14     20 ms    29 ms    26 ms   0.so-4-0-0.TL1.NYC9.ALTER.NET [152.63.0.173]
 15     46 ms    73 ms    44 ms   0.so-5-1-0.TL1.CHI2.ALTER.NET [152.63.1.129]
 16     63 ms    60 ms    60 ms   0.so-2-2-0.CL1.CMH2.ALTER.NET [152.63.68.93]
 17     81 ms    84 ms    62 ms   189.ATM5-0.GW3.CMH2.ALTER.NET [152.63.66.153]
 18     68 ms    70 ms    71 ms   thomsonlearning-gw.customer.alter.net [157.13
15.62]
 19     59 ms    58 ms    58 ms   nsu143010.thomsonlearning.com [198.80.143.10]
 20     63 ms     *       63 ms   nsu143055.thomsonlearning.com [198.80.143.55]
 21     64 ms    77 ms    63 ms   delmarlearning.com [198.80.136.28]
```

Exhibit

    A. Ipconfig
    B. Tracert
    C. Nbtstat
    D. Telnet

12. One of the workstations in the network cannot connect to the server. You direct the user to check to see if the light is blinking on the NIC. The user tells you that the light is not blinking. You then go to the wiring closet and check the cable that connects the user to the hub. You notice that the hub light is not blinking either, so you remove the cable and put it into a different port on the hub. The light begins to blink. The user reports that he can connect to the network. What was most likely the problem?
    A. The hub is bad.
    B. The NIC is bad.
    C. The patch cable is bad.
    D. The port on the hub is bad.

13. What command line utility will produce the following output?

```
Interface: 192.168.2.26 on Interface 0x1000002
  Internet Address          Physical Address          Type
  192.168.2.1               00-30-bd-c0-b4-94          dynamic
```

Exhibit

A. ARP
B. Tracert
C. Ping
D. Nbtstat
E. Netstat

14. What utility can you use to check the operation of any TCP/IP port?
A. PING
B. FTP
C. Telnet
D. Ipconfig

15. A user calls you complaining that he cannot log on to a server within the network. What are some of the steps you can take to troubleshoot this issue? (Choose all that apply.)
A. Have another user from the same segment attempt to log on.
B. Ping the user's computer from your computer.
C. Ping the server from your computer.
D. Tell the user to use a hardware loopback to test the port.
E. Have the user run IPCONFIG.

16. You have a home office with a cable modem connection to the Internet. Each time someone turns the microwave oven on in your house, your Internet connection is lost. What could this problem stem from?
A. The cable company.
B. Line voltage drop.
C. The telephone company.
D. Increase in line voltage.

17. You have recently reinstalled some cables in your network. You had to run the cables through a limited space in the ceiling. Several of the cables had to share tiles and space with the fluorescent lights. Now users are reporting strange activity in the network. What could this be caused from?
A. EMI.
B. ESD.
C. You used unshielded rather than shielded cable.
D. It is their imagination.

18. Examine the figure shown. Why can't this user reach a web site located on the Internet?

```
Windows 2000 IP Configuration

        Host Name . . . . . . . . . . . : workstation1
        Primary DNS Suffix  . . . . . . : TJCPlastics.com1
        Node Type . . . . . . . . . . . : Broadcast
        IP Routing Enabled. . . . . . . : No
        WINS Proxy Enabled. . . . . . . : No

Ethernet adapter Local Area Connection:

        Connection-specific DNS Suffix  . :
        Description . . . . . . . . . . : Realtek RTL8139(A) PCI Fast Ethernet
Adapter
        Physical Address. . . . . . . . : 00-E0-7D-C6-F9-14
        DHCP Enabled. . . . . . . . . . : No
        IP Address. . . . . . . . . . . : 192.168.1.126
        Subnet Mask . . . . . . . . . . : 255.255.255.0
        Default Gateway . . . . . . . . : 192.168.2.1
        DNS Servers . . . . . . . . . . :
```

Exhibit

A. Subnet mask is incorrect.

B. Missing WINS information.

C. Missing DHCP information.

D. Default gateway is on a different network.

19. You have consistently received error messages while trying to run a backup. What is a step to take to troubleshoot the backup device?

A. Buy a new tape.

B. Clean the tape drive.

C. Check the UPS.

D. Use the RAID device instead.

20. Your network has been running smoothly. You decide it is time to install a network software program. After the installation, server services and users begin to have problems. What is your first course of action?

A. Uninstall the program.

B. Contact the vendor of the software.

C. Bring down the troubled systems.

D. Procure a clean backup of the system in case of a devastating server crash.

knowledge TEST

21. You are the network administrator for an organization. The company installed a bus network several years ago and has not yet decided to upgrade the network. The building in which the network is located is old and has had rodent problems in the past. One morning you notice that a mouse has been nesting near a segment of the cable. Upon further examination, you notice the mouse has chewed through the cable. Utilizing the following exhibit, identify which nodes will not be able to access the network.

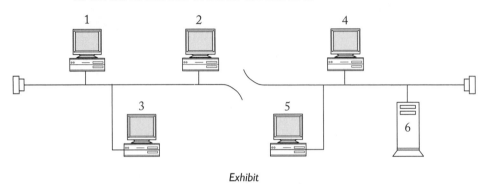

Exhibit

A. Nodes 1-3 will not be able to access the network.
B. Nodes 4-6 will not be able to access the network.
C. All nodes will be able to access the network.
D. None of the nodes will be able to access the network.

APPENDIX

a

Answers to Knowledge Test Questions

Chapter 1

1. **A.** A bus topology has a single cable in an open-loop format. The nodes are wired in a series from one node to the next.

2. **A.** The best choice here is a peer-to-peer because of the size. Inform the client if they grow to over ten nodes they should consider migrating to a client/server.

3. **D.** A mesh topology has the most connections per each node. It also has the most redundancy and fault tolerance associated with it.

4. **D.** Centralized computing involves a mainframe and dumb terminals. All of the processing takes place on the mainframe. The dumb terminals only feed the information to the central processor.

5. **D.** Mesh has multiple paths going from each node in the network. Because of the amount of connections, it is the most expensive to implement.

6. **C.** A star topology is easy to troubleshoot and allows for scalability.

7. 1 is a star, 2 is a bus, 3 is a mesh, 4 is a ring.

8. **A.** Because of the lack of security, a peer-to-peer network should not have more than ten nodes.

9. **C.** The server-based classification of distributed computing uses terminal services. There are several operating systems that offer terminal services, with Windows 2000 Server and Citrix being the most popular.

10. **B.** The server service handles requests from clients. It is also known as the provider. The client service requests data.

11. **A.** Directory services are used to allow users to authenticate to the network, at which time they gain rights to access resources on the network.

12. **D.** If users are having difficulty with printing, it is a good possibility that the print service is not working properly.

13. **A.** A LAN is often located in one building or one floor of a building.

14. **C.** The logical bus allows all nodes to compete for the wire, which causes many collisions. Although this seems less efficient than the logical ring topology, it is much more popular in the industry.

15. **A.** The logical ring topology is used to pass data from one node to the next. The logical bus allows the nodes to compete for access to the wire.

16. **B.** A virtual local area network would be used for this scenario.

17. **D.** The physical topology is the geometric layout of the components in a network. There are six primary topologies: Bus, star, ring, mesh, hybrid, and wireless.

18. **A.** The client service is also referred to as the requester. The actual service is not always named "client," depending on the operating system. The server service services the requests.

19. **B.** The logical topology defines how data is placed on the wire. The physical topology is the physical layout of the devices in the network.

20. **A.** Protocols define the standards used for a set of elements to communicate. In most situations, all nodes in a network must be using the same protocol for successful communication to take place.

Chapter 2

1. **C and D.** The NIC works at both layer 1 and layer 2. This is because it deals with the MAC address which is a layer 2 function, and it provides physical connectivity to the medium which is layer 1.

2. **A.** A hub operates in a single-collision domain. A bridge creates multiple-collision domains, and a router creates multiple collision as well as broadcast domains.

3. **B.** The switch being referred to in the question is a layer 2 switch. Layer 3 switches create separate broadcast domains. If given a question like this on the test and it does not describe the switch's function, assume it is a layer 2 switch since they are the most popular.

4. **D.** Hubs act as multiport repeaters. Bridges and switches also forward data to all nodes in certain situations. For example, if the data is a broadcast message or a multicast message, it will be forwarded to all nodes.

5. **C.** A gateway can connect independent networks. Gateways come in different variations, and they may work at any layer of the OSI Model. Gateways can be hardware components or software components. Routers often perform the functions of a gateway as well.

6. **A and D.** Bridges and layer 2 switches forward data based on the MAC address. Hubs simply repeat what they hear. Layer 3 switches forward data based on network addresses, and brouters use either the network address or the MAC address depending on the protocol.

7. **A.** Layer 2 switches can be configured to use VLANs, which act as separate networks.

8. **D.** Switches operate in a single broadcast domain, therefore a single broadcast message will be sent to all ports on the switch. Routers break up broadcast domains.

9. **A, C, D and F.** The NIC and the brouter are multilayer devices.

10. **B.** A layer 2 switch would increase the throughput in this scenario. Layer 2 switches can operate in full-duplex mode, which is much more efficient than a hub that only operates in half-duplex mode. Hubs are often associated with bottlenecks on networks due to their inefficient bandwidth and inability to manage traffic.

11. **C.** Brouters can route routable traffic and bridge non-routable traffic.

12. **B.** The data-link layer converts data into frames.

13. **C.** The network layer converts data into packets or datagrams.

14. **D.** The transport layer converts data into segments.

15. **A.** The physical layer. It also converts data into ones and zeroes before sending it onto the medium.

16. **F.** The presentation layer formats the data.

17. **B.** The transport layer deals with reliability of the end-to-end communication. Network addressing is done at the network layer, host-to-host sessions are at the session layer, and media access methods are at the data-link layer.

18. **C.** Category 5 UTP uses an RJ45 connector.

19. **D.** Coaxial cable uses a BNC.

20. **A and B.** ST connector is the twist-on connector, and the SC is the push-pull or snap-on connector.

Chapter 3

1. **C.** 10Base2 uses the BNC connector to connect nodes to the backbone or trunk.

2. **D.** 10BaseT uses unshielded twisted pair cable with a distance limitation of 100 meters per segment of cable.

3. **E.** 802.5 defines the token passing media access method which is used by both Token Ring and FDDI.

4. **A.** An RJ-45 is shown in the figure.

5. **C.** Category 5 unshielded twisted pairs is used in a 100BaseT implementation. RG58u is used in 10Base2, and RG62 is used in an ARCNet network.

6. **A, C and D.** SCSI is not a network connector, and MIC is used in a Token Ring implementation.

7. **D.** The 100BaseFX standard uses fiber optics as its transmission media.

8. **B.** In a Token Ring implementation, each MSAU has a ring in and a ring out port. The ring in port of one MSAU must be connected to the ring out of an existing MSAU.

9. **D.** 10Base5, also known as Thicknet, consists of a backbone that clients can connect to through the use of a component called a vampire tap, piercing tap, or a transceiver.

10. **B.** 10BaseT uses Category 3 UTP. Although there are eight wires in the cable, only four of the wires are used.

11. **C.** In this scenario, the only possible answers based on the problem are A and C. 'A' cannot be true because the user was able to print locally.

12. **A and B.** Category 3 does not support 100 Mbps, so new wire would have to be installed. New NICs would also be needed. Token Ring only goes four or 16 Mbps, and layer 2 switches are a good idea to increase bandwidth in a network only if the proper cabling infrastructure is there.

13. **C.** The most acceptable solution is to add some sort of a repeater to the network. Ensure it is closer to the node. Replacing the NIC would not help the distance limitation, neither would cable.

14. **E.** An AUI port is shown.

15. **B.** UTP is most susceptible because it has no shielding in it. Fiber is immune to crosstalk.

16. **D.** If the NIC has an AUI, it must be connected to a transceiver, which will be connected to the backbone of the network.

17. **B.** A 10Base2 cable segment has a limitation of 185 meters. However, there can be five segments connected by four repeaters. Only three of those segments can be populated. This is called the 5-4-3 rule.

18. **C and D.** 802.4 and 802.5 use token passing.

19. **A.** 802.3 uses CSMA/CD.

20. **C.** AppleTalk and wireless Ethernet both use CSMA/CA as their media access method.

Chapter 4

1. **C.** TFTP utilizes UDP only to transfer data. FTP uses TCP.

2. **D.** HTTPS is based on the industry standardized SSL, which is a security protocol developed by Netscape. SSL is based on a secure key pair algorithm.

3. **D.** SNMP is a management protocol that can be used to troubleshoot hardware devices.

4. **A.** Telnet uses TCP.

5. HTTP = 80, SMTP = 25, POP3 = 110, FTP = 21, Telnet = 23. FTP also uses port 20.

6. **C.** HTTP utilizes port 80. Therefore, if you block port 80 the HTTP protocol will not be able to reach the device.

7. **D.** SNMP uses the UDP port 161.

8. **A.** The Network Time Protocol operates at the Internet layer of the TCP/IP suite. However, it uses UDP port 123.

9. **B, D and E.** NetBEUI is a small, fast, self-configurable, self-tuning protocol that uses NETBIOS names rather than numbers to uniquely identify nodes on the network. NetBEUI is a non-routable protocol and should not be used on networks with more than 200 nodes. It is a broadcast-based protocol, and these protocols cause unnecessary amounts of network congestion.

10. **D.** The printer should be compatible with the AppleTalk protocol for this to work.

11. **A.** The Address Resolution Protocol maps IP addresses to MAC addresses. The Reverse Address Resolution Protocol (RARP) maps MAC addresses to IP addresses.

12. **D.** The AppleTalk Filing Protocol is used to transfer files. It is an application-layer protocol.

13. **C.** The top layer of the TCP/IP suite maps to the session layer, the presentation layer, and the application layer of the OSI Model.

14. **A.** The Internet Control Message Protocol sends Echo Request, Echo Reply, Source Quench, Destination Unreachable, and other messages.

15. **C.** This is a request to access an FTP site, therefore ports 20 and 21 would be used. However, only port 21 is given in the answers so the answer is 21.

16. **D.** Port 110 is the POP3 port. In this scenario it is assumed that the filtering device you have installed is blocking port 110.

17. **A and D.** Novell's proprietary protocol, IPX/SPX, utilizes the MAC address of the NIC as the host address. NWLink is Microsoft's version of IPX/SPX, therefore it uses the MAC address as well.

18. **B.** NWLink is Microsoft's version of Novell's IPX/SPX protocol. Novell did not begin to migrate its operating system to TCP/IP until NetWare 5.0.

19. **C and D.** Most e-mail programs today utilize POP3 and SMTP. Although IMAP is an e-mail protocol, it is not as popular as the other two mentioned.

20. **C and F.** Both TCP and SPX offer connection-oriented, guaranteed delivery with mechanisms in place to request data be resent if it is corrupted or lost. These mechanisms are considered connection-oriented services.

Chapter 5

1. **C and D.** On a private network the node addresses are not registered with ICANN. Therefore, the hosts are not accessible directly from the Internet. There are means, however, of accessing the Internet.

2. **B and E.** IPX is the protocol responsible for network addressing in the IPX/SPX suite. IP is the protocol responsible for network addressing in the TCP/IP suite. LocalTalk is a layer 2 protocol, DLC is a network printing protocol, and SPX is the transport protocol for IPX/SPX.

3. **D.** In this situation it is likely that you assigned a duplicate address. Remember, IP host addresses have to be unique on the network they belong to, just as IP network addresses have to be unique in the internetwork they belong to.

4. **C.** When a packet is sent to a network other than the one the node is located on, the packet will be accepted by the default gateway and then forwarded one hop closer to its destination network.

5. **D.** When you would like to set up a public IP network, the address will have to be assigned by then Internet authorities.

6. **A, B, C and D.** E is not correct because if nodes are on different networks they can actually have the same host address. For example, host A on network A has an IP address of 10.1.1.1, 255.0.0.0. Host B on network B has an address of 11.1.1.1, 255.0.0.0. Notice the host addresses are the same. The only difference is the first number which is the network address based on the subnet mask of 255.0.0.0.

7. **A, B and C.** Class D cannot be used to address hosts since it is used for multicasting. Class E is used for research.

8. **B.** Default gateway forwards packets to destination networks. However, the client must know the address of the default gateway. This is a parameter that is configured on the client when the IP address is assigned to the client, either dynamically or manually.

9. **D.** 209.41.87.9 is the only valid address on that network. All three of the other networks have been changed.

10. **B.** The correct answer is B. A is the network address only. C is the network and the host address, and D is the subnet mask being used.

11. **C.** 150.8.64.0 is correct because the /19 implies the subnet mask of 255.255.224. If that is the current mask, the lowest bit on in the mask is 32. Therefore, the networks must increment by 32. The possible valid networks become: 150.8.32.0; 150.8.64.0; 150.8.96.0; 150.8.128.0; 150.8.160.0; and 150.8.192.0.

12. **D.** The CIDR notation of /24 = 255.255.255.0 for the subnet mask. The gateway would receive host address 1 and the node host address 2.

13. **B.** Remember to use the powers of 2 chart, 2^9 equals 512. However, we have to subtract 2, which gives us a total of 510 possible host addresses.

14. **C.** A and B are incorrect because our networks have to increment by 32 in the last octet. Therefore, 47 is a valid host but not the end of the range. D is incorrect because the 32 in the last octet represents the network address.

15. **B.** The mask in this address is 255.255.224.0. The valid networks must increment by 32. Therefore, A is incorrect because they have the number 17 in the third octet. The first available network is 32. C and D are incorrect because the range of numbers is too far from each other in the third octet. If the networks increment by 32, the number can be no larger than 63 in the third octet. This is because the number 64 represents the next network address in the range.

16. **A.** This is the CIDR notation stating that there are 18 bits reserved for the subnet mask, which would be 255.255.192.0.

17. **B, C and F.** The /20 means 20 bits for the mask. This equals 255.255.240.0. Since 240 is the mask in the third octet, the networks have to increment by 16 because it is the lowest on bit in that octet. Therefore, our network numbers become:

    85.1.16.0   85.1.32.0   85.1.48.0   85.1.64.0, etc.

    The network address in the question would be 85.1.64.0. Since the network is 64, the host must be 2.245 because the number in the third octet of the question is 66. Subtract the network ID of 64 from the 66 and you will have 2.

18. **C.** Class C meets the description in the question.

19. **A.** Practice with more of these.

20. **D.** Practice with more of these.

Chapter 6

1. **C.** An ISDN BRI line has three channels; two of them are 64 Kbps and one is 16 Kbps. The 64 Kbps channels are B channels and transmit data. The 16 Kbps channel is a D channel and is used for signaling.

2. **D.** PPP is the successor of SLIP. SLIP is the Serial Line Internet Protocol, which was used for many years as a dial-up protocol. SLIP, however, did not support authentication, DHCP, or multiple protocols. It could only forward TCP/IP.

3. **B.** A DS1 line is a T1 line, and it has 1.544 Mbps.

4. **C.** An OC-3 line can carry 155.520 Mbps.

5. **A.** An ISDN BRI connection has a single 16 Kbps Delta channel used for signaling, call setup, and call termination.

6. **C and D.** TCP/IP and IPX/SPX both use a version of RIP. Both protocols do have the option of using link-state protocol as well. IPX/SPX uses NLSP, and TCP/IP uses OSPF. NETBEUI is a non-routable protocol, and DLC is a protocol used for network printing.

7. **B, D and F.** ISDN offers two rates: BRI and PRI. BRI offers two 64 Kbps lines for transferring data and one 16 Kbps line for transferring control and signal information. PRI offers much more bandwidth. Since ISDN is not a packet-switching technology, it does not use frame relay to encapsulate data. ISDN can encapsulate data using PPP or HDLC. ISDN supports voice and data; the data that it can carry includes video, and special services.

8. **C.** The sixteenth network is considered unreachable because RIP has a maximum hop count of 15.

9. **B.** A router must know all of the answers. To forward the packet it must know where the packet is destined for.

10. **B and C.** Static routing has less processor overhead and is well suited for small internetworks. When an internetwork becomes too large to manually configure routes, it is time to implement dynamic routing.

11. **B and C.** RIP uses several mechanisms to avoid routing loops: two of them are split horizon and route poisoning or poison reverse.

12. **B and E.** OSPF is an example of a link-state routing algorithm. Link-state routing algorithms have a higher processor overhead than static routing because they are dynamic. Link-state algorithms only send changes to their routing tables.

13. **A.** Frame relay is a packet-switching protocol.

14. **B and D.** ATM uses a cell relay technology. All of the cells forwarded by ATM are 53 bytes is size; 48 bytes is the payload, and the header is 5 bytes.

15. **C.** A T3 would be the best choice here. A T3 line can handle 44.736 Mbps.

16. **B and C.** CIR is the committed information rate, and it is the amount of bandwidth a customer pays for when leasing a frame relay circuit. A PVC is a permanent virtual circuit, which is the logical connection between two end points in a frame relay connection.

17. **D.** SONET is the North American standard for fiber optic connectivity. SDH, or the synchronous digital hierarchy, governs the fiber optic hierarchy for the rest of the world.

18. **C.** The problem seems to be located in the subscriber's network. If the provider's line is tested correctly that means from the CSU/DSU to the central office has full connectivity.

19. **D.** Route poisoning will falsely advertise the route. Split horizon does not advertise the route from the interface where it was learned.

20. **D.** Split horizon does not advertise a route on the interfaces in which it learned the route. Route poisoning advertises the route with a hop count of 16 to the interface where it learned the route. Holddown timers ensure that a route cannot change for the worse within a specified amount of time.

Chapter 7

1. **B.** Active Directory is the directory service for Windows 2000. NetWare 3.12 used the Bindery and NetWare 4.11 and better uses the NDS. The NT domain model is not a directory service.

2. **B.** In the scenario there are users that can access the data. The most logical assumption to this scenario is that the user's permissions are not set to allow the user to access the data.

3. **C.** PPP is the protocol that is supported by Windows 2000 and Windows NT. Microsoft clients can dial in to a SLIP server, but there is not a SLIP server available in the Windows NT/2000 operating systems.

4. **A, D and E.** Ctrl+Alt+Del will bring up the Windows Logon dialogue box.

5. **B, C and E.** User name, password, and the domain in which you are logging on to are the required parameters for a successful logon.

6. **C.** Winipcfg is the command that will return the IP parameters for the workstation. The command should be entered from the Run line off of the Start menu. The IPCONFIG command is used for Windows NT and Windows 2000.

7. **C.** TCP/IP is the native protocol of the Internet. NetWare 4.11's native protocol is IPX/SPX. Therefore, there must be a TCP/IP connection located in the network.

8. **C and D.** The user needs NWLINK and TCP/IP. Microsoft's protocol that is equivalent to the IPX/SPX protocol is NWLINK.

9. **B.** The resources on segment B will be available because NETBeui is non-routable. Therefore, all resources that the workstation had access to prior to the move will no longer be accessible unless a routable protocol is installed.

10. **A.** There can only be one primary domain controller per domain. However, there is no limit on the amount backup domain controllers.

11. **C and D.** To enable WINS on a Windows 98 machine, double click the Network applet in Control Panel, highlight TCP/IP, and click Properties. Choose the WINS tab and click the radio button to enable WINS, and then enter the IP address of the WINS server(s) in the network.

12. **D.** The first step would be to see if this is the only user having the problem. If so, check the user's permissions.

13. **C.** The screen shot consists of the output from the IPCONFIG /ALL command. IPCONFIG only returns three parameters: IP address, subnet mask, and default gateway. The /all switch ensures that more information is given, such as whether or not DHCP is being used, DNS information, and the MAC address.

14. **B and D.** CSNW is a Windows NT service.

15. **B, D and E.** The host name, domain name, and IP address of the primary DNS server are all required parameters.

16. **A.** Since TCP/IP is supported by all three of these operating systems, it only makes sense to use TCP/IP.

17. **E.** PPTP will allow users to dial in to the network and it creates a virtual private network to protect the integrity of the data crossing over the public Internet.

18. **B, C, D and E.** To authenticate to a NetWare network, the user must know the tree name, the context of the user object, the server name, the username, and the password.

19. **B.** The most likely cause of this problem is that the user does not have permissions to access the application.

20. **C.** RAS is loaded and configured from the Services tab of the Network properties, which is accessed through the Network applet of the Control Panel or by right clicking Network Neighborhood and choosing Properties from the drop-down menu.

Chapter 8

1. **A and C.** By using a single public address for all nodes, the proxy server hides the private, internal network from external users on the public Internet.

2. **B.** You should test your tapes by restoring the data annually, keep a copy of the backup off site, and clean your tape drive periodically.

3. **C and D.** The HOSTS file is used for host name-to-IP address resolution. The DNS is the automated process to complete host name resolution. LMHOSTS and WINS are used for NETBIOS names-to-IP address resolution.

4. **D.** Critical data should be backed up. This consists of users' data, registries of critical nodes, and directory services databases, among others.

5. **C.** The most likely cause is the DHCP server is down. When a node is configured for automatic IP addressing, it will sometimes receive an address of 0.0.0.0. Some workstations, however, support Automatic Private IP Addressing (APIPA). APIPA will give a node an IP address in the range 169.254.0.1 to 169.254.255.254 when a DHCP server is down. Windows 95 and NT do not support APIPA.

6. **D.** In this scenario, the HOSTS file would no longer be needed.

7. **A and D.** Fault tolerance is having the ability to continue to operate, and RAID is a fault-tolerant mechanism, therefore dual power supplies are considered fault tolerant. Keeping a backup of data in the event of a system crash will provide for disaster recovery.

8. **A.** WINS is used to map NETBIOS names to IP addresses. WINS is extremely important in a large Windows NT network because much of the NT architecture is based on NETBIOS names. If WINS is not being used, an LMHOSTS file may be used.

9. **B.** Incremental backups will back up the data used since the last incremental backup, which in this case should have been completed on Wednesday night.

10. **D.** DNS parameters can be sent out by the DHCP server. For users to renew their DHCP information, have them use the IPCONFIG /renew command.

11. **A.** PPTP can carry TCP/IP, NETBeui, and IPX/SPX over the Internet in a virtual private network.

12. **C.** You would accomplish the requirements for a disaster prevention plan. RAID 0 is not a fault tolerant RAID setup; it is only good to increase I/O speeds.

13. **A.** SSL is used to encrypt a session between hosts.

14. **D.** Routers filter broadcasts, therefore there must be a DHCP relay agent on the two segments where the DHCP server is not.

15. **B.** MX records list the addresses of e-mail servers in the network. When an e-mail reaches the DNS server it will forward the e-mail to the correct server, and then the server will hold the e-mail until an e-mail client requests it.

16. **D.** Installing a UPS will protect against power sags, surges, spikes, brownouts, and even blackouts. A surge protector will protect against spikes and surges, but the question states *amount* of electricity.

17. **B, C and F.** Packet filtering, NAT, and a DMZ would protect internal data from external threats.

18. **A, D and E.** RAID level 1 is a mirrored set, and only 50 percent of total disk capacity of the two disks used is available for storage. RAID level 0 uses two to thirty-two disks, and RAID level 5 uses parity when striping data.

19. **B.** DDNS stands for Dynamic DNS. DDNS allows DHCP to keep the DNS database updated by forwarding all IP addresses issued to the DNS server. This automates a once mundane process.

20. **B, C and F.** Having multiple copies of your data on site will not help disaster prevention if the building burns down. Stripe sets are used with fault tolerant RAID systems; and you should not bring down your entire network.

21. **B.** The DHCP server is not on the correct segment.

Chapter 9

1. **B.** The first step would be to replace the cable since the lights are not blinking. Utilizing the blinking lights as visual cues as to what a problem may be is a good trick of the trade. Normally, if there is a problem with the hardware it will be visible. If the lights were blinking the problem would be more difficult to troubleshoot, and it may be worth the time to check the workstation's default gateway settings.

2. **D.** Most NIC manufacturers include a diagnostic program that accompanies the network interface card. It is usually a software program found in the properties of the NIC.

3. **C.** The command is showing the active TCP/IP sessions open on the computer. Netstat –a will produce those results.

4. **A.** Although a crossover cable can be used to see if you can achieve connectivity with the NIC, a hardware loopback is more appropriate in this situation.

5. **C, D and E.** The odds that the cable or hub are causing this problem are very slim. However, there are viruses in the industry that propagate data throughout a network in an attempt to bring the network down. NICs can become chatty and continuously send data onto the network. To determine which NIC is faulty, use a packet sniffer or a network monitor. Finally, users that download large video and audio files often cause bandwidth problems within a network.

6. **D.** Nbtstat is used for troubleshooting NETBIOS over TCP/IP. Netstat shows network statistics, tracert tests connectivity between sites, and ipconfig shows a nodes IP settings.

7. **E.** IPCONFIG is used for Windows NT and Windows 2000. WINIPCFG is used for Windows 9x operating systems.

8. **B.** At this point in the troubleshooting process, there is not enough known about the problem to take drastic measures such as replacing NICs and fixing broken devices. Based on the question, we are not even sure what device may be broken. The best possible solution for this question is to identify the network segment the user is on and then move on to the next step, which would be to see if other users on that segment have lost connectivity.

9. **A.** The best answer here is to tell the user to log on on to another work-station. If the user logs on to another workstation and does not have access, there are two possible problems. First, there may be a problem with connectivity and second, the user may not have permissions to access the web site. The user should not give his password to anyone. In this situation the results of the PING will probably not resolve the issue.

10. **C.** This question is vague, however there is enough information available to find a logical answer. For example, we know there are thirty-five nodes in the network. That helps us determine that the only way all thirty-five work-stations are offline is because the default gateway TCP/IP parameter is incorrect, but that is not an available answer. Next, the failure of a single hub or switch would only result in some of the clients going offline. Finally, we know routers are often the entrance and exit points of a network. Therefore, this is probably where the problem resides.

11. **B.** The output is generated by tracert.

12. **D.** The most likely cause of the problem is that the port on the hub is bad. In this situation it would be a good idea to order a new hub to replace the existing hub.

13. **A.** ARP maintains an IP address-to-MAC address table.

14. **C.** Telnet allows you to check connectivity through all seven layers of the OSI Model. You can specify the port you would like to Telnet into on a remote server. For example, to test the e-mail server, it is possible to Telnet into port 25 which would test SMTP, or port 110 which would test POP3.

15. **A and B.** You should not have the user test his own configurations unless you are absolutely certain the user is capable of doing it without making the problem worse. You would not have to have the user run the IPCONFIG utility in this scenario because you would know if his TCP/IP settings were correct or not because you will PING his machine. If the PING is unsuccessful, there may be some additional troubleshooting steps necessary. If you cannot ping the server, go to the server closet and ensure it is functioning properly. Also, it is not a good idea to assume the user knows what a hard-ware loopback is.

16. **B.** The lack of or increase in electricity is known to cause problems with other devices. In this scenario there are additional factors that may come into play. However, the best answer is that there is a voltage drop and it causes the component you are using as your gateway to lose power. It may be the cable modem or the router losing the connection.

17. **A.** Electromagnetic interference generated by the fluorescent lights is proba-bly causing the problems. EMI is known to create strange problems in net-works.

18. **D.** The default gateway is incorrectly configured for this workstation.

19. **B.** Try to clean the drive before spending money that can be used elsewhere. Also, a UPS is related to power problems, and RAID is not a backup method. It is a fault-tolerant solution.

20. **B.** You should contact the vendor and ask them if there are any known issues with the software and the services you are having trouble with. The next step, if they cannot help you, is to uninstall the software and use a different software package.

21. **D.** None of the nodes will be able to access the network because once the cable is broken, termination of the signal will not be achieved and the entire network will be down.

Acknowledgement. Also known as an ACK. It is a confirmation of the receipt of data during peer transport-layer communication.

ACL. Access Control List. In Microsoft operating systems the ACL is the list on a resource that specifies what users can and cannot use the resource. The entries are access control entries.

Active Directory. The Windows 2000 directory services database.

Active hub. Network component that acts as a central device for multiple nodes to connect to. Active hubs require power and regenerate data signals before forwarding them. Another term for an active hub is a multi-port repeater.

Adjacency. A term used to describe the relationship between two neighboring routers.

ATM. Asynchronous Transfer Mode. A packet-switching technology that configures fixed-length packets 53 bytes in size called cells.

Autonomous system. A logical grouping of networks connected together by an interior gateway protocol, such as OSPF.

Backup. Process of making a copy of critical data.

Baseband. Communication technique utilizing a digital signal which is capable of handling one signal on the cable at any given time.

Bandwidth. Measurement in terms of bits per second. It represents the capacity of data transmittable over a network link.

BDC. Backup Domain Controller. A Windows NT server that maintains a backup copy of the directory services database.

BGP. Border Gateway Protocol. An exterior gateway protocol used to connect two autonomous systems together.

Bound media. Transmission media that is confined to a cable, such as copper cable or fiber optics.

BRI. Basic Rate Interface. ISDN standard that calls for two Bearer channels of 64 Kbps and 1 Delta channel of 16 Kbps.

Bridge. Network device that works at the data-link layer of the OSI Model and is responsible for segmenting an existing network into multiple collision domains through the use of a MAC table.

Broadband. Communication technique utilizing an analog signal which is capable of handling multiple signals on the cable at any given time.

Broadcast domain. Logical grouping of network components that will all receive a broadcast signal sent from any node in the group. Routers are capable of creating multiple broadcast domains because they do not normally forward broadcast signals.

Broadcast message. A data message sent to all nodes that are associated with the same network address.

Bus topology. A physical topology that uses a single cable in an open-loop fashion.

CAN. Campus Area Networks. A network that consists of several LANs connected together by high-speed links.

Centralized administration. Having the ability to administer a computer network from a single central location.

Centralized computing. Network computing model where one node (usually the mainframe) processes all data.

CHAP. Challenge Handshake Authentication Protocol. PPP authentication protocol that uses a three-way encrypted handshake.

CIDR. Classless Interdomain Routing. Provides an efficient method of allocating IP addresses. CIDR was developed to prevent the depletion of IP version 4 addresses. CIDR allocates addresses based on powers of two rather than using the classfull IP addressing scheme, for example Class A, B, C, etc.

Client. A network component or network service that requests data or information from the server.

CO. Central Office. WAN service provider's switching facility. Also known as point of presence (POP).

Collaborative computing. Network computing model where multiple nodes work together to complete the same task.

Collision domain. Logical grouping of network components that must compete for access to the network cable to send data. Switches and bridges can create separate collision domains through the use of MAC tables. A broadcast domain can contain several collision domains, but a collision domain cannot span multiple broadcast domains.

Computer network. An arrangement of computers that are connected together through some form of transmission media.

Connection-less communication. A data transfer standard that does not represent the reliable transmission of data. It is the opposite of connection-oriented communication. UDP is an example.

Connection-oriented communication.   A data transfer standard that represents the reliable transmission of data. TCP uses acknowledgements and flow control to achieve connection-oriented status.

Convergence.   The process routers in an Internetwork go through while learning about all networks. When all routers know about all other routers' paths to all networks, the internetwork is fully converged.

Count to infinity.   A routing loop that can occur while using a distance-vector routing algorithm.

CPE.   Customer Premises Equipment. Devices owned or leased by the subscriber of a WAN service. The devices are installed at the customer's site. Examples include terminals, modems, and telephones.

CSMA/CD.   Carrier Sense Multiple Access with Collision Detection. A media access method that allows the sending station to sense the wire before transmission to determine if it is clear to send.

CSU/DSU.   Channel Service Unit/Data Service Unit. Network device that modulates LAN signals into WAN signals before sending the data to the public network.

Cyclic redundancy check.   The value of a mathematical algorithm run through a frame and appended to the end of the frame before transmission.

DARPA.   Defense Advanced Research Projects Agency. A United States government agency developed to advance defense capabilities. Currently known as ARPA.

Datagram.   Term given to a logical grouping of data after it has been encapsulated by the network layer of the OSI Model. Also known as a packet.

Data packet.   Packet of data sent by a router that consists of information being sent from one node on a network to another node on a separate network.

DCE.   Data circuit equipment. In terms of routing, the DCE receives signals from a router and forwards them to the public network. DCE makes up a portion of the DTE/DCE communication channel. A typical DCE device is a CSU/DSU. DTE/DCE communication is governed by the RS232c standard.

DDNS.   Dynamic DNS. A service that allows DNS records to be automatically created and removed based on DHCP address assignments.

De-encapsulation.   The process a protocol data unit goes through as it travels up the OSI Model. Protocols at each layer of the model strip peer layer information off of the PDU before forwarding it to the next layer in the model.

Demarc.   The location between the CPE and the WAN service provider's equipment. Also known as demarcation.

DHCP.   Dynamic Host Configuration Protocol. A network service that allows for the dynamic allocation of IP addresses.

DHCP Relay Agent.   A routing and remote access service that will convert a client's DHCP broadcast into a unicast so the DHCP server can fulfill the IP address request over a router.

Differential backup.   Backup method that copies all files that have the archive attribute bit on but does not reset the archive bit after copying a file.

Distance-vector routing algorithm.   Algorithm that states that routers must forward their entire routing table to adjacent routers for route updates.

Distributed computing.   Network computing model where all nodes have the ability to process data.

Domain controller.   A Windows 2000 Server that maintains a copy of the directory services database.

DNS.   Domain Name System. Application-layer protocol of the TCP/IP suite used for domain name resolution. DNS utilizes the services of both TCP and UDP to transport data.

DTE.   Data terminal equipment. In terms of routing, the DTE is normally the router. It makes up a portion of the DTE/DCE communication channel. The DTE forwards data to the DCE which forwards the data to a public network. DTE/DCE communication is governed by the RS232c standard.

Dynamic routing.   A router configuration process of allowing routing protocols to update routing tables.

Dumb Terminal.   A node in a network that does not have the ability to process data.

Effective permissions.   The permissions applied to a user when all permissions are accounted for, including share permissions and NTFS permissions.

EGP.   Exterior Gateway Protocol. A category of routing protocols which includes BGP. EGPs are normally used to connect two autonomous systems together.

Encapsulation.   The process a protocol data unit goes through as it travels down the various layers of the OSI Model. Protocols at each layer of the model add layer-specific information to the PDU before sending it to the next layer.

Ethernet.   Networking standard created by Digital, Intel, and Xerox. It uses a baseband transmission and the CSMA/CD media access method. Ethernet has several physical-layer standards such as 10BaseT, 10Base2, and 10Base5.

FDDI.   Fiber Distributed Data Interface. Networking standard which uses fiber optic wire and a token passing media access method.

FECN. Forward Explicit Congestion Notification. FECN informs the destination frame relay device that the line the frame has just traveled is congested.

Firewall. A hardware or software component used to act as a single choke point for all data going in and out of a network. Firewalls are used to prevent hackers from breaking into network data.

Flow control. Method of ensuring that a receiving machine is not overwhelmed with data being sent to it during a network transmission.

Forest. A logical component of the Windows 2000 Active Directory. A forest can contain multiple trees and multiple domains.

FQDN. Fully Qualified Domain Name. The host name of a computer in the DNS structure. The FQDN lists all domains and subdomains, along with the computer host name.

Fragment-free switching. A switching method that checks the integrity of the first 64 bytes of a frame before forwarding the frame to its destination.

Frame. Term given to a logical grouping of data after it has been encapsulated by the data-link layer of the OSI Model.

Frame relay. A packet-switched protocol often used in a WAN that operates at the data-link layer of the OSI Reference Model.

FTP. File Transfer Protocol. Application-layer protocol of the TCP/IP suite used for transferring files. FTP utilizes the connection-oriented services of TCP for transport.

Full backup. Backup method that copies all selected files and resets the archive bit to zero.

Full duplex. A data transmission process that allows two end stations to have the entire communication channel available to them. Each station is capable of sending and receiving data at the same time. Communication may occur in both directions by both stations at the same time.

Half-duplex. A data transmission process that allows one station to transmit while the other station receives data. Communication may occur in both directions, but only one station at a time.

HCL. Hardware Compatibility List. A list provided by Microsoft that specifies which hardware components work with its operating systems.

HDLC. High-Level Data Link Control. A data-link layer protocol that was developed for transmitting data over serial lines.

Holddown timers. A timer used in distance-vector routing that will not allow a router to accept an additional route change unless it has a better cost.

Hop. A term given to the process of a packet being forwarded by a router.

Hosts File. A text file used to map host names to IP addresses.

IEEE. The Institute of Electrical and Electronics Engineers.

IGP. Interior Gateway Protocol. A category of routing protocols normally used within an autonomous system. Examples are OSPF, RIP, and IGRP.

Incremental backup. Backup method that copies all files that have the archive attribute bit on and resets the archive bit to zero.

IP. Internet Protocol. The network-interface layer protocol of the TCP/IP suite primarily responsible for network addressing.

IPCP. IP Control Protocol. Protocol used by PPP to establish IP communication.

IP address. Addressing scheme used by IP in the TCP/IP suite. It is 32 bits long and is represented in dotted decimal notation. An IP address is broken into four octets of 8 bits each.

IPX. Internetwork Packet eXchange. The IPX/SPX network-layer protocol and is primarily responsible for network addressing.

ISDN. Integrated Services Digital Network. A communication standard that allows telephone companies to carry voice, video, and data over existing telephone lines.

LAN. Local Area Network. A network that is usually confined to one building or one floor in a building.

LATA. Local Access Telephone Area. The geographic area serviced by a local exchange carrier.

LEC. Local Exchange Carrier. The local telephone service provider.

Link state routing algorithm. Routing algorithm that states a router must only forward the status of its own links to all routers in the internetwork.

Local backup. Process of backing up all critical data from the node in which it is located.

Local loop. The cable that connects the subscriber to the CO.

Local printer. A physical printer directly connected to a computer through its parallel or USB port.

Logical bus topology. Term used to explain that when data is placed on the cable in a network by one station, it will be partially read by all nodes on the local segment.

Logical ring topology. Term used to describe that when data is placed on the network, it will travel from one station to another until the destination station is reached and the data read.

Logical topology.   Term used to describe the rules of how data flows on a network.

MAC address.   Physical address burned into the ROM of a network interface card, 48 bits long, and represented in hexadecimal notation.

MAC table.   A database consisting of MAC addresses of nodes known by the bridge or switch storing the table.

MAN.   Metropolitan Area Networks. A network that is usually dispersed throughout a city.

Media access method.   How data is placed on the wire by a node in a network. There are three popular methods: contention, token passing, and polling.

Member server.   A Windows 2000 Server that is a member of a domain.

Mesh topology.   A physical topology where all nodes have a connection to all other nodes in the network.

Metric.   A value associated with the cost of a path to a network in a router's routing table.

Multi-port repeater.   See active hub.

NCP.   Netware Core Protocol. The IPX/SPX protocol suite upper-layer protocols.

Network address.   A hierarchical addressing scheme which allows for two identifications: host (node) and network (cable). Also known as logical address, protocol address, or layer 3 address.

Network printer.   A physical printer that is connected to the network cable.

NIC.   Network adapter board. A hardware component that allows for a node to physically connect to and send data onto a network cable.

Node.   Any device attached to the network, including: workstations, servers, printers, etc.

NTFS Permissions.   File access permissions that allow you to dictate which users can and cannot access files or folders locally or over the network.

OC.   Optical Carrier (OC) Standards. Also known as the SONET hierarchy, OC standards are written as OC-N where 'N' is equivalent to the bandwidth it supports.

Octet.   Term used to represent a series of 8 bits (byte) in an IP address.

OSI Model.   Open Systems Interconnect Reference Model. A seven-layered conceptual networking model, primarily used to ensure interoperability between multiple vendors.

Over-the-Network Backup.   Process of backing up all critical data from a single location.

Packet. Term given to a logical grouping of data after it has been encapsulated by the network layer of the OSI Model. Also known as a Datagram.

PAP. Password Authentication Protocol. PPP authentication protocol that uses an unencrypted two-way handshake.

Passive hub. Network component that acts as a central device for multiple nodes to connect to. Passive hubs do not require power and do not repeat data signals before forwarding them. Passive hubs are primarily responsible for wire management.

PDC. Primary Domain Controller. A Windows NT server that maintains the primary directory services database.

PDU. Protocol Data Unit . A unit of information that refers to data being transmitted between peer-layer protocols during network communication.

Peer layer communication. Virtual communication between peer layers of the OSI Model on two different end nodes in a networked environment.

Physical printer. Print device that produces the final printed product.

Physical security. The security measures taken to protect a network's physical equipment.

Physical topology. The physical arrangement of computers in a computer network.

Polling. Media access method used by mainframes. The centralized unit (mainframe) polls all nodes in the network based on priority and gives them the opportunity to transmit data.

Port(TCP). A decimal value that represents application-layer protocols in the TCP/IP suite.

Power sag. An unexpected decrease in the amount of electricity going to a device.

Power surge. An unexpected increase in the amount of electricity going to a device.

PPP. Point-to-Point Protocol. A dial-up protocol that is used over synchronous or asynchronous lines.

Preamble. A series of ones and zeroes included in the header of a frame to notify the destination station of the forthcoming data.

PRI. Primary Rate Interference. ISDN standard that allows for 23 Bearer channels at 64 Kbps and 1 Delta channel at 64 Kbps.

Print driver. Software that prepares a print job to be passed to the physical printer.

Print server. A computer that is used to manage the logical and the physical printer.

Protocol.   A set of communication standards that all entities must follow for successful communication to take place.

Physical topology.   Physical design of a network.

Protocol suite.   A group of closely-related protocols that allow for network communications to occur. Also known as a protocol stack.

RAID 0: Disk Striping.   It consists of connecting two to thirty-two hard disks together to act as one hard disk. It is used to improve I/O speeds.

RAID 1: Disk Mirroring.   Raid level 1 consists of having two hard disks with an exact mirror image of each other.

RAID 5: Disk Striping with Parity.   RAID level 5 consists of a striped set of three to thirty-two drives where data is striped across the drives in 64 KB blocks. As it is written, a parity block corresponding to the data that has just been striped is placed on a separate disk.

RAID 10: Mirrored Stripe Set.   RAID level 10 consists of a mirrored RAID 0 stripe set.

RAM.   Random Access Memory. The location where the IOS and the running-configuration file are loaded during boot up and executed from while the device is powered on.

Repeater.   Network component that works at the physical layer of the OSI Model. A repeater's primary purpose is to extend the distance a signal can travel.

Ring topology.   A traditional ring topology is a physical topology that uses a single cable in a closed-loop fashion. Newer ring topologies are wired as a star but use a logical ring topology to pass data.

RIP.   Routing Information Protocol. Distance vector routing protocol that broadcasts its entire routing table to its neighbors every 30 seconds. RIP has a version to route IP and a version to route IPX.

Route poisoning.   A process used by distance vector routing algorithms to prevent routing loops. Route poisoning advertises a downed route as unreachable once it learns that a specific network is down.

Routed protocol.   The routed protocol is the network-layer protocol that is responsible for transmitting the data throughout a network.

Router.   Network component that operates at the network layer of the OSI Model. Routers are primarily concerned with network addressing and allow two or more networks to interconnect with one another. Routers create multiple broadcast domains.

Routing algorithm.   The rules followed by routing protocols while gathering and distributing route information.

Routing loop.   An event that occurs when two routers forward inaccurate information to one another in an endless loop.

Routing protocol.   Algorithm-based protocol that generates routing paths, costs associated with those paths, and updates routing tables.

Routing table.   Table of information stored in a router's memory. It lists all network routes that the router knows about, including routes that are available through other routers.

SAP.   Service Advertising Protocol. An IPX/SPX protocol that allows for the advertisement of network services.

SDH.   Synchronous Digital Hierarchy. Equivalent to SONET, SDH defines the OC standards for the rest of the world.

Segment.   Term given to a logical grouping of data after it has been encapsulated at the transport layer of the OSI Model.

Sequencing.   A process of placing segments in order of sequence and adding a sequenced value to them before passing them down to the network layer. It allows for the segments to be reordered when they reach the destination machine.

Server.   A network component or network service that services requests from clients.

Share permissions.   File access permissions that allow you to dictate which users can and cannot access files in a folder over the network.

SID.   Security Identifier. A unique identifier used by Microsoft operating systems.

Simplex.   A transmission process that allows for one-way communication.

SMTP.   Simple Message Transport Protocol. An application-layer protocol of the TCP/IP suite used to send e-mail.

SNMP.   Simple Network Management Protocol. An application-layer protocol of the TCP/IP suite used to monitor network components.

Socket.   A virtual pipe created for two nodes to send data through. It consists of a service type (TCP, UDP), an IP address, and a port number.

SONET.   Synchronous Optical NETwork. Networking standard that was developed by the Exchange Carriers Standards Association (ECSA) for the ANSI. It governs OC *standards* in North America.

Split horizon.   A method used to prevent routing loops in distance vector algorithms. Split horizon does not allow routers to advertise information about a specific route out of the interface in which the information was learned.

SPX.   Sequenced Packet eXchange. The IPX/SPX transport layer protocol. It can be compared to TCP.

Standalone server.   A Windows 2000 server that is not a member of a domain.

Star topology.   A physical topology that requires all nodes to be connected together through a central device, such as a hub or switch.

Static routing.   The process of manually adding route information to a routing table.

Store-and-forward switching.   A switching method that receives a frame, copies it into its buffers, verifies the integrity of the frame by checking its CRC, and then forwards it to the destination address of the frame.

Subnet.   A subdivision of a current IP network.

Subnet mask.   A number that is configured along with an IP address to identify which portion of the IP address can be assigned to networks and which portion can be assigned to hosts.

SVC.   Switched Virtual Circuit. A virtual circuit that is created when transmission of data begins and terminated when the transmission is over.

Switch.   A network component that works at layer 2 or layer 3 of the OSI Model. Layer 2 switches are responsible for segmenting a network into multiple collision domains. Layer 2 switches maintain a MAC table and can support full-duplex transmissions. Layer 3 switches perform functions similar to routers.

TCP.   Transmission Control Protocol. The transport layer protocol of the TCP/IP protocol suite primarily responsible for connection-oriented, reliable, end-to-end communication.

TELNET.   TCP/IP suite terminal emulation protocol.

TFTP.   Trivial File Transfer Protocol. Application layer protocol of the TCP/IP suite used for transferring small files. TFTP uses UDP for transport. TFTP servers are often used to store router configurations.

Three-way handshake.   A process TCP goes through during the session establishment phase of data transfer. It consists of sending a series of requests and acknowledgements to establish a session.

Token.   Term used to identify a unit of data that primarily consists of control information that allows machines to communicate in a token passing network.

Token passing.   Media access method where a token is generated and passed from node to node on the network. A node is only allowed to send data when it has control of the token.

Token Ring.   Networking standard created by IBM. Token Ring uses the token passing media access method.

Toll network. A collection of WAN service providers' switches and cables that are used to forward data. Often represented as a WAN cloud.

Transmission media. The actual wire or technology that provides the path for electrical and other signals to flow between components linked together.

Tree. A logical component of the Windows 2000 Active Directory. A tree can contain multiple domains.

Triggered update. Allows a distance-vector routing algorithm to send update information to its neighbors without having to wait for its predetermined time to send.

UDP. User Datagram Protocol. A transport-layer protocol of the TCP/IP suite primarily responsible for unreliable connection-less communication.

Unbound media. Transmission media that is not confined to a cable such as infrared, laser, or microwave.

Virtual memory. A location on the hard drive that acts as RAM.

WAN. Wide Area Networks. A network that spans large geographical areas and sometimes crosses international boundaries.

Windowing. A process used by TCP to specify the number of segments that may be received during a data transfer before responding with an acknowledgement.

Wireless topology. A physical topology that uses wireless networking devices.

INDEX